DE VELOPI

An international comparison of local
and regional economic development

Edited by Andrew Beer, Graham Haughton and
Alaric Maude

The POLICY
P P
P R E S S

First published in Great Britain in November 2003 by

The Policy Press
University of Bristol
Fourth Floor
Beacon House
Queen's Road
Bristol BS8 1QU
UK

Learning Resources
Centre

Tel +44 (0)117 331 4054
Fax +44 (0)117 331 4093
e-mail tpp-info@bristol.ac.uk
www.policypress.org.uk

12715026

British Library Cataloguing in Publication Data
A catalogue record for this book is available from the British Library.

Library of Congress Cataloging-in-Publication Data
A catalog record for this book has been requested.

ISBN 1 86134 485 6 paperback

A hardcover version of this book is also available

Andrew Beer is an Associate Professor in the School of Geography, Population and Environmental Management at Flinders University, Adelaide, Australia. **Graham Haughton** is Professor of Geography at the University of Hull, UK. **Alaric Maude** is an Associate Professor in the School of Geography, Population and Environmental Management at Flinders University, Adelaide, Australia.

Cover design by Qube Design Associates, Bristol.
Front cover: photograph of vineyard supplied by kind permission of Clive Forster.
Printed and bound in Great Britain by Hobbs the Printers Ltd, Southampton.

Contents

List of tables, figures and case studies

Tables

Figures

Case studies

Acknowledgements

There are many people we need to thank for their contribution to this book. First, we wish to express our thanks to those who worked on various aspects of the data collection and analysis phases of this project, including Cecile Cutler and Louise O'Loughlin, Bridget Kearins and Robert Keane, all of the School of Geography, Population and Environmental Management at Flinders University, Adelaide. Our thanks also to Linda Love of the Geography Department, University of Hull, Emer Carlin of the Department of Community Sciences, University of Ulster and Lisa Gage of the Center for Economic Development at the University of North Texas.

Andrew Beer would like to express his sincere thanks to the Leverhulme Trust and to the University of Ulster. Andrew was a Leverhulme Fellow in 2001 and much of the planning and implementation of this project took place while he was based in Northern Ireland. Andrew would especially like to thank Professors Chris Paris and Jim Allan for their support and encouragement while he was in Northern Ireland.

Graham Haughton used his period as a Visiting Research Fellow at Flinders University in 2002 to make his contribution to this book. Many thanks therefore to the Faculty of Social Sciences at Flinders University for their financial support, and to the Geography Department, University of Hull for the sabbatical leave.

All members of the research team would like to express their thanks to the participants of a conference on Community Economic Development/Local Economic Development held in Derry in January 2002. Many of the ideas and concepts embedded in this book first took shape during that conference and we thank all participants for their constructive comments. Thanks also to the people and organisations that made that conference possible, in particular Conal McFeeley and Ann Molloy of the Social Economy Agency, the Foyle Development Organisation and the Department of Social Development.

We would like to thank the Local Government Association of South Australia, and in particular Chris Russell, for its financial support for this project through the Local Government Research and Development Fund. They, along with Flinders University, provided the monies that made the research reported in this book possible. As importantly, the Association has encouraged the research team, and emphasised the policy relevance of this work.

Finally, we would like to thank the 900 or so local and regional economic development practitioners who responded to our questionnaire. This book would not have been possible without their contribution of time and effort to respond to our survey. Many thanks to all of them.

Preface

This book reports on the findings of a survey sent to local and regional economic development (L&RED) organisations in Australia, England, Northern Ireland and the US. The aim of the survey, and of this research, was to shed light on the nature of L&RED in each country, to draw out both the common and divergent elements in the practice of L&RED across nations.

This book has been written against the backdrop of a burgeoning academic interest in L&RED and an equally explosive growth in policies, programmes and organisations directed at encouraging the growth of regions, cities and localities. Whole schools of academic thought have centred themselves on describing, analysing and theorising the emergence of local and regional development. Despite this growing academic concern, relatively little attention has been paid to cross-national comparisons. While there have been notable exceptions (Halkier et al, 1998; McNiven and Plumstead, 1998; OECD, 2001), there has been no systematic attention given to the differences and similarities in L&RED across nations. This absence is particularly puzzling given the substantial policy transfers between nations, particularly among English-speaking nations, and within the European Union. There is no doubt that the absence of a substantial body of comparative work reflects a number of factors. Much of the academic writing on L&RED comes out of either the UK or the US and national concerns arise first and foremost within that literature. Policy-focused research tends to be undertaken with funding from national or sub-national governments and almost inevitably the funding bodies are primarily interested in developments within their jurisdiction, not what is happening in another policy environment. Also, we need to acknowledge that systematic cross-national research is difficult and fraught with all sorts of methodological challenges. As will be discussed later in the book, even within the four nations covered in this book – which have very similar cultures and a common language – there are very substantial differences in their understandings of the terms 'local' and 'regional'. Perhaps for this reason, much of the comparative literature that has been published to date has been based on a series of case studies.

This book presents a comparative perspective on L&RED within four English-speaking nations. Through the survey we have been able to develop measures that allow the reader to compare the objectives, activities and partnerships of English L&RED organisations with those in Australia, Northern Ireland and the US. Through the analysis of the 900 or so questionnaires returned by practitioners we are able to develop insights into the institutional architectures for L&RED in each nation, the behaviour of L&RED organisations and the comparative strengths and weaknesses of how place-based economic development is pursued in individual nations. The latter is an important concern because we are mindful of recent criticisms of much contemporary research that it is divorced from policy and lacking in empirical rigour (for example,

Markusen, 1999). The policy and practice implications of this research are developed throughout this book. We consider what works, what does not work, why some things appear to be successful in some nations and not others, and the relative contribution of various factors to the apparent success of L&RED efforts. While this publication is not a recipe book for policy makers or practitioners about how to improve their performance, we believe that there is much within the book to interest practitioners, and that our ideas and conclusions will help them develop more effective agencies. Our findings are empirically grounded, and where appropriate we have used statistical analysis to test relationships.

Throughout the writing of this book we have been careful to consider the practical and policy implications of our work, but this has not meant that we have ignored the academic or theoretical dimensions of this study. Indeed, we believe it is not possible to fully understand the processes and dynamics of L&RED without reference to contemporary academic debates. While the data generated by our survey is an important starting point for our analysis, the information makes little sense unless informed by reference to our broader understandings of the social, cultural and economic processes that impinge upon L&RED. Throughout this book we have drawn heavily upon regulation theory, state theory, aspects of work on governmentality and the nature of discourse in constructing policy terrains. All have contributed significantly to our ability to comprehend the outcomes of our survey.

Any cross-national work is inherently difficult, but it is equally inherently enjoyable for the fresh insights it brings. This research has avoided being overwhelmed by that level of difficulty by using researchers based in each nation who are experts in L&RED in their country. It has been a collaborative effort, with input from all parties at each and every stage. While this is an edited volume, we have attempted to maintain the 'voice' of each author or set of authors. Each of the nation chapters therefore has a common format and considers broadly similar themes, but there are differences in the detail discussed and the emphasis awarded to particular topics. These differences reflect the variations in debate surrounding L&RED policy, and are an important element in accurately reflecting L&RED in each nation. The discussion of Northern Ireland, for example, pays particular attention to the peace processes and their impact on how community-based economic development has been promoted. In Australia, by contrast, community-based economic development receives relatively little attention because the social economy sector is weak and community development rarely addresses economic issues.

Local and regional economic development remains an important area of public policy in 'developed' and 'developing' nations. L&RED agencies will have an appreciable impact on the economic and social prospects of regions and localities for the foreseeable future and it is therefore important to ensure that how L&RED is framed, or set within the wider public sector, is appropriate and efficient. In addition, individual organisations need to be given the opportunity to employ effective economic development tools. We hope that this book will help policy makers, academics and economic development practitioners to develop a better understanding of the range of strategies and actions potentially available, to come to appreciate the strengths and weaknesses of the competing approaches, and through that knowledge make better informed decisions.

Andrew Beer, Graham Haughton and Alaric Maude

List of abbreviations

ACC	Area Consultative Committee
ACT	Australian Capital Territory
ALP	Australian Labor Party
BEC	Business Enterprise Centre
BSP	Building Sustainable Prosperity
CMSA	Consolidated Metropolitan Statistical Area
CNP	Creggan Neighbourhood Partnership
CVEDC	Cedar Valley Economic Development Corporation
IFI	International Fund for Ireland
IRB	Industrial Revenue Bonds
L&RED	Local and regional economic development
LEDU	Local and Economic Development Unit
LEED	Local and Economic and Employment Development Programme
LGA	Local Government Association
LSP	Local Strategic Partnership
MACCED	Metro-Atlanta Chamber of Commerce's Economic Development Division
MSA	Metropolitan Statistical Area
NSW	New South Wales
NT	Northern Territory
OECD	Organisation for Economic Co-operation and Development
PMSA	Primary Metropolitan Statistical Area
RDA	Regional Development Agency
RDO	Regional Development Organisation
RES	Regional Economic Strategy
SA	South Australia
SDRED	San Diego Regional Economic Development Corporation
SEA	Social Economy Agency
TEC	Training and Enterprise Council
TINA	There Is No Alternative
UDC	Urban Development Corporation
WA	Western Australia

ONE

International comparisons of local and regional economic development

Andrew Beer, Graham Haughton and Alaric Maude

Introducing local and regional economic development

Working to help create jobs and promote well-being at the local level – who could possibly object to that? Well many have, as critics from different perspectives have argued that the activities of local and regional economic development (L&RED) bodies are variously unnecessary, inadequate, ineffective, or even counterproductive. By contrast, there are others who argue that 'communities carry their future in their own hands', and that 'self-help' is the only assistance cities and regions can expect – and should wish for – within the global economy.

It is in this context that this book sets out to improve our understanding of how local economic development is currently practised in Australia, England, Northern Ireland and the US. The emphasis is on the institutional architecture of L&RED: which organisations do what, where, why, how, and in conjunction with which partners?

The main aims of the book are to:

- map the institutional landscape of L&RED in each country, emphasising how responsibilities are shared across scales of activity, from local, regional and national to supranational;
- examine the different governance structures for delivering L&RED in each country, and the partners with which institutions work;
- outline the main funding systems for local development in each country;
- examine the stated objectives of local and regional development institutions in each country, and the strategies and instruments used to achieve these objectives;
- analyse some of the main differences *within* each country in how local development activities are conducted;
- provide a critical analysis of the views of practitioners of the most and least effective approaches to economic development in each country; and

- develop an appreciation of the factors which practitioners consider are impediments to greater effectiveness, and of their views on what would increase effectiveness.

In addressing these issues the book provides a unique set of insights into some of the similarities and differences in the way in which local economic development is conceived, perceived and conducted in the four countries. Having a comparative component to the work is important as it helps highlight major differences in approach, which in turn helps in developing a better appreciation of the distinctiveness of each nation's experience. The comparative dimension of the work is also important because it raises some intriguing questions, such as, why is it that a policy approach which is considered mainstream in one jurisdiction may be virtually untried in others?

Alternative perspectives on the desirability of local economic development

The underlying premise of this book is that L&RED is an important area of policy, but that it is a relatively new area of policy which has much to learn from international experience. The rise of L&RED in recent years reflects the widespread acceptance of neoliberal ideas and rhetorical devices which argue that national governments no longer have the resources or the ability to counter the impacts of 'globalisation'. By contrast, powerful stories have emerged about the possibilities of constructing local and regional success stories, based on the claimed successes in supposedly paradigm-creating regions such as Silicon Valley in California, Silicon Glen in Scotland, Emilia Romagna in Italy, Baden Württemberg in Germany or the M4 corridor in England (DiGiovanna, 1996; MacLeod, 2002). Increasingly, therefore, the region is being seen as the appropriate level for strategies to improve business competitiveness and create employment. Local and regional actors are being encouraged to work together to revive the fortunes of their areas.

It is not just that in the context of public sector fiscal restraint national governments are unwilling to commit resources to support lagging regions or cities. More fundamentally, neoliberal ideology holds that large-scale government bureaucracies are too inflexible and too slow moving to deal with the demands of a rapidly changing global economic environment. By contrast, it is argued that locally based agencies can respond to economic opportunities as they arise. There are many commentators who would regard themselves as opposed to the prevailing neoliberal policy consensus but who would rush to agree with this statement. The argument here is that it is local and regional agencies which are often best placed to identify – and act upon – the critical impediments to growth, mobilise community resources to support development initiatives, build social capital within the local business community, and engage in strategic planning for the future of their region. Arguably, L&RED practitioners have at hand a potent set of instruments – industry clusters, business parks, networking strategies, place marketing, export development strategies –

for stimulating growth. Any region, any city, any town, it is claimed, has the capacity to improve its economy if it can get mobilised.

There are strong 'pull' factors encouraging cities and regions to engage in L&RED but there are also 'push' factors directing them down this path. Those communities which fail to organise and foster locally based development initiatives are at risk of being marginalised within the global economy, punished by the harsh discipline of market forces. National governments are more reluctant than ever to prop up locations or industries in decline and there is little room for sentimentality within the investment decisions of global corporations. L&RED has therefore moved from being a nicety to a necessity, from a peripheral to a central concern for those keen to ensure the survival of their locality in a neo-Darwinian fight for survival.

Critical views of local and regional economic development

While few would suggest abandoning L&RED altogether, it is not without its fair share of failings. Indeed there is an extensive critical literature that must make depressing reading for any practitioner who comes across it. From almost every ideological perspective it seems that L&RED practices have been found wanting.

Libertarian free market advocates have a specific range of concerns including the unacceptable use of government subsidies or tax abatements to support favoured businesses. They argue that these lead to higher taxes for other businesses, and help to put perfectly good local businesses out of operation. There is also a concern that local development professionals are facilitating government intervention in, and distortion of, free market processes. Libertarians contend that governments should focus on increasing national growth and let capital and labour flow to those places and regions where they can earn the best returns.

There are different concerns from a more liberal democratic perspective, the most trenchant of which focus on the problems of inward investment, also known as 'smokestack chasing' and 'industrial recruitment'. Criticisms of this approach question why taxpayers should subsidise private companies, are resentful of being forced to 'bribe' footloose employers to either stay in town if they are already there or to relocate to it if they are elsewhere, and are also concerned that once the subsidies dry up, companies will leave anyway. For such critics, local economic development is simply a form of 'corporate welfare' (Karmatz et al, 1998), where scarce government funds are diverted from social welfare to raising the profitability of businesses. At a more general level, there is a widespread concern that regional economic problems are for the most part the consequence of national and global decisions, and as such can only be addressed by actions at these levels. Environmentalists frequently challenge the conversion of greenfield sites to business use in the name of local job creation, criticising the negative impacts of some forms of economic development on the local quality of life. Across the political spectrum there tends to be a concern about public subsidies for incoming firms if this squeezes out local businesses, or leads to money leaking out of the region as a result of the trading patterns and profit repatriation of externally owned businesses.

Of course industrial recruitment is not the only – or even most – important tool in L&RED, but it is widely applied and is very important in some places. Independent assessments generally agree that using government money to attract firms to locate in one area rather than another is a 'zero-sum' game at the national level, subsidising job displacement rather than job creation (Industry Commission, 1996; Karmatz et al, 1998; but see Blair and Kumar, 1999, for a contrary view). Some companies have learnt to 'play the game', playing one region off against rivals elsewhere to extract the maximum value of subsidies or other incentives. There is also a widespread belief that many of the jobs that economic development practitioners claim to have created would have occurred anyway (Lenihan, 1999). Linked to this is the concern that there is considerable double counting of the jobs they claim to have generated (Hill, 2002).

As later chapters in this book show, contemporary approaches to L&RED embrace a wide range of strategies, including the promotion of small business start-ups, the provision of infrastructure, labour market training, streamlining the development approvals process, helping businesses export, and assisting in business planning and development. However, it is no more certain than with industrial recruitment that these other strategies are uniformly effective in promoting economic growth and generating jobs, as it is almost impossible to determine what would have happened in the absence of these interventions (Hughes, 1998). Some have suggested L&RED initiatives achieve limited 'real' outcomes but provide policy makers and politicians with a steady stream of media announcements (Rubin, 1988). There are grounds, therefore, for doubting the material value of some locally or regionally based economic development programmes.

Looking for success

Economic development practitioners should take some consolation in the fact that, far from retreating under the onslaught of its critics, L&RED activities are increasing all the time. Why should this be? One possibility is simply that the actions of practitioners actually do make a difference, helping regions and communities to grow. Politicians and practitioners travel extensively overseas in search of new ways of making a difference at the local level. Consultants are hired to help identify and transfer policies that are deemed to have been successful elsewhere. A mini-publishing industry thrives on publishing records of 'good practice' from local areas (OECD, 2001; DIIRD, 2002).

There is then an extensive literature on the achievements of L&RED together with an extensive literature on its failings. It is much rarer, however, to find a book such as this which has asked practitioners themselves to highlight both policies which have worked for them, and those which have been less successful, along with reasons for their evaluation.

Defining and redefining local and regional economic development

What constitutes L&RED needs to be seen as fluid and dynamic, changing over time. It varies both between and within countries (Reese, 1997; Danson et al, 2000). Despite this, there is a reasonable consensus about the broad parameters of what is meant by L&RED: it refers to a set of activities aimed at improving the economic well-being of an area. In some places these activities are organised and funded by the community, charitable foundations or the private sector, but in most cases it is governments that are the major supporters of these initiatives, increasingly in partnership with other funders.

Typically L&RED approaches include one or more of the following types of activity, some of which overlap:

- providing an agreed local economic development strategy, sometimes as a shared strategy between partners, sometimes as a single agency strategy;
- research on the state of the local economy and its wider economic context;
- place promotion, that is, marketing a region or locality;
- land and property initiatives;
- lobbying for a greater share of government funding for infrastructure and investment in regeneration or other schemes;
- direct business subsidies to entice jobs to an area or to retain jobs in an area;
- technology transfer, innovation, and cluster programmes;
- labour market initiatives;
- small firms support;
- development of cultural industries;
- flagship and 'icon' development projects;
- tourism promotion; and
- a range of other possible approaches, such as community economic development, local purchasing initiatives, anti-poverty initiatives, and targeted interventions for particular groups, such as indigenous communities, migrant communities, women, and young people.

It is worthwhile attempting to distinguish between L&RED programmes and other types of area-based redevelopment. In many developed economies governments have sought to regenerate run-down housing estates (see Taylor, 1998; Randolph and Judd, 2000) and other problem areas. However, housing renewal and neighbourhood-based regeneration schemes that are dominated by housing, social and environmental goals are not usually considered part of L&RED. This said, there are areas of ambiguity, not least as government agencies have increasingly sought to insert *economic* rationales and policy instruments closer to the heart of area-based regeneration initiatives. Alternatively, in some countries economic development practitioners are now being urged to take account of *social* and *environmental* issues in their work, in pursuit of what are often described as more 'holistic' and 'sustainable' approaches (see, for example, Regional Development Taskforce [South Australia], 1999).

As well as changing the boundaries as to what constitutes L&RED, there appear to be some interesting swings in terminology. To give an example, 10 years ago local initiatives were ascendant and the term 'local economic development' was becoming more widely known in England. It was the preserve of well-paid, smartly dressed practitioners talking of improving local competitive advantage and wealth creation. 'Regeneration', by contrast, was seen as a little bit dated, the preserve of underpaid, ill-kempt, underachieving but well-meaning individuals talking of locality specific social disadvantage and multiple deprivation. Ten years later, with a different government in power keen to address social exclusion and neighbourhood renewal, regeneration is once more a vogue word. Moreover, there is a growing elision between the practices and discourses of regeneration and local economic development, albeit with an interesting twist as regeneration comes to be seen as the 'palliative' side of local development, delivered at the neighbourhood level, while local economic development attempts to become more strategic, more regional, in the English usage of the word. A similar story could be told about community development in Australia. Where once the term was used almost exclusively by planners to refer to public participation in planning processes, more recently community development has come to embrace a range of 'self-help' strategies intended to revitalise and redevelop declining country towns (Kenyon and Black, 2001; Forth and Howell, 2002).

Same language, different meanings, different terminologies

Why include Australia, England, Northern Ireland and the US in this book? In large measure the answer is that the four are both similar and yet different. Each of the case study countries has developed distinctive approaches to L&RED, often drawing from the experience of other countries, with policy transfer to and from the US and England particularly prominent. While there are similarities in approach, however, there are also substantial differences, some of which relate to the divergent structures and traditions of government across the countries. Two of the countries operate within a federal system of government (Australia and the US) while in England and Northern Ireland it is essential to appreciate the powerful roles of the national government and the European Union. Each country also has its own sets of historically embedded and culturally specific political debates about central–local relations and the role of the state in relation to the individual. As such, while the dominant political economic context for all four countries in recent years has been the rise of neoliberal or market rationalist discourses, the resulting policy concerns and approaches in the area of L&RED have differed significantly.

There was also a pragmatic reason for choosing these four countries. The main results of the study are based on an English language survey, which, if translated into other languages, was likely to generate substantial problems in comparing terms. Indeed, we found many problems in interpreting words between countries using the same language. Even limiting the study to English-speaking countries, the international aspects of this study generated potential – and real – ambiguities in the use of certain key words and terms. For instance, is it possible to say the study is comparing four *countries*? With some reservations, the approach here is to accept the formulation of Northern Ireland and England as constituent nations or jurisdictions within the UK. Alternatives such as 'territories' or 'states' have the potential to lead to other confusions, as they refer to legally constituted jurisdictions in the US and Australia. And within Australia the territories – the Northern Territory (NT) and Australian Capital Territory (ACT, covering Canberra) – have a different legal standing to the states within the federation.

The words 'regions' and 'regional' also proved to be full of different resonances and meanings in each nation. This perhaps should not be too surprising, given the concern within the geographic literature with how alternative understandings of regions are constructed and contested (Paasi, 2002). All of the countries contained multiple ways of defining regions, from television regions, to water basin regions for environmental regulation, to 'official' or 'standard' administrative or statistical regions. In terms of the international study, however, there is a more immediate and pragmatic concern to the ways in which the words are used in everyday political discourse. In Australia, for instance, 'regional' is used rather differently by the two main political parties (Beer et al, 2003). For the conservative Liberal Party, in power nationally during the study period, 'regional' tends to be used to mean non-metropolitan areas, and rural and small town areas in particular. The Australian Labor Party (ALP), on the other hand, recognises a landscape comprised both of metropolitan and non-metropolitan regions. In the US, 'regions' and 'regional' are less prominent, tending to be found mainly in economic debates about initiatives that span two or more local government areas in a particular city-region. So, in contrast with Australia, US usage of regional is more likely to have an 'urban' rather than a 'rural' connotation.

Adding further complexity, 'local economic development' is a term not much used in Australia outside some urban areas, with 'regional economic development' instead the commonly used and understood term. Indeed, some practitioners feel that presenting their work as 'local economic development' somehow reduces its significance. In both Northern Ireland and the US 'local economic development' is the broadly understood term, with regional economic development far less commonly used. In England 'local economic development' is widely used, mainly but not exclusively covering activities at the neighbourhood or local government level. 'Regional economic development' has recently gained renewed salience, however, with the creation of Regional Development Agencies (RDAs) in 1999, which operate at the scale of the government's 'standard regions'. Rather than choose between local economic development or regional economic development, with their associated

7

ambiguities when applied to more than one nation, we use the term *local and regional economic development.*

Different political and institutional structures for local and regional economic development

Differences in terminology in some part reflect differing political and institutional structures. The intention here is to provide a very brief summary of some of the more distinctive aspects of the government and governance systems of each country in so far as they relate to L&RED.

L&RED in Australia is characterised by a large number of relatively small-scale agencies, with most dependent on either state government or local government funding (Beer and Maude, 1997; Beer, 2000a). Significantly, there is no one institutional architecture for L&RED as there are substantial differences between the states. In the State of Victoria, for example, L&RED is almost exclusively the responsibility of local governments, while in Western Australia the state government provides relatively generous funding to support nine Development Commissions. South Australia (SA) and New South Wales (NSW) both have Regional Development Boards, but in the former they are jointly funded by the state government and local governments, while in the latter they are solely funded by the state government. There are, however, some common features across the states. Non-metropolitan regions are the focus for L&RED initiatives in most parts of Australia and this reflects both current political debates (McManus and Pritchard, 2000) and the historical legacy of decentralisation programmes (Collits, 1995). Most agencies are relatively small and many depend on local governments for all or part of their income. State governments play a role in supporting some L&RED agencies, while the national government directly funds a small number of organisations and provides programme funds for many others.

While most accounts of L&RED in the US focus on the actions of local actors, particularly the literature on the emergence of local growth machines and urban regimes (Logan and Molotch, 1987; Stone, 1989), it is essential to appreciate the roles of federal and state government (DiGaetano, 1997). It is also important to recognise that, like Australia, there are significant differences between the states in how economic development initiatives are funded and organised. This variability is of a magnitude greater than that evident in Australia because there are 50 separate jurisdictions (not eight) and because the population of the US is 13 times greater than that of Australia. Since the 'New Federalism' of the Reagan years, federal governments have been keen to pass increasing responsibilities to the states for local development matters, while states in turn have been keen to pass the responsibility to local governments. These transfers of responsibilities have not necessarily been accompanied by similar transfers of powers and resources. Federal governments retain the capacity to intervene in local economies, most evident with the Clinton administration's creation of

Empowerment Zones (Lambert and Coomes, 2001). States also retain powerful economic development roles, particularly through their fiscal powers.

In the US local governments have greater responsibilities and stronger powers than their Australian or UK counterparts, including greater revenue-raising powers in the form of issuing bonds and the generation of specific local taxes, for instance, sales taxes (see, for example, Office of the Attorney General for the State of Texas, 2001). Local governments in the US are therefore more able to undertake substantial economic development programmes when compared with local governments in the other three countries examined here. Furthermore, some local governments in the US engage in economic development activities specifically to protect and increase the revenue base of the authority. In the other three nations local government powers are limited, and their funding is largely restricted to income streams either passed on by state and federal governments as grants, or defined by central governments (for example, property taxes). With powerful elected local mayors, local government in the US also tends to have stronger leadership and a stronger local profile than in any of the other countries, with local economic development activities often supported for their vote winning potential.

Northern Ireland presents a distinctive set of arrangements for L&RED because of its history of conflict and political agitation. It is not the purpose of this book to reflect upon the story of Northern Ireland and 'The Troubles', but we need to recognise some aspects of its political and administrative history. Beginning in the 1960s British governments based in Whitehall limited the powers of local governments in Northern Ireland and took control of those functions that related to the administration of the province as a whole. The provincial government was restored after the signing of the Good Friday Peace Accord in 1998. The Accord also paved the way for substantial investment by the EU and other bodies – such as the International Fund for Ireland – in initiatives that built links that transcended the Protestant–Catholic divide[1]. The goal of these initiatives was to strengthen local economies and enhance social relations between the Catholic and Protestant communities both within Northern Ireland and, in some instances, in the Border Counties of the Republic of Ireland. This history has resulted in an institutional architecture for L&RED characterised by relatively weak local government participation, direct involvement by provincial government agencies (for example, the Department for Social Development) and a large community sector made up of a myriad of small agencies heavily dependent upon the European Commission for funding. Importantly it is a framework that has emerged only recently and is likely to continue to change as Northern Ireland's constitutional and political circumstances evolve.

The English system is different again. There is a strong central government, which through to the 1960s, and arguably beyond, had the dominant role in L&RED, both directly through its own departments and indirectly through its funding of local government initiatives in this area. In formal terms, local government is the creation of central government in this system, which gives national government far-reaching influence over local government powers and responsibilities. Although primarily responsible for delivering a range of services at the local level, local governments since the mid-1970s have been increasingly involved in many aspects of economic development. Despite occasional concerns that budget constraints imposed by central government would squeeze out local economic development from local government activities, this does not seem to have happened. What has happened, however, is a broadening of the structures of local governance, as central government has created a wide range of alternative or parallel institutions for delivering aspects of economic development at the local level. Examples have included private sector-led bodies such as the Urban Development Corporations and Training and Enterprise Councils (both now abandoned), and the numerous local regeneration partnerships created in recent years.

Since the early 1990s two major trends have influenced the organisation of L&RED in England: the increasingly directive role of the EC in allocating its structural funds for local and regional development, and the attention to developing a stronger regional institutional fabric. At the moment, England still lacks elected regional government, but since the election of a Labour government in 1997 regional scale institutions have become increasingly important. In particular RDAs, created in 1999, have become major players in economic development, taking on responsibility for many of central government's programmes for local regeneration (Robson et al, 2000).

Methods

This book breaks new ground by reporting the results of an almost identical questionnaire sent to L&RED practitioners in each of the four nations in 2001[2]. The information obtained through this instrument has then been matched to deeper insights secured through the analysis of a number of case studies. The extensive data collected in the postal questionnaire survey provided the core empirical information on the ways in which L&RED was being conducted in each country, together with practitioners' own assessments of how effective some of their interventions had been. The intensive aspect of the work involved providing short case studies for each of the countries. The rationale for the local case studies was that with the growing division of responsibilities for L&RED activities across a range of institutions it would have been difficult to provide a sense of how institutions and policies come together at the local level without them.

While a number of researchers and organisations have compared economic development strategies internationally (Bennett and Krebbs, 1991; Wood, 1996a; OECD, 1997, 2001; Halkier et al, 1998; Danson et al, 2000), these analyses have not been able to compare nations on the basis of a common data set or evaluative criteria. The questionnaire helps draw out both the distinctive and common elements of the architecture for L&RED in each of the four nations. The questions asked of economic development practitioners in Austin, Texas, were the same as those asked in Hull and Plymouth in England, Wollongong and Broken Hill in Australia and Omagh and Coleraine in Northern Ireland. How and why their responses varied is one of the key themes addressed in this book.

Sampling frameworks

Ideally international comparisons should involve exactly the same sampling frameworks and exactly the same survey instruments. This study came close with the latter, but had to make some compromises on the former. The sampling framework proved difficult to standardise because of the very substantial differences in the geography, population and economies of the four nations covered here as well as the different ways in which the practice of L&RED is configured. In particular it was felt important to capture something of the recent growth in the range of approaches and types of institution in L&RED within the survey. Twenty years ago a study could perhaps have captured most L&RED activity with a survey of local governments, but today such an approach would tell only part of the story.

With differing sizes of country and differing governance structures, plus different databases of the institutions of governance in each country, it proved unworkable to use exactly the same sampling framework in each country. In the US random sampling was essential to make the survey manageable, while in Northern Ireland it was possible to attempt complete coverage of the main institutions. The differing sampling bases and techniques mean that the data here are not strictly comparable in the sense of a controlled scientific exercise. However, the data can provide a reasonably accurate picture of L&RED activities within each country, and a broad basis for comparing programmes and strategies across countries, particularly where we are using ranking for, say, identifying the most and least effective techniques. We are then able to compare like with like across nations. The data also enable us to build up a broad or indicative picture of what practitioners say they are doing, how their activities are funded, what their governance arrangements are, how effective they think their main activities are, and what constraints they think reduce their effectiveness.

In all nations except the US the questionnaires were sent to the chief officers of each institution, with a request that they be filled out by a senior officer. In the US they were sent to a named individual drawn from the sampling frame, but this person was not necessarily the chief officer of the organisation. Three main concerns arise about the sampling frame and these need to be taken into account when interpreting the questionnaire returns. First, we were seeking the views of the 'executive' rather than the board members of each organisation, and it is possible the two might have differed, particularly in interpreting areas of success (see, for example, Fulop and Brennan, 1997). Second, except in the case of the US, we had little control over who actually filled in the forms. On some occasions the chief executive officer was the respondent, on other occasions it was a more junior member of staff. Third, we had the views of only one

Table 1.1: Questionnaire responses by nation

Nation	Questionnaires sent out	Questionnaires returned	Approximate population (millions)
England	477	117	49
US	800	224	260
Australia	1,100	505	19
Northern Ireland	400	122	1.7

person in each organisation, so we could not capture the diversity of opinions about an organisation's activities.

Following on from this, it is worth emphasising that the study does not attempt to provide an independent evaluation of each organisation or of one particular policy approach. That objective would have required an altogether different approach centred on more intensive methodologies.

In Australia just over 1,100 questionnaires were sent to the chief executive officers of local governments, Regional Development Boards, Development Commissions, Business Enterprise Centres (BECs) and the federal government's Area Consultative Committees (Table 1.1). The sample frame was based on an update of a list of these organisations developed for previous research (Beer and Maude, 1997), and included all agencies that were part of a formal state or federal government programme. There was a second mail-out to respondents who failed to respond to the initial distribution of questionnaires, and this helped raise the response rate. The larger sample size, and the attempt to contact all organisations active in L&RED, was justified because of the considerable differences across states and programmes. An attempt to present a 'national' picture of economic development agencies based on a random sample would ignore the very real structural differences evident across Australia.

The size of the US economy and the number of L&RED agencies rendered a survey strategy based on a census of organisations – or of even one type of organisation – impractical. Individuals were selected randomly from a list of members of the American Economic Development Council, the professional association for local and regional economic developers, and came from all parts of the US. This sample was then screened to eliminate non-qualifiers such as private consultants and federal or state agencies, as well as multiple listings of people at the same organisation. In the latter case the person with the most appropriate job title was selected. Questionnaires returned within 10 days as undeliverable were replaced by random sampling.

Northern Ireland has a very small L&RED sector and it was therefore possible to include in the sample frame all 400 or so active organisations (Table 1.1). This included all local governments, the Local Economic Development Units, community groups active in economic development and related bodies. Organisations that did not respond to the first questionnaire were sent a follow-up approximately eight weeks after the initial mail-out.

In England, all local governments were mailed the questionnaire, plus all

Local Learning and Skills Councils, and local Small Business Services. These all tended to be actively involved with a very wide range of other local delivery bodies for which there was no comprehensive national database, for instance Single Regeneration Budget partnerships, training partnerships, various European-funded local partnerships, and other community regeneration initiatives. The result is that the English survey focused on the key strategic agencies at the local level, many of which also had strong operational dimensions. As all of these agencies conducted much of their work through partnerships with a wide variety of others, the approach captures much of the diversity of local activities. However, not surveying grass-roots organisations directly does mean that the views of their activities here are those of their funders and partners, rather than those of the organisations themselves.

Questionnaire survey and the local case studies

A common questionnaire format was used, developed between all the contributors to this book in a process of negotiation which took several months of reconciling different terminologies and institutional systems, and even paper sizes. The basic survey design and some of the questions drew on an earlier Australian survey (Beer and Maude, 1997), which meant some of the questions had been pre-tested. The questions used in that earlier survey had, in turn, been developed out of interviews with practitioners and government officials across Australia. Additional questions were developed from an analysis of a report of the Organisation for Economic Co-operation and Development (OECD) Local Economic and Employment Development Programme (LEED) on best practice in local development (OECD, 2001). Each national survey team was also allowed to add a limited number of specific questions of their own. An unanticipated problem emerged once the questionnaires were received and the data analysed. Many respondents reported staff numbers and agency budgets that reflected the totals for their organisation as a whole rather than for their L&RED activities alone. Some local governments, for example, reported their total budget and total staff numbers rather than the resources devoted to economic development, despite clear statements in the questionnaire asking for the latter. The result is that our information on the size and budgets of local economic development units contains too many inconsistencies to be used in the way we had originally hoped, and we have had to adopt proxy measures of agency size and resourcing.

The organisation of the book

This chapter has set out in some detail the questions that this book sets out to address, in the process seeking to be clear about the parameters of the work. In Chapter Two the academic grounding for the work is provided, focusing particularly on debates around institutions and L&RED. Chapter Three offers an analysis of key comparative data from the survey across all four countries, and this provides the background and introduction for each of the following four chapters, which provide separate overviews for each country. To a large degree each case study chapter applies a common format and common tables, thereby allowing for further comparative analysis. The detailed analysis of each country contains local case studies, which add flesh to the bones of the survey results. Finally, the concluding chapter returns to re-examine L&RED in international comparison and attempts to draw out the key findings for policy and theory.

Notes

[1] It is worth noting that in Northern Ireland the term 'community' is commonly used to refer to either the Protestant community or the Catholic community, and not both.

[2] Unless otherwise stated, this questionnaire is the source of the data presented in the tables and figures.

TWO

Understanding international divergence and convergence in local and regional economic development

Graham Haughton, Andrew Beer and Alaric Maude

Introduction

To get a sense of the scale and pace of the growth in L&RED activity, it has been estimated that worldwide the number of RDAs leapt from perhaps 400 in the mid-1980s to at least ten times that number by the late 1990s (Lovering, 1999). Lovering has almost certainly underestimated the number of L&RED agencies both in the 1980s and now, but his assessment does capture the rate and pace of growth in this field. At the local level, the change has been even more dramatic: in the late 1970s many places in the case study countries did not have a formal economic development agency, today most do. Moreover, in any area with more than 100,000 people there are likely to be several agencies engaged in complementary or competing activities. This in part reflects both specialisation among agencies and a broadening of L&RED policy (Haughton, 1999a).

This chapter sets out to examine four sets of interrelated issues. First, why has there been a growth in the number of economic development institutions? Second, why have we witnessed growth in the range and type of activities which constitute local economic development? Third, how and why do certain types of approach to local economic policy come to be dominant at particular points in time? Fourth, how can we best make sense of the similarities and differences across nations in the way local economic development is pursued?

Governance, institutions and the state

Most L&RED activity is sponsored by the state, which provides the legal framework, legitimacy and resources for most institutions, from direct funding and matched funding for government and various partnership bodies, to granting tax breaks and charitable status for independent private and community-based institutions. The state has long had an interest in supporting local development policies: what has changed over time are the rationales, expectations, magnitude and modus operandi of local development activity. This section examines how the state has operated strategically and selectively in the forms of approach that it has been willing to support, examining the rationales for these in the context of changing macro-level approaches to managing economic growth.

It is not our intention to provide a detailed history of local development, taking into account the many different national approaches. Rather, the more limited aim is to highlight how current approaches build from previous experience of local development. Our focus is on development in the last 100 years, but it is worth noting first some of the earlier examples of local development, such as Joseph Chamberlain's municipal development initiatives in mid-19th-century Birmingham, England; public and private elites pursuing 'boosterist' growth strategies in US cities such as Houston; and the 'colonial socialism' of 19th-century Australia which saw governments provide both infrastructure and labour market assistance in order to foster the growth of the colonies (Butlin et al, 1982).

In examining more recent tendencies in the development of capitalism, the approach here draws on regulation theory informed developments in state theory, focusing on Jessop's strategic-relational approach, which emphasises the importance of political strategy and contingency (Jessop, 1990a, 1990b, 1995, 2000, 2002). The advantage of this approach to state theory is that it represents a significant departure from the structural determinism of some earlier accounts, particularly certain forms of Marxist essentialism. Regulation theory usually takes as its starting point the work of Aglietta (1979) and his insights into the role of the state in creating 'regimes of accumulation'. From this perspective governments are involved in continuous efforts to create and maintain the conditions which allow businesses to achieve sustained profitability.

Regulation theory contends that periods of economic crisis, where the previously successful economic regime fails, trigger a search for new policy solutions to the dilemmas of managing economic growth (Goodwin and Painter, 1996). The state's role in local economic development has been held up as an important dimension of the search for a contemporary 'new institutional fix' to the problems of ensuring profitability, as part of helping to manage the spatial and social consequences of economic restructuring (see, for example, Tickell and Peck, 1995; Jessop, 1998). However, there are substantial dangers in over-reading regulation theory and related state theory developments as a form of explanation for local and regional change. While this approach can provide powerful insights into the large-scale processes that shaped growth in the immediate post-war period, it sheds little light on the processes of transition from one mode of regulation to the next (Amin, 1994). Regulation theory can identify useful broad-scale *tendencies* at a high level of generalisation: what it does not do is provide generalisable *explanations* of change (Hay, 1995; Jessop, 1995; MacLeod and Goodwin, 1999). As such this approach does not attempt to explain differences between nations and nor can it shed light on the specific circumstances surrounding L&RED in a single place – this requires taking into account the contingent circumstances of time and place through concrete empirical work. There is a need, therefore, for more grounded accounts of the complex geographically and historically specific economic, institutional and political processes that have shaped L&RED activities around the world (MacLeod and Goodwin, 1999).

Keynesian experiments in local and regional economic development, 1920s-1960s

In broad terms liberalism, with its emphasis on small government, dominated 19th- and early 20th-century political philosophy, leaving little scope for local state interventionism. However, levels of central government support for local development activities rose gradually and selectively, although sometimes erratically, from the 1920s to the 1940s. In part this can be traced to the wider changes in economic practices of the state, which in the case of Atlantic Fordism reflected the rise of the 'Keynesian welfare national state' (Jessop, 2002). The nation state assumed a central role in supporting a stable economic regime, taking an increasingly direct role in regulating and promoting national economic and social welfare. A combination of the economic instability of the previous economic system, changing technological and managerial practices, and political pressures help explain the state's assumption of a more interventionist role at national and regional levels. The 1930s Great Depression was particularly important in prompting a change of approach, and in the UK and US this included fears about the possible spread of communism as a consequence of rising social unrest in declining regions. Both Franklin Roosevelt's New Deal in the US, and the work of economist J.M. Keynes on using government spending to address unemployment, were influential in shaping approaches to state intervention.

It was after the Second World War that the more welfarist approaches to national economic management became dominant, although the approach was by no means universal. Work on 'welfare regimes' (Esping-Andersen, 1990), for instance, identifies three, sometimes more, types of welfare system within 'developed' economies. In Geddes' (1999) reformulation of this approach, nations can be classified into four broad approaches: comprehensive welfare systems, corporatist welfare regimes, liberal welfare regimes, and rudimentary welfare regimes. Significantly both Australia and the US are seen to have weak liberal welfare systems, while the UK has a mixed system that combines elements of the liberal and comprehensive models.

In the post-war years national governments tended to become more directly involved in economic planning, controlling financial markets, manipulating growth rates through their direct expenditures and fostering domestic industrial sectors selectively through tariffs and other forms of protection. The Australian, US and UK governments all aspired to raise incomes and achieve sustained economic growth. But while there were commonalities of purpose, there were also significant differences in how these policy goals were attained. An active immigration programme was a significant component of the economic growth strategy of Australia and the US through the post-war period, while the UK was a source of migrants to both these countries and a recipient of migrants from many other Commonwealth countries. Similarly, social security or welfare systems evolved differently. While UK Labour governments in the post-war period made a 'cradle to the grave' commitment to assisting individuals, Australian and US governments were much less ambitious.

Approaches to L&RED in the immediate post-war period were entangled in broader nation building efforts. The differences in approach tended to be affected by broader debates about the nature, purpose and structure of government intervention in the economy, a point amply illustrated by comparing the efforts of the UK and Australia over this period. The centralised government of the UK contrasts particularly with the federal systems of Australia and the US. During the 1950s and 1960s, UK regional policy was essentially run by central government departments in pursuit of national policy objectives, related to achieving stable growth and a more balanced national space economy. The main approach was to regulate the movement of industry through a system of subsidies and restrictions on industrial expansion in more prosperous regions in an attempt to redirect jobs into peripheral regions (Hall, 1989). National economic policy was also used directly to intervene in regional development, for instance in the provision of transport infrastructure and support for nationalised industries such as coal, steel and shipbuilding, which tended to be concentrated in the regions with the greatest economic problems.

The national tier of government in Australia, by contrast, was much less directly interventionist within regional economies, and this partly reflected the dominance of the conservative leaning Liberal Party which held power from 1949 to 1972 (Vipond, 1989). More fundamentally, however, the Australian constitution vests sub-national development responsibilities with state, not the national, governments. Regional development efforts were organised at the state level (Logan, 1978), and contained two often antagonistic elements. On the one hand, 'competitive Federalism' meant that state governments competed vociferously with each other for new manufacturing plants and other investment; they offered subsidies and other inducements to attract firms to their capitals. On the other hand, formal regional development policies emphasised the decentralisation of population and productive capacity away from the burgeoning metropolitan areas (Collits, 1995). Australia's single large-scale regional development initiative undertaken by the national government – the Snowy Mountains Hydro Electricity Scheme – was a unique example of what could be achieved when national and state governments reached consensus. However, the national government's impact on regional economies was more commonly limited to their application of nationwide policy instruments such as tariff policies.

Perhaps inevitably then, the differing structures of government in the UK and Australia have affected the regional growth priorities of governments with broadly similar objectives. The US, with its federal system of government, shared many similarities with Australia, as much of the growth of the 'sunbelt' states from the 1970s onwards resulted from state-level subsidies (Tietz, 1994). However, as Chapter One intimated, local governments in the US have long had a strong role in economic development.

Neoliberal experiments in local and regional economic development

Stalling national economic growth, rising inflation, high unemployment levels and mounting government debts provided the backdrop to a massive shift in the dominant ideas about the role of government in managing the economy during the 1970s. External pressures played a role, from the oil price shocks of the early 1970s to the decision of the UK government to call in the International Monetary Fund for support in 1976, which immediately prescribed its near universal medicine of fiscal restraint, involving cutting government spending and reducing taxes.

The transitional period, as the old regime entered a period of uncertainty and instability, saw a blossoming of experiments with alternative, more localised forms of economic development. While it is possible to dismiss this period as simply one of patchwork attempts to shore up the increasingly apparent failings of the previous economic system, some of the debates and approaches adopted in those days still resonate 30 years later. During the mid-1960s growing evidence of localised concentrations of high unemployment and riots in some inner cities in the US forced political attention onto local development policies, particularly in cities. It brought on a new set of rationales, mandates, agencies and tools. President L.B. Johnson's 'War on Poverty' (1963-68) funded over 1,000 projects in the major cities focused on skills development and training, community empowerment and public employment (Badcock, 1984). In Britain, the Community Development Project (1969-76) gave rise to local experiments in empowering local people. The subsequent Urban Programme was used to channel government funding into a number of areas selected on the basis of their multiple deprivation, with support for local economic, housing, environmental and social projects. Local governments in urban areas also began to extend their own funding for local economic development, in some cases breaking away from the constraints of government-funded programmes to explore alternative, more radical, approaches such as supporting cooperatives and community businesses.

The process of change was accelerated with the election of Margaret Thatcher in the UK (1979) and Ronald Reagan (1980) in the US. Both rejected the Keynesian view that the state could spend its way out of a crisis. Instead, drawing inspiration from economist Milton Friedman's monetarist doctrine, the newly elected governments led the way in reforming both national and sub-national economic management. New policies were introduced which sought to promote less government not more, lower personal and business taxes, greater trade liberalisation, deregulation of financial and labour markets, and privatisation rather than nationalisation of industries.

At the sub-national level, the rise of neoliberalism during the 1980s saw the emergence of a more economic oriented approach to development at the local or regional scale. In the new approach priority shifted to promoting greater local competitiveness and private wealth creation, rather than propping up 'lame duck' industries with public money.

For Jessop (1997, 2002) the shift away from Keynesian welfarism has involved four major tendential shifts. First, a shift from the centrality of hierarchical forms of govern*ment* to more porous forms of govern*ance*, a trend which is evident at all scales, with the rise of global governance bodies, plus national, regional and local governance institutions (Jessop, 1997; Pierre and Peters, 2000). Increasingly policies have been devolved to cross-sectoral partnerships, networks and other forms of policy coordination. This shift has seen businesses and civil organisations more formally integrated into the decision-making and implementation activities of the state. Private sector partners have become particularly important in economic development. Public sector financial restraint has resulted in an emphasis on using state funding to 'leverage' private investment to support economic development. This in turn has influenced which types of approach have come to be regarded as viable and desirable. New institutional forms were generated to encourage and direct private sector funding in pursuit of public policy objectives. Increasing volumes of government funding were directed to these new policy delivery vehicles rather than through local governments. The business-led Urban Development Corporations (UDCs) in the UK were paradigmatic examples, as are the Local and Economic Development Units (LEDUs) in Northern Ireland and the Area Consultative Committees (ACCs) in Australia.

As indicated earlier, many regions now have two, three or more agencies working to promote their well-being. Australia's experience highlights this phenomenon as state, federal and local governments all support L&RED organisations and initiatives, and their efforts are additional to community or business-led agencies. In the US private property investors reacted to falling city centre property values by forming or participating in alliances to promote redevelopment to revive land and property values, and also to create new commercial opportunities.

Inspired by development in US and UK cities in particular, there has been a rise in interest in the urban political economy, evident in the literature on growth machines, growth coalitions and public–private partnerships (see Judd and Ready, 1986; Stone, 1989). These frameworks depict local actors, such as property owners, retailers, financial institutions, small businesses, utilities, and local government leaders and key officials, as being financially dependent on the health of the local economy, and therefore motivated to engage in activities to improve that economy. In this sense, some businesses are place dependent, in that they cannot easily move elsewhere, and are therefore tied to the economic fortunes of their local area (Cox and Mair, 1989; Wood, 1996a). As a consequence, in some places local economic development has tended to be driven by local business interests, involving an approach that emphasises private sector investment and public–private partnerships. These insights are particularly useful in the US, where business is often quite localised, and local government is heavily dependent on revenue from the local economy (Wood, 1996a). They might also usefully be applied in Australia, with modifications, to explain the wide variety of locally initiated development organisations, especially in Queensland. These perspectives are less appropriate as business becomes less locally integrated and more nationally organised. In England and Australia, for example, the greater centralisation of capital and political power (among other differences) has meant that local economic development is more likely to be driven by, and dependent on, the public sector than in the US (Axford and Pinch, 1994; Harding, 1999).

More recent work in this vein has implicitly or explicitly critiqued its narrow 'economism', seeking to build a more central role for neighbourhood and community groups in pushing for their interests, whether for environmental programmes, improved quality of life, employment, or social justice issues. For example, in non-metropolitan Australia significant support for local economic development comes from parents who want better local educational and employment opportunities for their children, as large numbers of young people leave their home town for post-secondary education and employment. For the US, Miranda and Rosdil (1995) show how city administrations have followed a variety of economic development strategies, some of them involving redistribution programmes for minority groups. In England, Haughton and While (1999) demonstrate how the local authority of Leeds shifted in the mid-1990s from an entrepreneurial approach to city development to a more community oriented vision of social regeneration, reflecting changes at both the local and the national levels. As their analysis highlights, local changes needed to be seen in the light of their intersection with changing national politics and ideologies.

This brings us back to the second of Jessop's tendential shifts, the subordination of social policy to economic policy, as exemplified in the rhetoric of 'responsibilities' that has replaced the language of 'entitlement' in welfare systems (Jessop, 2002). This is perhaps most associated with the enormous experimentation with workfare schemes in the US and the UK (where the preferred nomenclature is New Deal), and the bluntly titled 'work for the dole' scheme in Australia. Here local experimentation is being encouraged in the design of workfare programmes, prompting a period of frenzied policy experimentation and policy transfer, allied to auditing systems of disciplinary surveillance (Peck, 2002).

In related vein, growing social and geographical inequalities have been unleashed by changing economic policies from the 1970s on, as the goal of full employment was abandoned and the social security safety net lowered. With national governments disinclined to intervene directly, the emphasis has been on passing responsibilities to communities themselves. This has been evident in the proliferation of community economic development, or social economy, initiatives in run-down urban areas in the US (Shutt, 2000), England (Haughton et al, 1999) and Northern Ireland (Greer et al, 1999). At the same time, the emerging strength and diversity of civil society groups has resulted in a growing diversity of approaches and institutions within L&RED. Reacting against the dominant paradigm of publicly subsidised, private sector 'flagship' projects, neighbourhood groups have often been associated with a demand for greater attention to neighbourhood level initiatives, developing alternative rationales and policy approaches (Clavel, 1986; Nickel, 1995; Haughton and While, 1999).

The third tendency which Jessop (1997) notes is the shift from the pre-eminence of the nation state in economic management, with powers, responsibilities and resources being reworked vertically, both up to bodies such as the World Trade Organization and, in the case of the UK, to the European Union, and down to local and regional governance bodies. Taken together with the horizontal shift of powers to non-government institutions, the result has been a 'hollowing out' of the nation state. However, the state has retained its capacity to dictate how it deploys its powers, including the potential to withdraw from arrangements and create new ones. In this sense, the state has retained power through its 'strategic selectivity'.

Fourth, there has been a tendency towards the internationalisation of policy environments. Policy making has also become more international. Following up work on successful regional growth models, such as Silicon Valley in California and the Cambridge Phenomenon in England, attempts have been made to transfer aspects of successful regional experiences internationally. They are offered up as quick fix solutions to local problems, borrowing selectively or wholesale from 'best practice' exemplars elsewhere. Improved communications have helped stimulate greater and more effective sharing of information about new approaches between policy makers. Evidence of this includes the rise in science and technology parks in the 1980s, and the growth in social economy initiatives across the UK since the mid-1990s. In addition, as we will see later, there have been a number of internationally active, high profile academics and consultants who have promoted particular approaches to L&RED, shaping both public debates and the agendas of local, regional and national governments.

These four tendencies have underpinned a 30-year period of massive institutional experimentation, with new institutional arrangements having been criticised, reformulated or abandoned with great regularity. Alternatively, the experiments with new policy tools (for example, cultural policy in cities, community banks and credit unions) have led to a growing repertoire of approaches, not all of them in favour at any one moment in time, but few abandoned wholesale. The scope of local economic development has therefore increased and with this has come a degree of specialisation among agencies, some focusing on small business issues, some on labour market initiatives, others on the social economy, and so on. Intriguingly, while there has been growth in agency types and agency approaches, there has also been a tendency towards conformity around a narrow range of government-sanctioned institutional forms and policy tools.

Part of this conformity reflects the strategic and spatial selectivity of the state. Central governments have maintained a degree of control over the new institutional architectures for L&RED through their decisions about which scales of policy intervention to favour – neighbourhood, local government or regional – and which institutions and approaches to support. Discipline has been maintained through the growth of competitive funding regimes for distributing monies for local development, serving to bring local agencies into line with the aims of the funding providers. Similarly, target and audit culture has created a sharper focus on delivering measurable outcomes against the criteria set by central governments. Along the way it has provided funding opportunities for a widening array of local delivery agencies, from private sector providers to community organisations.

While it is important to recognise the role of state selectivity it is also critical to note that central governments do not directly control processes, agencies and outcomes at the local level. Organisations excluded from funding by one tier of government may be supported by another tier, or by the local community. This occurred in Australia when a newly elected federal government withdrew funding in 1996 from the network of Regional Development Organisations (RDOs). In some places the RDOs continued to operate with funding from state governments, local governments or other sources. In the case of the UK, funding sources might include the EU, while charitable and religious foundations and the use of local bonds and taxes are important in the US. There is almost universal dependence on private sector funding to back large-scale property developments and this adds to the diversity of outcomes, processes and institutional forms 'on the ground'.

In short, we have seen a proliferation of experimental local delivery arrangements, often relying on a range of short-term, highly conditional funding arrangements. What has united them has been that most have been involved in delivering central government programmes to centrally approved, if not determined, goals and delivery targets. It is possible to argue that the rise of neoliberalism since the late 1970s has set in train not so much a new settled order, as a period of continuing experimentation. This experimentation has involved a fluidity and multiplicity in the reworking of state approaches to managing both the national economy and the issue of local economic development (Jessop, 1999; Brenner, 2000; Peck, 2002; Peck and Tickell, 2002). From this perspective, experimentation with alternative approaches to local economic management is a critical feature of the current period of regulatory transformation. Local, national and transnational approaches are being mutually and continuously reworked, top-down, bottom-up, across scales, across national boundaries, and across institutional boundaries.

The implications for this study are threefold. First, we must recognise the dangers of attempting to 'read off' general social and economic dynamics affecting L&RED based on the experience of one nation, or even one set of nations. A considerable amount of work linking regulation theory and local economic development has been based in the UK and there are dangers in assuming that this experience will always be relevant to other 'developed' nations.

Second, in charting the different institutional architectures in each country, it is important to establish their different political and legal frameworks, and also their different institutional traditions and trajectories. Third, the fragmentation and specialisation of activities means that locality-wide case studies are needed to show how the growing multiplicity of local institutions link together, duplicating or competing in some functions, while not engaging in others. This requires attention to how economic development functions are articulated across different scales, including neighbourhood, regional, national and even supranational institutions.

Local and regional economic development and the social construction of knowledge

Having mainly focused so far on the institutional aspects of L&RED, this section broadens the discussion to provide a more diffuse examination of how alternative approaches to L&RED are constructed and contested. The emphasis here is less on the dominant strategies that are imposed on local areas but instead on how communities and regions resist and react to these hegemonic approaches. Their responses create strategies that are unique to their circumstances. In particular, we want to emphasise how widely accepted approaches to policy become rooted in dominant narratives, which work in part by seeking to refute both previous paradigms and potential contemporary alternatives. While not wanting to reject the insights of state theory, the aim is to go further in developing an understanding of how policy regimes emerge out of local, regional and national debates. Reflecting aspects of the broader cultural turn in the social sciences, the focus here is on power/knowledge (the two are interdependent), and the processes of selectivity in the ways in which ideas are developed, articulated, contested, circulated and adopted.

Governmentality and technologies of government

The starting point here is the notion of governmentality, or the art of government, which involves the study of complex processes of self and collective discipline which influence people's actions (Foucault, 1991; Dean, 1999). The art of government in this sense is not the way in which the state enforces its rules in a coercive sense, but rather the more generalised construction of rationalities, knowledges and norms that influence people's behaviour and practices. In this approach, notions of truth are embedded in particular discourses, which are ordered and structured frameworks of language, signs and symbols through which people understand and interpret the world, in order to define what constitutes a problem and the range of ways of addressing these problems.

   Associated with this work on governmentality has been a growing interest in the 'technologies of government', which sets out to question "by what means, mechanisms, procedures, instruments, tactics, techniques, technologies, and vocabularies is authority constituted and rule accomplished?" (Dean, 1999, p 31; see also Murdoch, 2000; Painter, 2002). For the present analysis, thinking about governmentality and its associated technologies draws attention to how governments and others involved in contemporary governance structures – such as the Boards of Management for an economic development agency – construct their own political and administrative rationalities (Murdoch, 2000), drawing on particular 'scientific' knowledges and discourses. In particular, it suggests that it is important to think about how our ideas about a problem are constructed: that is, how we recognise and label an issue as a problem, how we decide whether an issue warrants policy action, how our selection of policy instruments are determined, and how we measure and evaluate success in dealing with the issue.

Painter's (2002) work illustrates the value of notions of governmentality in this area. He examined how the Regional Economic Strategies (RESs) produced by English RDAs represent a particular 'technology' to assist in the art of government. He emphasised how the RESs are based on selective knowledges, statistical and theoretical, which help shape their purpose. Using the case of equal opportunities he is also able to show how the potential of this issue to upset the status quo is addressed by absorbing it into the RESs in particular ways. It is probably true to say that notions of sustainable development were similarly selectively interpreted and absorbed into the dominant discourses of the RESs, losing their capacity to disrupt their work.

Discourses and policy choices

A discourse, in its contemporary academic usage, is a specific language of terms, symbols, concepts and assumptions that people use to define issues, identify appropriate actions, dismiss opposing views and justify the correctness of their viewpoint. The importance of discourse is frequently evident in the way it identifies some policy options as appropriate and others as inappropriate. These choices will partly reflect 'evidence and experience', but the parameters of choice will also reflect ideas of what is 'common sense' and what is not, what is acceptable and what is not, that are contained in competing discourses. A successful change in policy direction requires that old approaches be subject to critique, in order to assert the legitimacy of new approaches. In inserting new policies, discourses need to be developed which are sufficiently strong that for a time at least they can convince many, if not all, that There Is No Alternative (the TINA approach).

To give an example, during the early 1970s regional policy in the UK was able to rationalise subsidising businesses not as a subsidy to capitalists, but as helping modernise the national economy while supporting jobs in local communities. With a change in government such policies came to be portrayed as 'propping up' 'lame duck' industries and were no longer seen as 'common sense'. In Australia the rhetoric of neoliberalism condemned past approaches that were seen to 'pick winners' among industries, and instead new policies were promoted to create a 'level playing field' for all segments of the economy. In justifying changing approaches, the choice of 'evidence and experience' will also rely on a selective use of tools and information to evaluate a particular approach. In the case of regional industrial policies, economic evaluations tended to be preferred, using techniques such as cost per job and 'deadweight' to reveal high costs. Alternative evaluation approaches such as social audit (Haughton, 1987) failed to find favour, their emphasis on the economic and social costs to individuals, communities and governments of unemployment no longer deemed to be appropriate. In effect the new approach proclaimed that 'There Is No Alternative' to going with the grain of market forces rather than seeking to intervene to change the market.

Discourses manifest themselves in various ways, including meta-narratives which frame particular ideologies, institutional narratives which translate these into particular local contexts, and more personal narratives which embed them into everyday practices (Jessop, 1997). With governments seeking to draw business leaders into economic development institutions and programmes, the language of local economic development began to change to take on something of the meta-narratives, the language and the outlook of business. For instance, the work of the Harvard Business School guru Michael Porter on 'competitive advantage' found a receptive audience, particularly once he began to focus on regions and cities and started to promote the notion of industrial clusters. Work on sector studies returned to fashion, albeit with a different way of operating than in earlier incarnations, and focused on identifying growth clusters rather than problem sectors (Haughton and Thomas, 1992). With Porter's ideas finding rapid acceptance in New Zealand, Australia, the UK and the US in particular, cluster building became an accepted strategy in local economic development.

It is interesting to contrast the discourses and practices of cluster policies with those of the not dissimilar notion of growth poles, which had been popular 30 years earlier. Indeed, the rise to prominence of 'growth pole' thinking in the 1960s provided a precursor to later work on technopoles, science parks, 'clusters' and 'industrial districts'. Growth poles were intended to provide economic propulsion outside the main economic centres of a country, based on new large-scale industries, archetypically chemical or steel works, and sometimes relocated government functions, which would attract upstream and downstream users to locate close by, creating a growth pole effect. Policies were based on a specific narrative about the role of the state in developing the national space economy using the language of regional economic science, allied to discourses about the role of the state in working with large industries in the national interest. Growth pole policies quickly spread around the world, including to Australia, France and several Latin American countries, with policy makers drawing on a selective reading of the academic literature in this area. In contrast to contemporary work on clusters, growth poles were essentially state-centred investments, with the major propulsive operations at their core tending to be state-owned enterprises. Essentially Keynesian in nature, such large-scale state initiatives are no longer deemed acceptable or even feasible. Alternatively, as we write, cluster policy is extremely popular in Western nations; not only is it given credence by Michael Porter, it is less costly and works in ways which seek to influence and reinforce market trends rather than attempting to redirect market forces. In essence, discourses on the beneficial impacts of national planning and accords between business, government and labour unions have given way to those focused on the need to facilitate private enterprise. In terms of economic management, the state has shifted from rowing to steering, metaphorically at least.

The receptiveness of local economic development practitioners in the 1990s to the ideas of Michael Porter reflected an established trend for adopting language which emphasised a business oriented approach: Enterprise Zones were created, Task Forces set up, Development Corporations established. Allied to this was a 'can do' approach which saw problems as limited and resolved by the application of 'common sense' business approaches, which 'cut through' to the core of the problem. In the UK and the US local regeneration problems were portrayed as largely economic in nature and therefore amenable to market-based solutions. Social issues could be dealt with through 'trickle-down' benefits arising from wealth creation. Time-limited, locally applied business oriented agencies could move in, identify problems, establish solutions, make quick decisions, implement them, then pull out and move on. Mission accomplished. Except of course it rarely happened like that, given that the problems were rarely purely economic in nature, with intractable social and environmental issues rather messing up the neat business oriented view of economic and social renewal. With time the 'accepted wisdom' moved on again, with social criteria reinserted into regeneration efforts (Shutt, 2000; Shutt et al, 2001).

In a sense, 'business speak' has become the language of the all-pervading discourse of business first approaches to local economic development, and is also expressed through signs, symbols and other practices. Documents have become increasingly glossy, punchy, and business-like. As Chapter One suggested, practitioners assumed the garb of business and consultants, with designer clothing, well pressed for the 'business dynamos' or fashionably crumpled for 'creative types'; clothes made a statement. To be taken seriously by business, and by fellow practitioners, appearances became increasingly important. These discursive practices are critical in terms of how they consolidate and embed a sense of what is acceptable and accepted practice, and also for how they interpret alternative discourses as marginal, ephemeral, 'academic', 'woolly' or 'political'. Opposition can be neutralised in many ways, by counter-critique, by partial incorporation of alternative ways of doing things, or by requiring participants to adopt the practices of the dominant group in order to gain a voice.

Pre-eminent philosophies and practices are themselves always open to opposition and subversion. Experimentation and innovation are pivotal in the practice of L&RED, and this demands a degree of openness to new players, new ideas, new funding, new resources, and new policy approaches. In particular, grass-roots groups with their alternative perspectives and practices frequently possess a local legitimacy and community backing which makes it difficult to reject them out of hand. In each nation these processes are played out and give rise to suites of practices that fit within, and are predisposed by, each nation's institutional architecture. For example, the greater prominence of industrial recruitment within L&RED in Australia and the US compared with the UK is partly a function of the greater policy distance between national, state and local governments within federal systems. The practices that constitute L&RED in any nation arise out of four processes. First, L&RED activities are the product of learning and experiences. Individual agencies build upon their own experiences, but also learn from the success and failures of comparable organisations. This learning may be formalised through conferences, mentoring and conventions, or may arise spontaneously through casual interaction. Second, L&RED may reflect the ideologies and philosophies operating at a larger scale, with the UK's UDCs a prominent example. Third, conflict and dispute shape the pattern of L&RED activities. Conflict may be manifest in the form of community groups arguing for more direct control of the economic development agenda or may be more oppositional, directly challenging the projects and strategies of development agencies. Fourth, policy transfer is significant. Nations, regions and communities seek out international 'best practice' in framing their strategic plans and in selecting more effective mechanisms for encouraging growth.

England: community economic development versus 'trickle-down'

As an example of how discourses pervade policy choices, it is helpful to examine the European Commission's approach to competitiveness, in particular the Delors Competitiveness White Paper (EC, 1993). Rather than the prevailing Anglo-American emphasis on competitiveness as a process of wealth creation driven by private enterprise, where social benefits would arise from 'trickle-down' effects, in the European interpretation competitiveness meant more jobs as a means of addressing social exclusion and/or social inclusion. Inclusion and economic performance, and cohesion and competitiveness, were seen as complementary not conflicting issues. The term 'social exclusion' in particular was strongly resisted by Conservative UK governments in the early and mid-1990s, which saw it as a term which placed too much emphasis on negative processes and reflected an unpopular continental European philosophy. In order to find favour, writers of local economic development documents had to find ways of gaining the approval of European funding bodies without alienating the UK government. This called for a sparing use of social inclusion (never exclusion) and liberal use of terms such as 'wealth creation', 'competitive advantage' and promoting the interests of 'UK plc'.

The heated debates over inserting community economic development into the UK's regional structural plan submissions for European Commission funding very much reflected these debates. The central issue in this case was the UK government's resistance to the Commission's attempts to create a more community-oriented approach to run alongside more conventional economic measures in an effort to bring greater benefits to targeted local communities (Haughton et al, 1999). Operating here was a battle over both the language and the substance of how policy should be delivered. At an ideological level, the issue was whether to continue to wait for economic policy to 'trickle down' to the communities most in need, as neoliberal ideology suggested should happen, or to intervene more directly to ensure the benefits of regeneration were felt in the most needy areas. In practical terms the key issue was who should be the recipient of European funding – central government-appointed agencies at the local level, operating to a national rule book, or grass-roots community organisations using economic tools to address local social needs. Selective understandings pervaded these debates, influencing perceptions of what the problem was, economic or socioeconomic, which approaches were valid and which were not, and who might be considered as legitimate practitioners of the art and science of local economic development. In an interesting case of 'scale jumping', it was the EC which played the lead role in asserting a community based logic to programme delivery, aided by a team of English academics. At the time, after years of funding withdrawal, community economic development did not possess a strong institutional architecture, so it was supranational government that took the lead in arguing for a neighbourhood focus.

Australia: compete globally, lead locally

The discourse on L&RED in Australia remains in dispute because there are a number of competing ideologies. On the one hand, federal governments, and the economists that work for them (Industry Commission, 1996; National Commission of Audit, 1996), have argued that L&RED distorts markets, misallocates scarce public sector resources, and has little real impact. On the other hand, the 'realpolitik' of economic restructuring propels governments to intervene (McManus and Pritchard, 2000). Substantial shifts in policy are a recurring theme in the history of L&RED in Australia. In 1994, for example, Australia's federal government re-entered regional policy after a prolonged absence through the introduction of its Regional Development Program. In large measure this initiative was designed to kick-start regional economies made moribund by a government-induced recession (Beer, 1998), but rather than engaging in a conventional 'pump-priming' exercise, the government changed the nature and the direction of its assistance to focus on providing regions with the tools needed to compete in global markets. Overnight L&RED policy debates were transformed as the federal government used the mantra of 'Lead Local Compete Global' to encourage regions to embrace an ethos of self-reliance and global competitiveness (McKinsey & Co, 1994). State-based L&RED agencies quickly adopted similar philosophies and the face of L&RED in Australia was transformed.

The tension between neoliberal ideology and grass-roots political pressure for government intervention affects debates on L&RED in many and complex ways. For example, since the early 1990s state and federal government officials charged with implementing a neoliberal policy agenda have supported L&RED agencies because they are perceived as contributing to micro-economic reform and economic restructuring. On the ground, however, such niceties of economic theory tend to be irrelevant for the communities and regions that host these agencies. Instead they perceive L&RED agencies as important conduits for securing government grants. In this way the neoliberal discourse is combined with the practical concerns of regional communities to produce agencies that are seen to be legitimate both within broader policy frameworks and at the local level. The concerns of these communities are mainly in employment, incomes and service provision, and unlike in England or Northern Ireland, the community development movement has had limited involvement with economic development, and the social economy movement is weak.

US: from industrial recruitment to 'third wave' policies

In the US, L&RED is closely aligned with business. While community economic development is important, local economic development as such is focused on employment and investment growth. L&RED in the US is big business: the practitioner's professional association boasts over 10,000 members and virtually every local government, state government, and many Chambers of Commerce are active. L&RED in the US represents an interesting juxtaposition between neoliberal ideologies and corporate engagement, with many utilities (for example, electricity and gas) financially supporting economic development efforts as a mechanism for boosting their own markets. Moreover, corporations appear willing to participate in L&RED processes because they can see benefits for themselves (Henton, 1994; Saxenian, 1994). Neoliberal ideologies remain prominent, with conservative think tanks arguing against public sector handouts for business. Despite these arguments, locally based economic development efforts remain prominent, and L&RED as business is a powerful discourse in its own right. As will be shown in Chapter Four, this discourse exerts a significant influence on how practitioners frame and assess their actions.

L&RED in the US is directed at business, but what type of business, and how can the agencies best meet the needs of their communities? There has been a long battle over the meaning and purpose of L&RED, as advocates of 'third wave' policies (Eisinger, 1995) such as Ed Blakely (1994) have sought to replace industrial recruitment with policies and programmes that build the economic capacity of regions. Interestingly, 'third wave' approaches have enjoyed qualified acceptance at best (Isserman, 1994; Tietz, 1994), and the existence of competing paradigms of economic development highlights the contested and changeable nature of this field.

Northern Ireland: the rise of the social economy

The discursive construction of the terrain of L&RED takes on a new dimension when Northern Ireland is considered. Political activity in Northern Ireland reflects, in major part, historical differences between the Catholic and Protestant communities. The landscape for L&RED is made more complex by the fact that the two communities largely live apart and have separate concentrations of disadvantage marked by low incomes and high unemployment rates.

In the 1960s and 1970s Northern Ireland was one of the main UK regions that received regional assistance, mostly in the form of support for its traditional heavy industries plus money for attracting new businesses. An example was the use of substantial UK government funding for the short-lived DeLorean car venture near Belfast. In this case the Northern Ireland Development Agency was able to attract the company away from a deal nearing completion with Puerto Rico by providing substantial state funding. A key justification for this major government subsidy was the decision by the company to recruit equally from Catholic and Protestant communities in a deliberate attempt to build bridges between them. The resulting factory was established in 1975, and at its peak it employed 2,600 workers; all were laid off when the company went broke in 1982.

The outbreak of peace during the mid-1990s ushered in a new era for L&RED in the province, with EU and British government programmes explicitly changing approach, as the emphasis shifted to the support of local or community economic development and initiatives designed to build social capital within and across the two communities (Greer et al, 1999). This rapid rise of community-based groups in recent years reflects both local historical issues and also the influence of European Commission ideas, backed by its funding. As in England, the Commission's support for community economic development has been pivotal in changing approaches. It has directed funds into community organisations rather than through the departments of local, provincial or national government.

Discourses, narratives and international policy comparison

The approach adopted here suggests that one way of understanding the diversity of approaches in contemporary economic development practices is that they are rooted in a range of sometimes conflicting, sometimes complementary, discourses. Indeed, one of the implications of central government relinquishing its substantive role in the direct delivery of local economic policies is that this has opened up the space for alternative discourses and alternative practices to emerge.

While dominant discourses and practices have certainly arisen, these have not entirely displaced alternatives, which can be called on selectively to legitimate new policy regimes as circumstances permit. In fact, one of the interesting things about policies in this area is how alternative ideologies, rationales and discursive practices can combine to provide support for very similar policy approaches. But they can also be used to bring about change. Since gaining additional land rights in the early 1990s the Aboriginal and Torres Strait Islander people of Australia have challenged many assumptions about the nature, value and processes of economic development in non-metropolitan regions. Their capacity and willingness to block new developments, and their desire to achieve greater prosperity for their own communities, has forced a paradigm shift in how, and with whom, L&RED agencies consult, the issues they consider in developing projects, and the outcomes they seek to achieve. Significantly, a stronger role for Indigenous Australians has brought an additional impetus for L&RED.

For an international comparison such as this, a particularly intriguing issue concerns which approaches are *not* pursued in a particular nation. Different traditions and discourses can in effect deny legitimacy to a policy approach in one country that might be mainstream in another. For instance, in the US the principles of local tax raising powers and bonds are not questioned, although some of the projects they support are. In the UK by contrast, such approaches would be regarded as unacceptable by national policy makers, reflecting the different constitutional position and traditions of local government there, and also the resultant discursive techniques for rationalising the limitations on local government powers. Similarly, gambling – that is, the building of casinos – is an accepted mechanism for boosting the local economies of First Nation North Americans but comparable strategies have never been considered or conceived for Aboriginal Australians.

The issues raised in this type of analysis have some important implications for this research. First, the emphasis on discourses and the selectivity of ideas may help to explain some of the similarities and differences in approach that emerge between and within nations. While all four nations have L&RED policies, there are significant differences in the detail of their execution, application and objectives. Second, the dominant discourse will shape how practitioners responded to our survey. This is most evident in the individual's self-assessment of their organisation's activities and effectiveness. In nations where the economic development discourse is tightly focused on narrow economic objectives – such as the US – respondents are more likely to respond positively. Places where the discourse is broader and more complex are likely to result in a greater number of qualified evaluations. Alternatively, awareness of the material limitations imposed by a particular policy discourse may lead to more critical self-assessments. Third, it is helpful to highlight how L&RED discourse varies from nation to nation, time period to time period, and from region to region within nations.

The advantages of regional development organisations

L&RED organisations have a number of advantages for governments wanting to promote, or to be seen to promote, regional development. These advantages reflect the shifts in capitalist development, the rise of new policy instruments, the discourses used to promote particular courses of action, and the changing roles of governments. Governments garner at least three clear advantages through the delivery of L&RED programmes via specialist agencies. First, L&RED organisations are compatible with the neoliberal approach to economic management, in that their activities can be described as addressing local market failures in areas such as access to market information, training, capital, technological information or the provision of infrastructure (Danson and Whittam, 1999). This has not, of course, stopped many organisations from also providing subsidies for new investment, despite the heavy criticism of this type of development activity. Second, businesses often find it easier to work with agencies that are separate from the bureaucratic structure of state and national government departments, and independent agencies are often able to act more swiftly and more flexibly than a government department. Regional development organisations are therefore suited to the emphasis on public partnerships with the private sector, and on private sector-led local development. Their documents illustrate their adoption of the current dominant discourse. Third, an RDO is a visible symbol of a government's commitment to the development of a region, and can serve a useful political purpose (Halkier et al, 1998, p 18).

Recent work on institutions in regional economic development has emphasised issues such as the diversity of practices through which institutions and businesses can collaborate at the regional scale, in the process promoting the overall competitiveness of their regions. Typical themes in the 'new regionalist' literature include the role of L&RED institutions in promoting collaboration, innovation and learning; the need to develop regional social capital; and a recognition of the economic advantages of proximity and clustering. While it is often argued that nation states are losing their primacy in economic management, it is also contended that regions have become the level at which public policy can most effectively contribute to the growth of competitive industries and firms. Consequently, RDOs which can work across sectors and agencies are needed to bring together the ingredients required to support successful and competitive firms (Morgan and Nauwelaers, 1999; Keating, 2001; MacKinnon et al, 2002).

In particular, it is now widely argued that collaborative associations between L&RED agencies and professional associations, universities, business groups, trades unions, government departments and community-based bodies can all be positive features in promoting local development (Cooke and Morgan, 2000). Of particular interest is Amin and Thrift's (1995) work which suggests that productive regions are characterised by 'institutional thickness'. The argument here is not that it is necessary to create a particular critical mass of regional bodies, but rather that successful regions contain a set of interlocking working relationships that bind a diverse array of actors to the region. It is the functionality or success of the relationships that is important, rather than the presence or absence of particular types of institutions. These associations are important in that they facilitate learning, sharing and other forms of information flows, helping to mobilise responses to threats to the region, and embedding trust and social capital into collaborative ventures. The concept of institutional thickness can be criticised for creating a 'black box' that masks more fundamental processes (McLeod and Goodwin, 1999). However, it is a useful construct in this instance because it highlights the strong role institutional interrelationships can play in helping to strengthen local economies and in embedding firms into their regions.

Conclusion: local experimentation is conditional, learning is partial

This overview of the considerable literature on L&RED has necessarily been selective, focusing on two main themes. First, it has examined the changing approaches of the state to managing sub-national economies, highlighting the state's 'strategic selectivity' in reordering sub-national institutional architectures for L&RED activity. Second, debates about the social construction of knowledge have been linked to local economic policy, exploring how choices are made about what constitutes an appropriate problem area for policy intervention, and the appropriate range of policy instruments. We have argued that this approach is particularly helpful in understanding some of the differences between nations, while also helping to explain the different – and sometimes competing – approaches found within nations and indeed within local areas.

The analysis presented in this chapter has developed from Jessop's strategic-relational approach to state theory. Jessop's approach goes further than most in recognising the importance of political struggle and local contingency in understanding how and why different areas adopt different policy approaches. He recognises that it is important to look in more detail at how opposition to dominant ideologies is mobilised and how alternative discourses which challenge these ideologies and practices are articulated. Scale jumping and the diffusion of influence is one way that centralised power is challenged. A good example is the European Commission support for a neighbourhood-focused approach to local economic policy in the UK, an approach which went against the views of both national, provincial and local government officials in England and Northern Ireland. In this case supranational support could be used by community groups to overcome or bypass national opposition. In both countries, a vibrant social economy sector has now emerged which is actively engaged in ensuring that its voice is heard in policy debates at all scales, local through to supranational.

Australia and the US present somewhat different situations. Australia is similar to England and Northern Ireland in that central governments (state and federal) are able to control much of the L&RED activity in the nation, through the control of funding and their sponsorship of a number of organisations. It differs in that the community economic development movement has had limited involvement in economic development, and the social economy movement is poorly developed. While this may be changing, opposition to the dominant discourse is not as evident as in the UK, and grass-roots organisations tend to have the same objectives as central governments. In the US the strength of local government, the role of place-dependent economic interests, and the lack of strong involvement by the federal government has produced more independent L&RED organisations than in the other nations in this study. These organisations, however, are tightly focused on business development, and as the account of the US survey sample shows, community development is not seen as part of economic development. There are therefore contrasts between the nations in the degree to which organisations at the local and regional levels are able to set their own priorities and determine their own activities. Chapter Three shows that these priorities and activities vary considerably from nation to nation. However, all organisations are constrained by the wider tendencies within capitalist development – and their articulation within communities and regions – and we will only fully understand the processes shaping L&RED when we account for both broader trends and locality specific dynamics.

THREE

Local and regional economic development organisations in international comparison

Andrew Beer, Graham Haughton and Alaric Maude

This chapter discusses the commonalities and differences in L&RED across England, Northern Ireland, Australia and the US. It introduces the survey results with a broad-ranging overview, with more detailed analyses following in the individual national chapters. The focus of this chapter is on four themes: the institutional characteristics of the respondents; governance, partners and partnerships; the objectives, regional capacity building and business service activities of responding agencies; and the assessment of effectiveness. The emphasis here is on the aggregate data, with the national chapters providing more detailed breakdowns in order to analyse in greater depth some of the differences within each nation. In many instances in this chapter and subsequent chapters we separately discuss local government agencies and non-local government L&RED agencies. This distinction reflects the very substantial differences between the two in some nations.

Institutional architectures for local and regional economic development

The size of area served, the structure of the local or regional economy, organisation type, funding levels and staff resources can all in different ways influence how L&RED agencies set about developing their local economies and assessing their performance in this task. These institutional factors vary across nations according to historical and political circumstances, the structure of the economy and the system of government.

Some notable differences emerge when we examine the type of region served by respondents to the survey. This partly reflects the differing institutional approaches in each country and partly the differences in our sampling in each country. In Australia and Northern Ireland 40% of responding L&RED agencies were based in predominantly rural areas, compared to 23% in England and 36% in the US (Table 3.1). Australia's high rural response rate reflects the fact that regional development there has focused on non-metropolitan regions (see Chapter One), a political imperative reinforced by the traditional importance

Table 3.1: Types of area served by agencies (%)

	Australia	England	US	Northern Ireland
Predominantly rural	40	23	36	40
Predominantly urban	20	29	29	22
Mixed	40	48	35	38

of primary production and also discourses of non-metropolitan disadvantage and accusations of bias against 'country' areas (NSW Country Mayors Association, 1993).

Local governments were the most common *institutional type* to respond in Australia and England, accounting for around 60% of the total, while regional or local development boards/committees were the largest group of respondents in the US and Northern Ireland. The profile of L&RED respondents is discussed in more detail in the individual country chapters, but it is worth noting that in Australia and England the institutional landscape is dominated, at least numerically, by local governments, while in the US local government and regional development boards appear to be equally important. After years of domination from Whitehall and Stormont, recent years have seen a growth in independent organisations in Northern Ireland, many focusing on the social economy. The Northern Ireland responses pick up on this very diffuse institutional framework, which includes local or regional development boards, not-for-profit organisations, district partnerships and community forums.

The differences in formal *legal structure* across nations reflected the variation in broad types of organisation: most of the respondents in England and Australia came from agencies formally constituted as part of local government, while in the US not-for-profit companies and parts of local government were equally important. In Northern Ireland, not-for-profit companies were the most significant legal entity, followed by registered charities and local governments.

In terms of both *funding* and numbers of *staff*, English non-local government agencies tended to be the largest (Table 3.2). In part this reflected the focus in the English sample on the larger strategic players, but also the simple fact that English L&RED agencies tended to have a different orientation to their counterparts elsewhere, with responsibilities and budgets for regeneration programmes devolved to them from the national government and the European Commission. As has been discussed elsewhere (Gleeson, 2001; Beer et al, 2003), both the UK and the EU have regional development programmes far larger than any found in Australia and the US, resulting in relatively well-funded agencies. By contrast, agencies in the Northern Ireland sample tended to be much smaller, reflecting the inclusion in the sample frame of a large number of social economy agencies, many receiving European Commission funding. While Northern Ireland has participated in the regional programmes of the UK and the EU, its political and administrative history has meant that the mechanisms and agencies used to deliver L&RED vary between Northern Ireland and other parts of the UK. Almost one third of respondents from

Northern Ireland had a budget of less than one full-time salary. The low level of resources available to the agencies within their sector must challenge their capacity to achieve growth, a theme that will be pursued further in Chapter Seven. The US sample showed a substantial proportion of respondents came from mid-size to larger agencies, with 57% having budgets equivalent to between four and 50 salaries. Australian agencies exhibited a similar pattern, although generally smaller. Typically, Australian agencies had budgets equivalent to between two and 12 salaries. The larger size of the US agencies relative to those in Australia and Northern Ireland reflects the taxing autonomy of local governments, the considerable emphasis afforded economic development by governments, businesses and community groups, and the participation of infrastructure providers.

The sources of L&RED funding are dealt with in more depth in the individual national chapters. For each country the set of responding agencies reported a suite of funding sources, but that package of funding varied significantly across nations. International funding was especially important for agencies in the Northern Ireland sample, reflecting the levels of European structural funding in the province. However, funding from the provincial government and the

Table 3.2: Annual agency expenditure: % of respondents for local government and non-local government agencies

Average salary equiva-lents	Local government				Non-local government			
	Australia	England	US	Northern Ireland	Australia	England	US	Northern Ireland
<1	2.4	0.0	7.4	11.1	8.7	0.0	2.7	29.4
1-2	4.4	0.0	3.7	11.1	5.6	0.0	5.5	9.8
2-4	4.4	1.6	9.3	11.1	20.9	0.0	11.0	21.6
4-8	5.8	1.6	13.0	0.0	27.0	2.0	13.7	11.8
8-12	5.8	4.8	16.7	0.0	11.7	4.1	15.1	5.9
12-25	5.4	7.9	22.2	33.3	9.2	2.0	17.1	7.8
25-37	5.8	7.9	9.3	0.0	5.1	0.0	7.5	4.9
37-50	3.7	9.5	1.9	11.1	1.0	2.0	3.4	2.0
50-75	9.9	9.5	3.7	11.1	3.6	8.2	6.2	4.9
75-125	5.4	4.8	3.7	0.0	3.6	0.0	6.2	2.0
125+	46.9	52.4	9.3	11.1	3.6	81.6	11.6	0.0
Total %	100.0	100.0	100.0	100.0	100.0	100.0	100.0	100.0
Total *n*	294	63	54	9	196	49	146	102
Missing/ not stated	107	2	8	5	5	2	6	6

Note: 'Average salary equivalents' refers to multiples of the average annual salary in each of the survey countries, a device used to attempt to create a degree of cross-national consistency in measuring size. Respondents were asked to respond solely on the L&RED aspects of their organisation; however, not all took this into account, especially those in local government. The figures therefore overestimate the size of L&RED agency budgets, especially in the local government sphere. The data in the non-local government agency categories appears to be reasonably robust by comparison.

UK government was also important. Compared to Australia and the US, where very little funding came from international sources, English agencies too were often able to draw on international funding, mostly from the European Commission. National government funding – either directly or via RDAs – was important, and, to a lesser degree, local government funding. The most singular feature of the US funding regime was the extent to which local government actors were able to develop their own funding sources, in contrast to the heavy reliance on delegated budgets which marked the English and Northern Ireland sample in particular. This includes funds raised from the sale of goods and services, income received from property, and subscriptions. Interestingly, national government funding was unimportant in the US, but local government funding was significant. Australian respondents reported funding from a range of sources, with all three tiers – national, state and federal – making a significant contribution to the funding of the sector. These differences in how agencies are funded across nations are substantial, and, as we shall see later, had a bearing on the degree to which respondents felt that their effectiveness was hampered by funding restrictions of one kind or another.

Governance, partners and partnerships

As Chapter Two highlighted, there has been a growing proliferation and fragmentation of actors within L&RED, requiring the growth of improved processes of interaction between the multiplicity of agencies. The survey sought to examine these issues in a variety of ways, including studying the composition of the boards of agencies, the diversity of partners, and also the scoring of the relative importance of partners by individual respondents.

Most L&RED organisations have a board of management or equivalent body responsible for overseeing agency operations. The composition of these boards of management varied significantly across nations, reflecting their different jurisdictions, objectives and funding sources. A number of authors (McKinsey & Co, 1994) have argued that the composition of these boards can critically affect their prospects for success. Variation across nations in their composition may therefore affect outcomes. In England just under 60% of agencies had boards dominated by the government sector, although this may reflect the nature of the organisations we surveyed. By contrast, only 12% of respondents from Northern Ireland had boards dominated by the government sector, with mixed representation most common (39%). Importantly, however, the voluntary sector dominated the board of management for just over one third of organisations in Northern Ireland. By contrast, in Australia and the US representation was relatively evenly balanced between public sector, private sector and mixed representation.

Partners and partnerships were important in all four nations, with most respondents indicating that they work with a variety of types of partners. Overall there is a high degree of convergence in the emphasis given to particular broad categories of partners across nations (Table 3.3). In all four nations other

Table 3.3: Mean importance of partners, by type of partner

	Public sector	Other RDAs	Business sector	Community sector	Education, training and research sector	All partnerships
Australia	2.0	2.2	1.7	1.5	1.4	1.6
England	2.8	1.7	1.3	1.7	2.0	1.7
Northern Ireland	1.9	2.3	0.9	1.8	1.4	1.5
US	1.9	2.0	1.7	1.5	1.1	1.6

Scale: 0 = Not a partner, 1 = Mildly important, 2 = Moderately important, 3 = Very important.

L&RED organisations were important partners, suggesting a high degree of 'institutional thickness' under most circumstances. English respondents, however, were more likely to work with government bodies and placed a far greater emphasis on partnerships with education, training and research institutions. This reflects the prominence of the Local Learning and Skills Councils within the sample, and the very substantial efforts of the UK government to develop strong links between universities and their regions. Respondents from Northern Ireland were less likely than agencies from other nations to have partnerships with the private sector and, in common with England, were more likely to work with the community sector. This pattern of partnerships is consistent with the social economy focus of Northern Ireland's agencies and the flow of funding for EU and UK programmes.

In terms of the range of partners, over half the respondents from the US and Australia, and nearly half in England, worked with 16 or more types of partner. In all three countries less than 5% of agencies worked with fewer than five types of partner. This is a very high level of interaction between L&RED agencies and other organisations, and is indicative of a considerable level of information exchange and partnership, as many would work with multiple partners within each type. By contrast, broadly constituted partnerships appeared to be much less important among Northern Ireland respondents, with 12% reporting fewer than five types of partner and only 34% having more than 16 types of partner. The more restricted range of partners in Northern Ireland may well reflect both the small size of L&RED agencies in Northern Ireland and also the relatively narrow remit of many of those within the sample framework.

There are appreciable differences between the nations in the specific *types* of bodies L&RED agencies partner (Table 3.4). Across the four countries, local government emerged as the most important partner, with between 92% and 99% of respondents working with, or within, this tier of government. The strong relationship with local government is inevitable given that many agencies are part of local government, or are funded by local government. However, the strength of the relationship also seems to emphasise the important role of local legitimacy conferred by working with or within this tier of government (see Beer and Maude, 1997). National governments were important partners in

Table 3.4: Percentage of agencies reporting particular groups as 'partners' in promoting local and regional development

Partners	Australia	England	US	Northern Ireland
International organisations	32	41	29	56
National government departments/agencies	97	95	89	82
State/provincial government departments/agencies	99	17	99	94
Local government	98	92	99	97
Other regional/local organisations	97	97	93	94
Local venture capital providers	59	89	58	37
Banks and other financial institutions	63	36	89	57
Property developers and/ or retailers	78	52	85	42
Manufacturers	71	75	87	45
Public utilities (private or public ownership)	81	85	89	50
Other private businesses	90	76	85	75
Business groups (eg Chambers of Commerce)	93	91	95	76
Environmental groups	83	85	58	83
Indigenous groups	79	81	46	94
Other community groups	93	80	81	98
Universities	75	97	86	74
Technical education and further education agencies	86	90	82	86
Research and development organisations	77	97	62	76
Local political representatives	94	84	93	87
Trades unions	53	89	39	46

England and Australia, where they fund L&RED projects either directly or indirectly, but were of lesser importance in the US and Northern Ireland. State (US and Australia) and provincial (Northern Ireland) governments were important, but only 17% of English respondents indicated that they worked in partnership with regional government offices. Because of the international construction of the questionnaire we did not specifically ask about RDAs, and are therefore unable to comment on their role as partners of the responding organisations.

As might be expected, US agencies were the most likely to report private sector partners. The US had the highest percentage of positive responses with respect to banks, property developers and retailers, manufacturers and public utilities. Respondents from the US were also least likely to have partnerships with environmental groups, international organisations, research and development bodies and trades unions. There is an unequivocal business sector focus within L&RED partnerships in the US.

In England, the most distinctive finding is the high percentage of organisations having partnerships with further education colleges, universities and research organisations. It would probably surprise many environmental organisations to find that 85% of responding agencies regarded them as partners, and likewise the finding of high levels of partnership with trades unions is a slight surprise, perhaps revealing something of the extent of changes under the New Labour government. These remarkable findings are indicative of a broad attachment between L&RED agencies in England and public sector actors. As a group, respondents from England reported fewer partnerships with Chambers of Commerce, property developers, banks and other private businesses than for the US or Australia.

Partnerships in Australia were most notable for the strength of the links with government bodies with a direct influence on regional development outcomes, as well as the business sector. For Australian agencies key partners included Chambers of Commerce, private businesses, property developers, retailers and institutions of technical and further education. In contrast to the UK, where many of the partnerships with bodies such as universities, trades unions and research and development organisations were likely to generate substantial benefits in the long term, there is a greater sense of immediacy to the public sector partnerships of Australian agencies. State, federal and local government partnerships are important because they are central to agency funding and as sources of investment for their regions. Universities and research and development organisations are less important partners because it can be difficult to identify direct benefits from the relationship and any benefits accrue relatively slowly. Local political representatives were also very important in Australia – as elsewhere – with 94% of respondents indicating they were a partner. This high response reflects the centralised nature of government in Australia, and the need to influence federal and state politicians in order to secure funding and investment. Australian agencies, like those in the US, appear to have relatively weak connections beyond their national boundaries, although 32% reported a partnership with an international body.

Northern Ireland's L&RED agencies were leaders in their partnerships with international organisations, with 56% working with an international body. They also had near universal interaction with other community groups. These two key sets of relationships reflect the structure of the sector as a whole, since a substantial percentage of L&RED agencies in Northern Ireland are community groups who use EU and other international funding sources. Intriguingly, Northern Ireland had the lowest percentage of agencies working in partnership with national government departments, and relatively low levels of engagement with universities, research and development institutions and the property sector.

The objectives and activities of local and regional economic development agencies

This section introduces the survey findings on agency objectives, the services L&RED agencies provide to businesses, and regional capacity building activities. Once again, the section highlights only the broad patterns in evidence and leaves the more detailed analysis to the individual nation chapters.

Objectives

In many respects the objectives or goals of L&RED agencies are their most important characteristic: it is the objectives that largely determine the strategies employed, the partnerships that are established, the funding sources used and the criteria for assessing success or failure. All other dimensions of L&RED behaviour flow out of their objectives which are, in turn, shaped by the broader debates on public policy and the role of locality-based development.

Respondents were provided with a long list of possible objectives that they were asked to check and, if necessary, add to. Across all four of the study countries, promoting economic growth was an important objective of L&RED agencies (Table 3.5). In the US virtually all agencies reported that they held the promotion of economic growth as an objective, reflecting the strong pro-growth ethos of most US agencies. In contrast, in Northern Ireland only 65% of respondents cited the promotion of economic growth as an objective, which seems to reflect a greater concern with the *quality* of growth, in terms of both equity and the transparency of processes. This is perhaps not too surprising when it is remembered that community-focused agencies constituted a larger part of the Northern Ireland sample than in other nations. These are agencies that inevitably operate within rather different discourses about the meaning and values of L&RED. In England just under three quarters of respondents reported that promoting economic growth was an objective. While at a lower level than the US and Australia, it remained the most frequently cited goal. Like Northern Ireland, the lower priority awarded economic growth per se among English respondents relative to the US and Australia reflects the more complex debates surrounding L&RED.

Not only were US respondents strongly focused on economic growth, but they also tended to favour explicit employment and income growth objectives. Compared to the other countries, fewer US agencies were directly concerned to address the specific needs of low-income residents, or achieve broader 'quality of life' enhancements for their population. The US sample also showed the greatest percentage of agencies reporting that protecting or increasing the revenue base of local government was an objective. Given that both England and Australia had a higher percentage of returns from local governments, the priority awarded to this objective in the US does not simply reflect the population of agencies submitting returns. Instead it is indicative of the intense competition between local governments in the US, and the funding of L&RED

Table 3.5: Percentage of agencies reporting adoption of nominated objectives

Objective	Australia	England	US	Northern Ireland
Promote economic growth	81	74	93	65
Increase local incomes	26	35	51	33
Promote employment growth	65	48	75	58
Improve the quality of life of regional/local communities	68	61	67	79
Regenerate/revitalise regional/ local economy	54	67	55	61
Diversify regional/local economy	48	42	63	33
Protect/increase revenue base of local government	35	9	46	6
Retain/increase regional/ local population	44	12	27	27
Attract/recruit new businesses	61	47	75	41
Develop local businesses (start-ups, expansion, retention)	54	58	72	47
Build local partnerships between public agencies, private sector and community	61	66	56	69
Stimulate involvement of local people and entrepreneurs	50	44	39	68
Build capacity of the region/local area for development	53	37	54	44
Improve employment, incomes, welfare of disadvantaged groups	27	58	35	67
Promote environmentally sustainable regional/local economy	53	46	32	44
Advocate for/lobby governments on behalf of region/local area	57	40	26	41

agencies from local government taxes to both 'grow' businesses endogenously, and recruit firms into the region.

The pattern of objectives among Australia's economic development agencies exhibits a number of similarities with the US data. For example, in Australia there was a strong focus on promoting employment growth; agencies aspire to attract and recruit new businesses as well as develop local businesses. Australian agencies, however, tended to have broader goals than their US counterparts. Fully 44% of Australian agencies reported that retaining or increasing the population of the region was an objective, a far more common response than in the other surveyed nations. In large measure the relative importance of this objective reflects the rural basis of many agencies, the history of decentralisation initiatives, and contemporary debates about population loss from the country (Forth and Howell, 2002).

Few Australian L&RED agencies appeared to focus on meeting the needs of disadvantaged groups within their regions, and nor did they report playing a major role within local labour markets. In part this reflects broader factors – such as the functioning of the JobsNetwork, the national system for providing employment assistance – and the fact that urban regeneration initiatives in Australia focus narrowly on replacement of the housing stock, with only minimal attention to economic and labour market issues (Beer and Maude, 2002). This absence within the suite of objectives also reflects the very distinctive discourses and practices of 'economic rationalism', with its emphasis on market-led economic growth and low levels of state engagement with local economic development.

The objectives of English L&RED respondents proved to be more broadly focused than in either the US or Australia, in particular with more agencies awarding priority to meeting the needs of the poorer members of their communities. Importantly, when compared with the US and Australia, promoting economic and employment growth was seen to be a less important pathway to improving community well-being. English agencies tended to be concerned to revitalise or regenerate their local economy and saw the building of public/private/community sector partnerships as an important pathway.

As might be expected, there were many commonalities between the objectives of the Northern Irish and English agencies. Like the English, Northern Ireland respondents did not emphasise simple economic growth objectives but instead sought to improve the quality of life of local or regional communities. This was the most common objective among the agencies from Northern Ireland and reflects the manner in which the discourse on L&RED in that nation has been embedded in broader debates about community development and reconciliation. Objectives that are inclusive of the broader community are more important in Northern Ireland than in the other nations, including partnership building. There is a strong social economy sector in Northern Ireland and this was reflected in the two thirds of respondents who sought to improve the welfare of disadvantaged groups.

Business-related assistance

The survey focused on two types of L&RED activity. One set of questions focused on what we term 'business development', that is, those actions whose primary purpose was to either bring firms into the region, or assist the growth of existing firms. In essence the agencies were asked to indicate the range of services they provided to businesses. The second set of questions related to the broader 'capacity building' role of development agencies. These are interventions in the region's economy and governance that are not specific to individual firms or groups of firms, but instead have a more diffuse impact which it is intended would help build a region's capacity and improve its overall levels of well-being. While recognising that there are sometimes overlaps between the two categories of activity, this chapter – and subsequent chapters – considers each of these broad types of activity separately.

As with the data on objectives, there was considerable variation across nations in the business development activities of L&RED organisations (Table 3.6). However, unlike the objectives, no single business development activity or function stands out as the dominant approach across nations. This said, a high percentage of respondents from all four nations indicated that they assisted firms to gain access to government funds, and there was a comparable level of convergence around providing assistance with major events.

In contrast to the distinctive property/technology focus of English L&RED development agencies, 'facilitation' is the term that best describes the pattern of activities pursued by Australian respondents. In Australia the dominant activities were those which could be undertaken with modest expertise and resources: Australian respondents marketed their region; streamlined development approval processes; provided information on government programmes; helped in gaining access to government funds; assisted with major events; undertook urban business district development; and promoted tourism. Similar to the US, Australian respondents had relatively high levels of involvement in offering reduced taxes to firms and subsidising relocation, a finding reinforced by government analysis (Industry Commission, 1996). They had the smallest percentage of respondents engaged in the training and recruitment of labour.

The 'business first' ethos that pervaded the goals of US L&RED agencies was reflected in their day-to-day activities. Industrial recruitment is clearly a more important part of the work of US L&RED agencies than in the other nations. In other respects, US respondents tended to mirror trends in Australia. For example, Main Street or urban business development projects were important (with just over half of all respondents active in this field), and provision of information on government programmes was significant as was coordinating public sector processes. Overall, the 'flavour' of L&RED in the US was one centred on a combination of the provision of direct subsidies to firms and low-cost market facilitation roles. Policy activities which could be high cost or yield diffuse collective benefits, and those which have benefits that are difficult to measure – supply chain associations, business incubators and so on – were not favoured. The similarities between the US and Australia in the actions of L&RED are not coincidental: both have federal systems of government, and both societies favour market-based solutions to questions of economy and society. Moreover, as discussed in the previous chapter, there has been substantial policy transfer between the two nations, especially from the US to Australia.

In many respects, English agencies reported the most distinctive set of L&RED business development activities. They were far more likely to be involved in property-led developments and the types of assistance to firms discussed in the 'new regionalism' literature. For example, there was a high level of involvement with supply chain associations; a strong commitment to the development of industry clusters; assistance with ISO standards; and widespread application of small- and medium-sized enterprise support. English respondents were also much more likely to be involved in labour market training and recruitment than their counterparts in other nations. It is worth noting that many of the business service activities of English L&RED agencies are relatively high-cost

Table 3.6: Percentage of agencies reporting participation in business-related assistance within the previous two years

Function performed	Australia	England	US	Northern Ireland
Marketing the region and its facilities to prospective businesses	78	68	86	49
Operating a business incubator	20	43	19	27
Operating industrial estates or science parks	21	48	29	19
Other provision of land or buildings	40	55	45	26
If you are a government agency, offering reduced government rates, taxes or charges to attract or retain business	23	13	32	0
Subsidising relocation costs for businesses moving to the region	10	9	18	3
Assisting businesses with training or recruitment of labour	36	68	58	38
If you are a government agency, providing streamlined approval/ development processes	39	9	27	0
Coordinating the activities of public sector agencies to support business development	51	73	69	28
Providing general small and medium enterprise business support programmes	46	70	53	48
Assisting firms to access venture capital	25	24	37	20
Providing information on programmes of government departments and other agencies	74	69	81	58
Assistance in accessing funding and support services from governments at all levels	75	71	72	63
Assistance with technology transfer/innovation	31	33	35	33
Assisting firms to meet quality standards, whether those of their customers or ISO standards	14	27	15	14
Assistance, either financial or advisory, with marketing nationally	39	36	40	26
Assistance, either financial or advisory, with marketing internationally	21	26	20	20
Promoting supply chain associations	23	42	8	16
Assisting the development of industry clusters	36	56	33	24
Tourism promotion	74	64	56	46
Assistance with major or special events in the region	82	64	58	63
Urban business district development (Main Street)	62	33	54	25
Programmes to help people establish their own small business	44	65	52	53
Other local employment creation programmes	55	62	45	60

policy instruments geared to meeting the needs of emerging industries such as information and communication technology industries, research and development-based employment and office-based administration. The ability and willingness to fund such activities reflects the more substantial public sector intervention in the UK economy when compared with Australia or the US.

The prominence of community organisations exerted a profound impact on the types of business development activities undertaken by respondents to the survey from Northern Ireland. They indicated relatively little engagement with those aspects of L&RED work where economic development needs to be integrated with the formal processes of government. No respondents from Northern Ireland, for example, reported that they offered tax abatements, and nor did they have a role in streamlining development approval processes. Northern Ireland had the lowest percentage of respondents participating in a science park or industrial estate and in the provision of land or buildings. Many of the prominent activities in Northern Irish were also prominent in England. For example, some 60% of Northern Irish respondents were involved in other employment creation schemes, but in no cases did Northern Ireland record the highest percentage of responses for any activity. This suggests a relatively diffuse model of service delivery to businesses. Data on the number of business development activities showed that Northern Ireland's agencies had the smallest number of activities. It would appear, therefore, that the L&RED sector in Northern Ireland is comprised of a number of relatively small bodies that in total encompass a diversity of approaches to L&RED development, but individual agencies focus on a relatively limited number of activities. In short, it is a wide-ranging sector comprised of small, fragmented actors.

Regional capacity building

The nationally evident patterns within business services were not as pronounced when we examined the data on the types of regional capacity building activity undertaken by responding agencies. Some activities – such as analysis of the local or regional economy – were important in all four nations. But in other spheres of practice the administrative and political circumstances of each nation have resulted in a distinctive pattern of activities (Table 3.7). In some areas the US and Australia have similar patterns of responses, but in other types of capacity building activity there is greater commonality between Australia and England, or the US and England. There is, however, evidence of convergence around governance issues for the three largest nations, with comparable responses for England, Australia and the US. Northern Ireland's respondents were less likely than agencies from the other three nations to be involved in issues of local governance, reflecting both the nature of the sample and the administrative circumstances of the province.

US and Australian respondents were far more likely to be involved in the provision of local or regional infrastructure and telecommunications than those

Table 3.7: Percentage of agencies reporting participation in nominated forms of regional capacity building within the previous two years

Function performed	Australia	England	US	Northern Ireland
Improvement of regional/local physical infrastructure (eg roads, railways, utilities)	73	49	79	25
Improvement of regional/local telecommunications infrastructure	55	23	51	8
Improvement of regional/local service provision (such as education or medical services)	50	50	36	33
Development of planning for business sites and premises	50	65	73	28
Education and training for youth not targeted to a specific firm/enterprise/business	37	66	32	58
Education and training for minority groups not targeted to a specific firm/enterprise/business	24	53	22	23
Education and training in general not targeted to a specific firm/enterprise/business	34	69	42	56
Improving regional/local economic development strategic planning and implementation capacity	71	72	81	51
Analysis of the regional/local economy	61	80	67	47
Developing cooperation and networking between firms and relevant public and private sector agencies and institutions	58	68	62	49
Coordinating government programmes	55	63	61	25
Acting as a lobbyist for the region/local area with governments	70	60	46	43
Identification of business opportunities or gaps in the regional/local economy and implementation of strategies to fill them	54	51	51	46
Attempting to influence land use regulations and planning decisions that impact on business	45	43	49	19

from Northern Ireland or England. Respondents from England and the US were most likely to plan and develop business sites and premises, reflecting the long engagement with property-led development in both nations.

Skills development and labour market training is clearly a more dominant discourse and activity within the UK than in Australia or the US, with respondents from England heavily engaged in education and training for young people and minority ethnic groups. In Australia and the US, labour market training was relatively unimportant, while respondents in Northern Ireland engaged in education and training for youth and generally, but not for minority groups. Northern Ireland's political circumstances may make the targeting of programmes to specified groups difficult.

The processes of local governance and the development of land drew considerable convergence across nations, with approximately half of all respondents from Australia, England and the US indicating that they attempted to influence land use regulations and planning decisions that affected business. This applied to both local government-based respondents as well as those outside local government. Roughly 60% of respondents from the same three nations attempted to coordinate government programmes locally, and between 71% and 81% sought to improve local or regional strategic planning. Between 58% and 68% of respondents from this group indicated that they sought to foster stronger networking between firms and public and private institutions. Approximately half of respondents from England, Australia and the US – and 46% from Northern Ireland – said that they attempted to identify gaps within their regional economies, and develop strategies to fill those gaps.

Overall, Northern Ireland has the most distinctive pattern of capacity building activities and this, no doubt, is tied to the number of community sector respondents. The data suggest that the small size of many agencies in Northern Ireland, and possibly the community focus, may limit the capacity of many agencies to engage in regional capacity building. This impediment was less evident in the provision of services to businesses.

The impact and effectiveness of agencies

Despite the vast consulting and academic industry claiming to evaluate the impacts of economic development programmes in objective and value-free ways, the quasi-scientific measurement of effectiveness in L&RED is largely an illusion, a fact reflected in the evaluation criteria applied by some government programmes (Hughes, 1998; Mack Management Consulting, 1998). In this book we eschew the usual technical apparatus of multipliers, deadweight, opportunity costs, and even social audits, in favour of a much simpler approach of asking those directly involved what works best for them and what does not. Intriguingly, while there are many examples of surveys which ask what types of policy work best, and why, there are very few that have ever before asked what does not work, and why. The result is some fascinating insights, which go some way beyond those in previous studies. Using this information base we draw conclusions about how 'success' in L&RED is perceived and constructed in each nation, and whether the differing national perceptions of success and impediments give rise to policy lessons that can be transferred across and within nations.

At the core of the analysis is a consideration of the practitioners' own assessment of their organisations' impact, along with an examination of the range of factors that respondents see as limiting their effectiveness. This analysis is combined with questions on the evidence base used in forming these judgements, as well as the data on the types of business service and regional capacity building activities undertaken, to triangulate, or cross-check, the results. This said, there are limits to this approach. In presenting this data we do not claim that self-evaluations provide definitive insights into the effectiveness and operations of L&RED agencies. They do, however, shed light on the perceptions of practitioners about what works best, and what impedes successful action.

Self-assessment

The questionnaire asked practitioners to make an assessment of their agency's effectiveness 'in achieving its local or regional development objectives, on a scale of 7 (major impact) to 1 (no impact)'. The same question was asked in all nations thereby allowing comparison across borders and types of L&RED agency. Clearly this question will elicit subjective responses. Variations will reflect not only individual prejudices, but also differences in the discourse of L&RED across nations, as well as institutional factors. Practitioners are likely to rate their effectiveness according to their day-to-day understanding of L&RED and its objectives; the mission statements and objectives of their organisation; their perception of their agency's standing; and evidence to hand of their level of achievement.

Across the four nations there was a relatively high degree of commonality in the practitioner assessments of effectiveness (Figures 3.1 and 3.2). Most respondents in all four nations reported that they had an appreciable impact on their region, with a small percentage offering a negative evaluation, and a somewhat larger group assessing their effectiveness very highly. There were, of course, variations across nations. Critically, the variation between and within nations suggests that respondents were discriminating in their assessment of their effectiveness, and did not simply award themselves the highest possible assessment.

Our discussion of the objectives of agencies noted the tightly focused attention to economic concerns and the interests of business among US respondents to the survey. This business focus was reflected in the assessments of the impact of their organisation: more than 15% of respondents from both local government and non-local government agencies reported that they had a major impact on their region. By contrast, the L&RED discourse is more complex in England, based on a wider engagement with the problems of local areas, meaning that the assessments of practitioners tended to be more qualified and judged against

---

Figure 3.1: Respondent assessment of effectiveness, local government

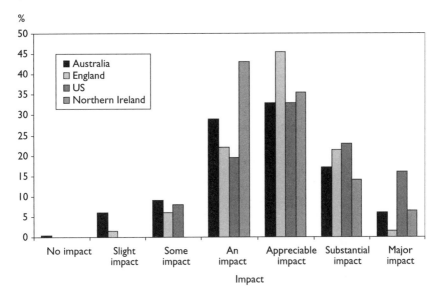

Figure 3.2: Respondent assessment of effectiveness, non-local government

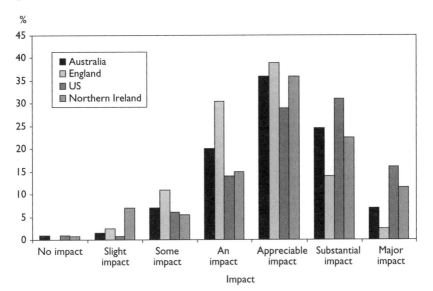

wider ranging criteria. It is therefore not surprising to find that only 2% of English respondents felt that their agency had a major impact on their region.

Respondents from Northern Ireland had a positive attitude to the effectiveness of their agency. No respondents based within a local government rated their agency's effectiveness as less than 3 (no impact, slight impact, some impact) while 6% felt they had a major impact on their region, and 14% reported a substantial impact. Those working within the non-local government sector were more self-critical in their evaluations, with 12% placing their agency's effectiveness within the bottom three categories. On the other hand, an equivalent percentage of respondents from this sector felt that their agency had a major impact. The key issue here is the substantial scale of the local economic problems faced by some agencies and the relatively low levels of funding and staffing with which they were able to address these issues.

Australian respondents generally reported that their agencies had modest achievements, and local government respondents were more critical than those working within the non-local government sector. This pattern is the reverse of the outcomes for England. The more positive attitude of non-local government respondents reflects the fact that many local governments in Australia have an ambiguous relationship with L&RED, with relatively limited funding and equivocal community support for efforts in this area. It is also worth noting that Australian practitioners considered their agencies had a more positive impact in 2001 than five years previously (Beer and Maude, 2002).

Impediments to effectiveness

Respondents were asked to indicate from a list which factors impeded the operations and effectiveness of their agency. The list of potential impediments presented to respondents included the level of funding provided; the duration of funding; skill shortages among the agency's staff; the absence of regional leadership; and the presence or absence of local businesses in the management of the agency.

There were significant differences between nations in how commonly respondents recognised problems in achieving their goals. Respondents from Northern Ireland were almost twice as likely as those from the US to report problems, while Australia and England fell between the two (Table 3.8). The lower recognition of problems among US agencies may reflect the much greater ability of some agencies to generate their own funding, most notably through the local tax base in the case of local governments.

Overwhelmingly, and across all nations, financial matters were seen to generate the greatest barriers to achieving the agencies' objectives. Some 60% of Australian respondents indicated that the lack of untied funding and the absence of funding for 'core business' limited their effectiveness. Too much time spent seeking funding and the short duration of funding were also significant problems. The other nations reported a similar mix of impediments, although there were notable variations in order and magnitude. In Northern Ireland, and England

Table 3.8: Most significant impediments to agency effectiveness

Rank	Impediment	% of respondents[a]
	Australia	
1	Insufficient untied funding to use as leverage with other agencies	60.2
2	Lack of funding for core business	60.1
3	Short duration of much of the funding	53.2
4	Too much staff time spent seeking funding	48.5
5	Priorities of funders have more influence on organisation than region's needs	47.4
	England	
1	Short duration of much of the funding	65.2
2	Inflexible rules and guidelines of funders	59.5
3	Insufficient untied funding to use as leverage with other agencies	54.9
4	Lack of funding for core business	52.7
5	Priorities of funders have more influence on organisation than region's needs	48.6
	US	
1	Lack of funding for core business	45.2
2	Insufficient untied funding to use as leverage with other agencies	41.3
3	Short duration of much of the funding	36.1
4	Priorities of funders have more influence on organisation than region's needs	29.3
5	Inflexible rules and guidelines of funders	28.9
	Northern Ireland	
1	Short duration of much of the funding	80.7
2	Lack of funding for core business	69.4
3	Inflexible rules and guidelines of funders	67.9
4	Too much staff time spent seeking funding	67.6
5	Insufficient untied funding to use as leverage with other agencies	65.7

Note: [a] % of respondents agreeing that each represents an impediment.

too, funding issues dominated concerns about impediments to effectiveness. Factors such as inadequate skills among the organisation's staff, an absence of regional leadership, and the capacity of the agency to offer itself as an independent and legitimate representative of its region were not among the most significant impediments to effectiveness in any nation.

The influence of funding concerns on the self-evaluations of practitioners becomes more apparent when the questions are summarised into three types of response: problems in the funding of agencies; problems in coordinating regional interventions; and limitations in the capacity of agencies (Table 3.9). Funding constraints were perceived to be the greatest impediment to effectiveness in all four nations, followed by problems in coordination at the regional level, and limitations in the capacity of agencies. Respondents from Northern Ireland recognised greater dimensions of difficulty in all three areas of their work.

Table 3.9: Constraints on effectiveness, by type of constraint

	Funding constraints	Regional coordination constraints	Capacity constraints
Australia	4.3	3.4	3.4
England	4.3	3.3	3.1
Northern Ireland	5.1	4.5	3.6
US	3.4	3.0	3.1

Note: 1 = 'Strongly disagree' or 'Not a problem' and 7 = 'Strongly agree' or 'Major problem'.

It would be reasonable to expect that larger agencies that are engaged in more activities, working with more partners, and seeking to achieve a greater range of objectives, would rank their effectiveness more highly. We were able to use correlation analysis to show that this held true for some nations: in Australia there was a strong and statistically significant relationship between the self-evaluation and the number of agency objectives, the number of business service activities, the number of regional capacity building activities, and the number of partners[1]. These relationships were also evident in the US, although to a lesser degree. Respondents from US local government L&RED organisations did not relate assessments of effectiveness to the number of partners or the number of objectives, and the relationship between the number of services provided to businesses and the evaluation was significant but at a lesser level. In all other instances there was a statistically significant relationship between activity levels and the self-assessment of effectiveness. In Northern Ireland there was a statistically significant relationship between self-assessment and the number of business service activities for all respondents, and for respondents based outside local government, but no other relationships were significant. There were no statistically significant relationships between levels of activity and evaluation scores in England.

Essentially, the statistical analysis shows that in Australia the more objectives, functions and partners an organisation has, the higher the self-evaluation of effectiveness. In the US, similar relationships apply but to a lesser degree; in Northern Ireland respondents tend to rate themselves more highly if they offer a larger range of business-related services, although this did not apply in the community sector. In England, the number of partners, objectives and activities had no observable influence on how respondents rated the effectiveness of their organisation.

The differing relationships and outcomes across the four nations are potentially subject to a range of interpretations. It may simply be the case that the survey instrument was more effective in measuring the performance of Australian and US agencies than those in England, and that this measurement error has masked fundamental relationships. Alternatively, we might tentatively argue that for any respondent, success in L&RED is a social construct and the understanding of what constitutes success differs substantially between Australia at one extreme, and England at the other. English respondents, working in an environment that takes a broader and longer-term view of L&RED, might be less likely to equate levels of activity with achievement. Australian respondents, with their focus on the need to secure funding which is often only available in the short term, and their use of multiple public sector income streams, might be likely to equate greater activity levels with success in securing funding and a more prominent profile within their region.

Assessments of most and least effective actions

Self-reporting can be used to determine which actions or strategies are perceived to be most effective. Respondents were asked to nominate their most and least effective activities. These responses were written on the questionnaires and then encoded during data input. Multiple answers were recorded for each respondent and the number of times each strategy or action was mentioned then calculated (Table 3.10).

There is a remarkable degree of consensus among practitioners from all nations about what constitutes the most effective L&RED activity. In all four nations practitioners most frequently nominated the provision of business advice and services as their most effective activity. This outcome is entirely consistent with writings on 'third wave' approaches to L&RED (Isserman, 1994; Tietz, 1994), but the level of convergence is surprising. Respondents to the survey also clearly valued networking and partnership building, ranking it in the top five most effective actions in all instances. As would be expected given their concentration of effort in this field, respondents from Northern Ireland and England considered training and labour market programmes were effective, as were property-related initiatives, such as business incubators and site development. In both England and the US, inward investment and the promotion of the region were ranked in the top five effective activities. However, the tensions inherent in industrial recruitment were reflected in the fact that in both nations a higher percentage of respondents (24% and 18%) nominated inward investment and marketing their region as their least effective activity. As Loveridge (1996) has argued, industrial recruitment is a high risk, potentially high return activity, and some will be successful while others will fail.

Respondents were less clear on what constituted their least effective activities. Many indicated that they could not identify ineffective activities, or nominated actions specific to their own circumstances. Marketing was clearly a challenge for many respondents in the US. Some types of activities were perceived to be very effective in one nation, but ranked among the least effective in others. Labour market programmes were among the most effective activities reported by respondents from Northern Ireland and England, but were seen to be one of the least effective activities in Australia. Similarly, land preparation and site development was a highly regarded activity in England, but considered a less effective strategy in Australia. Differing institutional contexts, and widely varying opportunities to act within the economy clearly influence how respondents evaluated individual strategies.

Table 3.10: Five most commonly reported most and least effective activities or strategies

Rank	Most effective activity	% respondents[a]	Rank	Least effective activity	% respondents[a]
	Australia			*Australia*	
1	Business support/advice	21	1	Other	16
2	Infrastructure development/service provision	15	2	Inward investment/ promotion of region	14
3	Networking/partnerships	14	3	Some types of business assistance	10
4	Sector planning/ development	10	4	Land preparation/site/ premises development	6
5	Tourism promotion/ special events	10	5	Training skills/labour market programmes	5
	England			*England*	
1	Business support/advice	23	1	Inward investment/ promotion of region	24
2	Training skills/labour market programmes	18	2	Other	16
3	Land preparation/site/ premises development	10	3	Can't say, unable to determine	11
4	Networking/partnerships	10	4	Training skills/labour market programmes	7
5	Inward investment/ promoting the region	10	5	Business support/advice	7
	US			*US*	
1	Business support/advice	19	1	Marketing generally	22
2	Land preparation/site/ premises development	16	2	Inward investment/ promotion of region	18
3	Provision of grants or loans for development (including to businesses)	15	3	Other	17
4	Networking/partnerships	13	4	Some types of business assistance	6
5	Inward investment promoting the region	11	5	Business support/advice	5
	Northern Ireland			*Northern Ireland*	
1	Business support/advice	27	1	Other	32
2	Training skills/labour market programmes	24	2	None	7
3	Working with the community sector	19	3	Working with the community sector	7
4	Networking/partnerships	14	4	Inward investment/promotion of region	4
5	Managed workspaces/ business incubators	10	5	Tourism promotion/special events	4

Note: [a] % of respondents to include this activity as one of their responses.

Conclusion

This chapter has considered some of the key findings from the survey of L&RED agencies, and considered the similarities and differences between nations. While the institutional architecture and practice of L&RED in each nation is unique, there is a remarkable degree of commonality across nations. There is no more telling indicator of the convergence in L&RED than the fact that in all four nations the provision of business support and advice was considered the most effective strategy available to the respondents, and networking and working in partnerships was also important in all four nations.

The responses from the survey suggest that in all four countries there are unique elements in the way L&RED is pursued. In Northern Ireland the community sector was prominent among respondents; in the US there was a clear focus on meeting the needs of business and achieving economic growth, and limited attention paid to other dimensions of well-being. The institutional architecture and practice of L&RED in England was characterised by longer-term agendas, a property focus and the adoption of sophisticated techniques for encouraging endogenous development. L&RED in Australia shared some features with the US, but its system of funding and the focus on facilitating development within its region distinguished it from the others. The differences across nations are particularly evident when the regional capacity building and business service activities of agencies are considered. Australian and US respondents, for example, were more heavily involved in Main Street or urban business development activities, while English and Northern Irish respondents were largely unfamiliar with this approach. Respondents from England were more likely to report the use of 'new regionalist' business capacity building approaches to L&RED, including the development of supply chain associations, business clusters and business incubators.

The self-assessments of practitioners demonstrated broad convergence in how responding practitioners rated their performance across the four nations, but significant differences in detail. We cannot escape the conclusion that in large measure the differences in evaluation between nations reflect the very different discourses surrounding L&RED and the degree of autonomy available to organisations. The relatively uncomplicated business orientation of L&RED efforts in the US result in clearly defined strategies and actions and self-confident evaluations among practitioners, while the broader aspirations for local economic development in England seemed to result in more cautious assessments. Funding regimes cut across and reinforce these differences. In the US, L&RED organisations typically enjoy a relatively high degree of autonomy in their funding and this contributes to their positive self-assessments. By contrast, the centrally controlled funding regimes of England and Australia limit the independence of L&RED organisations and contribute to a more cautious assessment of achievement. Effectiveness in L&RED, therefore, may be an issue of governance.

The practitioner assessments of effectiveness also force us to re-evaluate our assumptions about what constitutes good practice and capacity within L&RED. The small size and limited resources available to the respondents to the survey in Northern Ireland might imply that these bodies are relatively powerless and, potentially, ineffectual. The positive self-evaluations from Northern Ireland, however, suggest that there are dimensions of community-based models of economic development that appear to compensate for the small size of the individual actors. Smaller, community focused approaches to L&RED may represent a genuine alternative, or at least parallel, to large-scale organisations. Their relative independence in funding and political control may be one contributor to their apparent effectiveness, although this may come at a cost, as reflected in the substantial challenges reported by respondents from Northern Ireland.

Note

[1] Significant at the 0.5 level, for a two tailed test, using Spearman's Rho.

FOUR

Local and regional economic development in England

Graham Haughton

Introduction

Background to local and regional economic development in England

L&RED activity in England has grown enormously since the 1970s, emerging as a professionalised field of activity employing substantial numbers of people in a growing range of organisations. From its initial roots in central government regional policy in the immediate post-war years and the 1960s, the focus began to shift in the 1970s towards local activities as regional policy was reduced in scale and area coverage. In these early years local economic development functions tended to be linked to local government planning departments, reflecting the strong emphasis at that time on land and property development. Quite quickly, however, separate economic development departments started to be established during the 1970s and early 1980s (Sellgren, 1989), while the range of activities began to broaden to include other approaches, including small business support, skills and training, and providing loans and grants. The most strongly developed local economic development functions tended to be in the larger metropolitan local governments.

Following a change in national government in 1979, some of the larger Labour-controlled urban local authorities began a short-lived experiment with radical local initiatives, which aimed to act as an intellectual counterweight to the national policies and also as a local palliative to growing local unemployment problems. The result was a series of innovative experiments, from supporting cooperatives to loans and grants for firms willing to work with local authorities to create or protect local jobs (Cochrane, 1987). Government cutbacks in funding for local government, increased centralised control of government-funded programmes, restrictive legislative changes, the use of alternative local delivery agencies and the shift towards highly audited competitive funding regimes all meant that this challenge to the dominant national approach was short-lived. That said, this period left a substantial intellectual legacy that continues to influence policy through to today. For instance, the Sheffield

Employment Department was a pioneer in creating a local cultural quarter in the city during the early 1980s, an approach that would now be regarded by many as mainstream, yet at the time was regarded as a radical departure.

As Chapter Two highlighted, the 1980s and 1990s saw a proliferation of new local economic development bodies, acting as alternatives to local government in many instances, with funding and powers diverted particularly to private sector-led bodies with very different intellectual agendas from those of the previous pioneers in local economic development. Of these, the best funded agencies were the property-oriented UDCs and the Training and Enterprise Councils (TECs), the latter responsible for allocating central government funds for labour market support and small firms advice. Almost inevitably, local 'turf wars' sprung up between these new institutions and the existing institutions of local economic development, especially the local authorities (Haughton et al, 1997; Haughton, 1999b; Imrie and Thomas, 1999; see also Case Study 4.1).

In the early 1990s the national political climate started to change, with more open partnerships becoming the preferred policy vehicles for centrally funded programmes of local economic development. In broad summary, this process has seen the position of local government strengthened somewhat after a decade or so of struggling to retain its power base in this policy area. Meantime, the private sector has remained important but lost the assumption of primacy, while the community sector has gradually moved closer towards centre-stage.

Case Study 4.1: Turf wars in Leeds, 1988-2003

Through most of the early 1980s the dominant L&RED agency in the city was Leeds City Council's in-house economic development unit. Then in 1988 central government designated a UDC to cover parts of the city, a proposal initially opposed by the local authority, which in retaliation vested much of its land in the designated area in a public–private partnership of its own creation, the Leeds City Development Company, run with private bodies sympathetic to its aims. The advantage of this manoeuvre was that the UDC could take land from the local council fairly readily, but not from a private body. Responding pragmatically to the imposition of a UDC in its boundaries, the council quickly decided to work with it, with some representation on its boards (Haughton and Whitney, 1994; Haughton, 1999b). In similar vein, in 1989 the government created a private sector-led TEC for the city, which again the city council opted ultimately to work with, although an undercurrent of fractious relations remained through its early years.

In an attempt to ease some of the frictions emerging, in 1990 the city leaders established a city-wide regeneration partnership, the Leeds Initiative. This was intended to be a strategic venture alliance of the local council, Chamber of Commerce and other key major institutions of the city, including the two universities and the local media (Haughton, 1999b). Later in the decade, with a change of local leadership, a change in national government, plus local challenges to its legitimacy, the board of the Leeds Initiative was broadened to include community organisations and others (Haughton and While, 1999).

Added in to this, despite attempts to rationalise the number of funding regimes during the early 1990s, since 1997 there has been a proliferation of initiatives under New Labour, including both full-blown programmes and a series of 'pathfinders', 'pilots' and 'prototypes'.

Different agencies have assumed the lead role in different forms of policy intervention, in part reflecting a growing specialisation within the field, for instance with Business Links taking the lead role in business advice services. Where once strategy and delivery both tended to be undertaken within the large institutions of L&RED, increasingly delivery is contracted out to a range of delivery agencies in the public, private, education and voluntary sectors, many of which have sought to broaden their base to become 'partnerships' in some form or another. An early Audit Commission (1989, p 1) review of urban economic regeneration had talked of the "patchwork quilt of complexity and idiosyncrasy" and the confusion this caused. Likewise, the rules of the game were argued to be "over complex and sometimes capricious", encouraging compartmentalised rather than coherent approaches. The support for more partnership working and the rationalisation of government programmes in the early 1990s were intended to bring some greater coherence to this policy area. However, nearly a decade later in its revisit to local economic policy the Audit Commission (1999) still found massive complexity, creating a maze of policies, strategies and actors, intimidating to clients and time-consuming for those engaged in delivery.

The Audit Commission (1999) further argued that the proliferation of partnerships and cross-cutting strategies has not always been productive, with many strategies and partnerships superficial in nature. This finding resonates with those from Wong's (1998) survey of local economic practitioners, which highlights how partnerships are often rather ill-balanced affairs, with private sector partners bringing little in the way of financial resources, leaving central government and the European Commission as the main funders of local economic development, both acting in highly conditional ways. Wong (1998, p 477) aptly summarises the current situation as being one where: "local partnerships in Britain are very much led by the public sector under a semi coercive framework from central government".

It is in this broad context that contemporary L&RED activity in England needs to be situated, where the rhetoric remains of a flexible and business-led approach, while the reality is one of centrally imposed frameworks and limited, highly conditional private sector engagement. Despite such concerns, L&RED is now a relatively mature and geographically widespread policy area, which has a wide range of tools at its disposal. These have tended to become associated with a range of specialist agencies, not just local government, meaning that there is a range of sometimes competing, sometimes complementary strategic and delivery agencies on the scene in most localities. The growing range of policy tools has been accompanied by an intriguing growth in the intellectual rationales for particular types of policy intervention, 'market failure' in land and labour markets, to 'social exclusion' approaches to addressing local areas of deprivation. Linked to this, different types of agency tend to have different mandates handed down from central government, often linked to quasi-independent organisational 'vision' statements. In the case of local government, their role has been strengthened under New Labour, including a new duty to promote the economic, social and environmental well-being of their areas (Audit Commission, 1999), a rather general statement which has the advantage of justifying a relatively wide range of activities, including local economic development.

The survey

Of the 477 organisations contacted, 117 returned completed forms. The response rate of 25% was rather lower than in similar surveys, such as the Audit Commission's (1999) 37% for its survey of local authority economic development and the 31.5% for the similar Local Government Association (Bennett and LGA, 1998) survey in England and Wales. A mixture of survey fatigue and the lack of official backing may explain the slightly lower response rates.

Of those responding to the survey, 61% (n=71) were from local government, while 39% (46) were non-local government agencies. Following the abolition of TECs in early 2001, much of the national funding for local labour market initiatives is now channelled through a newly created national network of Local Learning and Skills Councils and a similar network of Business Links. In the survey, 19% (22) of respondents were from Local Learning and Skills Councils, which administer funding for adult and youth training, including further education. A further 9% (10) of respondents were from Business Links. Neither type of organisation has a wide-ranging direct mandate for local economic development in the way that TECs felt they had, but both undertake specialised aspects of local economic development activities. Because of this, both Local Learning and Skills Councils and Business Links are almost inevitably involved as partners in other local economic development activities in their areas. Of the remaining respondents, 9% were local regeneration or local strategic partnerships, involving a wide variety of local organisations and 2% were either Chambers of Commerce or a similar business association. Because of the sampling framework adopted, community-based initiatives are not included directly, although all of the other organisations will be involved in working with, and in most cases helping fund, community economic development organisations.

Thinking about organisational status in a different way we asked about the legal status of each organisation. This found 55.6% (n=65) were part of local government, slightly down on the proportion which had claimed they were part of local government in the earlier question, a response which may have come from the option to count themselves as a statutory authority. Just under 12% (14) of responding organisations had private company (not-for-profit) status, while 3% (4) were constituted as private companies for profit and one was a company limited by guarantee. Of the remainder, four were informally constituted groups while 29 classified themselves as some variant of a statutory authority, non-departmental public body or government-established board.

To give a sense of longitudinal development, reference is occasionally made to findings from previous surveys of L&RED, notably those in 1981 and 1987 (Sellgren, 1991) and 1998 (Bennett and LGA, 1998; Audit Commission, 1999). However, it must be stressed that these studies are referred to for indicative purposes only. All of these earlier studies only covered local government activities, none used exactly the same terminology and questions as our survey and indeed most of them extended their remit beyond England to cover Wales or the whole of Britain. Their value then is to provide a broad indication of contrasts and similarities, rather than as precise indications of change.

Governance and partnership

The rise of local economic governance is most immediately evident in the increasing range of organisations involved in L&RED. Case Study 4.2 illustrates how partnerships proliferate and interrelate, using Hull as an example.

The trend towards partnership in English L&RED is reflected in the growing emphasis on the interaction at board level and also patterns of engagement with local partners. In the English survey 57% (n=67) of respondents had a board of management mainly from the public sector, just 13% (15) had boards mainly from the private business sector, while 30% (35) had a variety of groups present without one group dominating. Partners were important to all of the organisations surveyed, with all of them working with a broad range of types of partner, in most cases over 10 (Table 4.1). This finding implies actual numbers of partners well above this, since for some categories, such as community partners, this may have involved a large number of individual groups.

Simply being a partner is one thing, being an active partner is another. In consequence respondents were also encouraged to indicate the relative importance of their partners (Table 4.2). The emergent importance of 'other local/regional government agencies' probably reflects the emergence of RDAs and regional assemblies in recent years, while the various departments of local government are key partners for local government and non-local government agencies alike. Many environmental groups might be surprised to find themselves seen as important partners by both local government and non-local government agencies. It is possible that their views are more important than they might have thought, or perhaps that their incorporation into partnerships is a key form of legitimacy in the current political climate, not least as environmental groups have a tendency to go public on any disagreements with 'the authorities' when not incorporated. Universities are also ranked quite highly, reflecting the recent concern with knowledge transfer, plus their role in training within the labour market and indeed as major institutions in their own right, in terms of both employment and student numbers.

Case Study 4.2: L&RED agencies in Hull, 2003

As one of the most deprived cities in England, with an urban population of 261,000, Hull has attracted a whole raft of programmes over the past 20 years, including an Urban Task Force and a Housing Action Trust, although never a UDC. At present, the key ingredients of regeneration activity in the city include: a New Deal for Communities pathfinder area and European Objective 2 area funding, managed through the Government Office for the Region. The later successful initiatives under the Single Regeneration Budget are currently working through the system, following five successful bids since 1995. Hull City Council also runs its own Economic Development Agency, while the Chamber of Commerce is an active player in many local regeneration activities. Operating at the sub-regional level of the Humber, there is also a Local Learning and Skills Council and a Business Link, plus an economic development partnership, the Humber Forum. Training is also funded for various New Deals (for example, for youth, single parents) from the Employment Service.

At the regional level, the RDA is an important funding source, with the Humber one of its four sub-regions. As the current dispenser of central government regeneration funds, the RDA is now a key player in the city. However, the Government Office for the Region remains important for its role in European structural funds and more recently for its role in Neighbourhood Renewal Funding, of which Hull will be a major beneficiary. Seeking to coordinate these activities since 1994 has been Cityvision, a public–private partnership run as a separate entity, but chaired by the leader of the council. Cityvision was also responsible for Cityimage, a company set up to improve the external image of the city with investors.

In addition to these agencies there exists a whole range of other key players in the city, most notably perhaps the University of Hull, local colleges, and a handful of larger businesses, including Kingston Communications, the powerful local telephone company. In regeneration terms, delivery is frequently contracted out to a range of organisations, including cross-contracting between the major partners in the city, plus smaller private companies and voluntary sector agencies, increasingly those working in the social economy. Until recently community economic development tended to be viewed suspiciously by the local authority, making it difficult for agencies pursuing this approach to establish financial stability and political legitimacy, even where external funders were being supportive. The legacy of this is that this sector remains underdeveloped within the city.

Two recent government initiatives have led to a reworking of the regeneration partnership structures of Hull. First, like all local authorities, the city council was charged with creating a Local Strategic Partnership (LSP), which was expected to act as a forum for coordinating all the strategies of key agencies in the area, including L&RED institutions but also key statutory bodies such as the police, local university, colleges, and community groups. A key function of the LSP was to develop an agreed Community Strategy for the whole area, in conjunction with partners. The second critical event in 2002 was the city's successful bid for Urban Regeneration Company status. The resulting strategic partnership structure of the city now looks like this:

Cityvision: the LSP, with a widely constituted board, plus eight thematic sub-boards.
City Venture: operates the funding programmes formerly associated with Cityvision. Its board is drawn from the public, private and community sectors.
City Build: the urban regeneration company for the city, with a three-year lifespan.

Other 'good examples of partnerships' cited in the Hull Community Strategy (Hull Cityvision, 2002, p 3) include: Health Action Zone, Education Action Zone, New Deal for Communities, Sure Start, Sure Start Plus, Children's Fund, Community Safety, Cityimage, and Citylearning.

For Hull, as in most other cities, there is a danger of partnership fatigue, particularly for underfunded community groups asked to sit on a variety of partnership boards.

Table 4.1: Number of partners, local government and non-local government agencies, England

Number of types of partner (range)	Local government (% of respondents)	Non-local government (% of respondents)
0	0.0	0.0
1-5	4.6	5.8
6-10	4.6	11.5
11-15	36.9	40.4
16-20	53.8	42.3
Total	100	100

In contrast with the US in particular, 'banks and other financial institutions' emerge as the least highly rated partner for local government agencies and among the least important for non-government agencies, reflecting the different legal frameworks and different recent traditions of local banking in the two countries. Despite the importance of the European Commission as a funding provider, 'international agencies' were among the lowest scoring partners, reflecting that local agencies tended to see the Commission simply as a funder, not a partner.

Size and funding

Almost all of the responding English L&RED organisations appeared to be substantial in size, but, as Chapter One highlighted, the survey generated a large number of responses to this particular set of questions which had to be treated as invalid, mainly from local governments. In addition, there was a bias within the sample framework towards the mainstream providers of L&RED,

Table 4.2: Importance of key partners, local government and non-local government agencies, England

Rank and type of organisational partner	Non-local government: rank (mean)	Local government: rank (mean)
'Other' public local/ regional partners	1 (2.95)	2 (2.55)
Local government	2 (2.77)	1 (2.60)
Trades unions	3 (2.44)	10 (1.54)
Environmental groups	4 (2.35)	5 (2.06)
National government departments/agencies	5 (2.30)	3 (2.52)
Universities	6 (2.16)	6 (1.94)
Research & Development organisations	7 (2.11)	4 (2.35)
Local venture capital providers	8 (2.06)	9 (1.63)

Notes: Rank: out of 20 categories

Mean scores: based on a ranking of 0 = Not a partner, 1 = Mildly important, 2 = Moderately important, 3 = Very important partner.

which might be expected to be larger than other organisations in this field. To add further confusion, it is almost impossible to disentangle the budgets of the various agencies involved to find out how much regeneration money is coming into an area, not least because of the considerable cross-funding between agencies, which raises issues of double counting or even triple counting. As an example, when an RDA gives money to a local regeneration partnership, which then passes the money on to a community agency, it is possible for the same money to be counted three times in the different institutions' annual accounts.

There is useful material available from other recent surveys on local authority economic development funding. The Audit Commission's (1999) survey found that spending in 1999 varied considerably across authorities, from £5.6 million to £7,500 per year, or from £24 per head of population to 9p, with a national average of £4.21 per head. Some of this money came from local authorities' own revenue base, but most of it came from bidding for government regeneration funding. In the 1998 Local Government Association (LGA) survey (Bennett and LGA, 1998), the average expenditure by local governments was £4.2 million, with funding almost 10 times higher in London boroughs and in metropolitan districts than in other areas. From the same survey, the average number of people employed in economic development sections of local government was 13.8 full-time equivalents, averaging 38.9 in the metropolitan districts, but just 3.6 in non-metropolitan districts.

Both the survey data on funding for non-local government agencies (see Chapter Three) and our own experience suggest that English non-local government agencies tended to be larger in size than those in the other survey countries. This mainly reflects the relatively large amounts of funding which central government opts to channel through agencies such as the Local Learning and Skills Councils and Business Links.

In the 1998 LGA survey, external funding bids accounted for an average 29% of local economic development spending. Our own findings provide further insights into the tied nature of funding in L&RED. Of the 98 responses to a question on the percentage of the organisation's income which is government grants tied to specific projects, 33 (33.7%) had 10% or less of their income tied in this way, while 34 (34.7%) had over 70% of their income from government for specific projects.

The survey also asked about the sources of funding, a question which revealed the greater reliance of England and Northern Ireland on international sources, reflecting the importance of the European Commission to the UK's regeneration efforts. More than half of the responding English agencies relied on international sources for at least 20% of their funding. Perhaps surprisingly, there was a stark difference between local government and non-local government agencies in terms of their reliance on national government funding. Over half of local governments obtained less than 20% of their income from national government. Alternatively, over half of non-local government agencies received more than 80% of their income from central government. In comparison with the US, very few organisations gained substantial funding from business memberships, private foundations or from sales and rental income from their activities. The main point here is that, as Chapter Two intimated, notions of the autonomy of L&RED need to be treated cautiously, given the extent to which their finances are tied to central government and EU funding programmes.

These funding programmes are substantial. The main national funding programme in 1998/99 was the Single Regeneration Budget, which provided £564 million, while EU structural funds allocated £10 billion to the whole UK for the period 2000-06 (Audit Commission, 1999). More recently, RDAs have had their funding and spending flexibility increased, and considerable funding has been introduced for the Neighbourhood Renewal Fund, not to mention programmes such as the Coalfields Regeneration Trust, Community Fund, Community Empowerment Fund, New Deal for Communities, the various labour market New Deals, and countless other programmes. Interestingly, in light of subsequent findings in this chapter, preparing bids to these external programmes in some cases accounted for 8% of the economic development budgets of local governments (Audit Commission, 1999, p 18). Finally on this theme, funding for different types of economic development activity varied between different types of local government, with metropolitan authorities spending proportionately more on bid preparation and community enterprise than county or district authorities, but less on tourism promotion (Audit Commission, 1999, p 19).

Objectives and activities of local and regional economic development organisations

The objectives adopted by local and regional economic development organisations

The main objectives found in English L&RED were to promote economic growth and to generate the local economy, which, as Chapter Three illustrates, is in line with the findings in the other survey countries. However, building regional and local capacity was much less frequently cited than in other countries, as was the objective of retaining local population. Population retention and growth was particularly important in rural Australia, with concerns about rural depopulation, and in the US, where there are concerns about out-migration leading to a loss in the local tax base. Alternatively, in England, while there is some central government support for rural population retention, this is frequently seen as interwoven with housing and agricultural policy. Likewise, since changes to the business property tax in the late 1980s centralised the process, measures to increase the local tax base do not have quite the same immediate impact on local government revenue in England as in the US.

Reflecting the diversity of local economic development in England, most respondents reported a wide range of objectives, typically between 6 and 15 for local government, while non-local government agencies tended to be more focused, with 60% having just 1–5 objectives (Table 4.3). This difference in part reflects the breadth of local government activities in local economic policy, but also the expectation that as the elected tier of government they would be represented in most local partnerships. In consequence, even if local governments were not directly delivering in a particular policy area they would be likely to be involved at the strategic level in helping coordinate activities.

Table 4.3: Number of objectives, local government and non-local government agencies, England

Number of objectives (range)	Local government (% of respondents)	Non-local government (% of respondents)
0	0.0	0.0
1-5	16.9	59.6
6-10	32.3	21.1
11-15	30.8	13.5
16-20	20.0	5.8
20+	0.0	0.0
Total	100	100

Range of local and regional economic development activities in England

Business support activities

The survey collected information on types of L&RED activity under two broad headings: business support activities and more general regional development activities, which we refer to here as 'capacity building'. We asked firms to indicate from lists under each category which types of activities they had been involved in during the past two years, allowing them to add other responses if they saw fit.

In terms of numbers of business support activities (Table 4.4), local governments tended to be involved in a wide range of types of activity, while non-local government agencies were more focused on fewer activities, as might be expected of the more limited remits of Local Learning and Skills Councils and Business Links. The exception was the small number of non-local government agencies recording more than 20 activities, which commonly were the more widely based regeneration agencies. As Chapter Three has already highlighted, the dominant business support activities for English L&RED institutions were: coordinating public sector processes (73% of all respondents), helping gain access to government funding (71%), small- and medium-sized enterprise support (70%), provision of information on government programmes (69%), marketing the region (68%) and training and recruitment of labour (68%). Of the top six activities, three were essentially coordinating functions, a fact that largely reflects the fragmented nature of the governance arrangements for English local economic development.

Chapter Three also highlighted that, relative to other nations in this survey, English L&RED organisations were far more likely to be engaged in cluster development (56%), business incubator activity (43%), supply chain activities (42%) and land and property development (provision of industrial estates or science parks (48%). English organisations were also much more likely to be

Table 4.4: Number of business support activities, local government and non-local government agencies, England

Number of activities (range)	Local government (% of respondents)	Non-local government (% of respondents)
0	0.0	3.8
1-5	6.2	30.8
6-10	18.5	23.1
11-15	47.7	21.2
16-20	26.2	13.5
20+	1.5	7.7
Total	100	100

engaged in small- and medium-sized enterprise support activities and labour market interventions.

By contrast, along with Northern Ireland, English organisations were less likely than their Australian and US counterparts to be involved in facilitation work, such as streamlining approval processes, and in fiscal intervention, from tax reduction to subsidising relocations. This reflects the fact that in England taxation and subsidy issues are largely controlled by national rather than sub-national governments.

Capacity building activities

In terms of capacity building activities, which covers actions aimed at building regional capacity rather than direct assistance to firms, some interesting variations emerged between local government and non-local government actors (Table 4.5). For local government, developing business sites was undertaken by most local authorities, along with analysis of the local economy. The emphasis on physical development among local authorities is consistent with earlier surveys of local authorities in England and Wales (Sellgren, 1989) and Britain (Sellgren, 1991). However, in relation to these earlier surveys, local authorities are now much less likely to be involved in 'loans and grants' and providing 'key worker housing', reflecting wider political and legislative changes in the intervening period. In particular, local government grants to businesses have been very heavily restricted since new legislation in 1989, while much of the country's local authority housing stock has been sold off, especially that in more desirable areas.

In addition, changes in national labour market policy mean that while many local authorities still support training courses as part of their economic development function, they are now rarely the main provider or funder, in contrast to the mid-1980s. Since 1989, the lead role in providing funding for training activities was handed first to the business-led TECs, which tended not to favour local authorities in deciding which training courses to support, instead preferring 'independent' or private sector providers. At the time of the survey it was not yet clear how closely Local Learning and Skills Councils would work with local authority economic development sections. Despite this, the percentage of local governments involved in education and training in 2001 (63%) was actually very similar to the 59% found in Sellgren's 1987 survey of local authorities in England and Wales (Sellgren, 1989). Perhaps more importantly, the present (2001) survey found high levels of activity among non-local government agencies in this area, mainly reflecting the presence in our survey of Local Learning and Skills Councils.

Table 4.5: Ranking of capacity building activities, local government and non-local government agencies, England

	Local government			Non-local government agencies	
Rank	Capacity building activity	% of respondents[a]	Rank	Capacity building activity	% of respondents[a]
1	Development of or planning for business sites	87.7	1	Education and training for youth (not targeted to specific firm/enterprise)	76.9
2	Analysis of the regional/local economy	83.1	2	Education and training, general (not targeted to specific firm/enterprise)	76.9
3	Improving regional/local economic development strategic planning/implementation capacity	76.9	3	Analysis of the regional/local economy	75.0
4	Developing cooperation and networking between firms, and/or firms and public/private sector agencies	76.9	4	Education and training for minority groups (not targeted to specific firm/enterprise)	69.2
5	Acting as advocate or lobbyist for the region/local area	72.3	5	Improving regional/local economic development strategic planning/implementation capacity	65.4
6	Improving regional/local physical infrastructure	67.7	6	Coordinating government programmes	65.4
7	Education and training, general (not targeted to specific firm/enterprise)	63.1	7	Improving regional/local service provision	57.7
8	Coordinating government programmes	61.5	8	Developing cooperation and networking between firms, and/or firms and public/private sector agencies	57.7
9	Attempting to influence land use regulations and planning decisions impacting on businesses	61.5	9	Identifying and implementing strategies to fill business opportunities, gaps in region/local economy	50.0
10	Education and training for youth (not targeted to specific firm/enterprise)	56.9	10	Acting as advocate or lobbyist for the region/local area	44.2
11	Identifying and implementing strategies to fill business opportunities, gaps in region/local economy	52.3	11	Development of or planning for business sites	36.5
12	Improving regional/local service provision	44.6	12	Improving regional/local physical infrastructure	25.0
13	Education and training for minority groups (not targeted to specific firm/enterprise)	40.0	13	Attempting to influence land use regulations and planning decisions impacting on businesses	21.2
14	Improving regional/local telecommunications infrastructure	27.7	14	Improving regional/local telecommunications infrastructure	17.3

Note: [a] % of local government or local and regional agencies indicating involvement in each activity.

Institutional effectiveness

Overall organisational effectiveness

Figure 4.1 illustrates that most organisations rated themselves as having made an appreciable, substantial or major impact, with only a minority feeling that their impacts were limited. Around two thirds of local governments rated their impact as appreciable or better, compared with around a half of non-local government agencies. This difference in self-assessment may reflect the limited lifespans of many of the non-government organisations in the survey, although as some of these felt unable to provide a response to this question, their responses are not included here.

A related reason for local government's higher self-assessment may be that as more established agencies, they had over time moved away from activities which they felt were least effective. It may also be the case that while newer non-local government organisations had some autonomy in how they delivered a programme, they had very little control over the basic design of the programmes they had to deliver. This is an issue that also turned up in the qualitative comments (see below).

A series of correlation and regression exercises seeking to identify links between levels of impact and various variables were undertaken. Although

Figure 4.1: Respondent assessment of effectiveness, local government and non-local government agencies, England

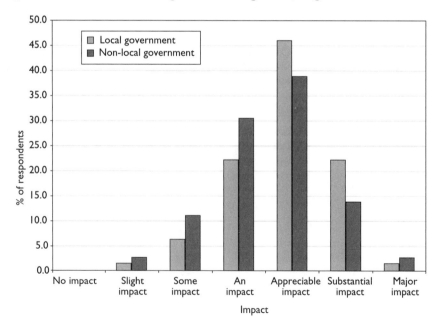

these were similar in scope to those described in the chapters on Australia and the US, unlike those case studies only weak associations emerged.

In international comparison the fact that English L&RED organisations tended to be much better resourced than elsewhere raises the fairly awkward question of why their self-assessment scores did not tend to be higher than, for instance, their US counterparts. Could it simply be put down to the stereotype of English reticence and diffidence? Only in small measure is the most likely answer, as English local economic development practitioners tend to operate in an environment where discourses of success, benchmarking against international best practice and so forth are part of the daily process of psyching up staff and clients alike. Or, to put it another way, economic development practitioners are not known for being backward in coming forward with a positive view of their achievements. (One English practitioner did score an organisation as having no impact. Maybe just a bad day, maybe just an unusually candid assessment.) The more likely reason for the relatively low scores of English practitioners is the much wider range of objectives which they typically had (see Chapter Three), which meant they were often trying to tackle a much more widely drawn set of problems than their counterparts in the other survey countries. Particularly important has been the recent broadening of the scope of regeneration under New Labour, as the dominant discourse has shifted from an economy-led view of local economic problems and policies to a much more nuanced understanding of the social and environmental aspects of local economic development. For many practitioners this has been a challenging period, of coming to grips with the language and policies of social exclusion, economic inclusion and sustainable development. This new approach introduced a greater awareness that local economic development meant more than the 'big hits' of inward investment and assisting a targeted number of small firms, instead revealing a series of complex, interrelated and ingrained problems of a magnitude which four years of New Labour policies were unlikely ever to have had sufficient time to address.

How organisations made their assessments

In order to develop an overview of some of the complexities of how effectiveness was achieved and impeded, the analysis now turns to the basis of respondents' assessments. For most respondents, the assessments of their organisation's effectiveness tended to be based on partial or impressionistic accounts, with few seeming to have undertaken holistic overviews of this issue. This may link to the Audit Commission's finding that evaluation was relatively underdeveloped in this area. This is not to say that there is no evaluation, but it tends to be project-based rather than for whole organisations.

Impediments to organisational effectiveness

Having asked about the organisation's overall effectiveness, we probed further by asking respondents to highlight what they felt were the most important impediments to improving their organisational effectiveness. As Table 4.6 indicates, for English agencies the dominant concerns were funding-related, accounting for the top six impediments for both local governments and non-local government agencies. The short duration of funding programmes, mainly from central government, were seen to be a particular obstacle. Interestingly, however, for the non-local government agencies, mainly comprising the supposedly autonomous agencies set up by central government, their main concerns were that their main funders' priorities had more influence than regional needs, while being tied to inflexible rules and guidelines. This finding gives some empirical substance to the discussion in Chapter Two of the growing importance of the 'strategic selectivity of the state' and of its emerging mechanisms for continuing to exert influence over the activities of local development agencies. In similar vein, it is noteworthy that the more competitive funding environment introduced since the early 1990s probably contributed to the finding that over half of all local government respondents felt that too much staff time was devoted to seeking funding.

It is worth noting that the most frequently cited five impediments to effectiveness involved much higher percentages in the English case than in the US in particular, giving a sense of the greater frustration among English practitioners relative to their counterparts. More positively, it is not surprising to find that most English organisations felt that they had adequate access to information on best practice, given the attention of recent governments to this issue. While it might be expected that local governments would regard themselves as legitimate representatives of their area, it is a slight surprise to find that non-local government agencies also tended not to regard this as an issue for them.

'What would make your organisation more effective?'

In order to triangulate responses on agency effectiveness, we asked a related open-ended question on what would make each respondent's organisation more effective, an approach which generated a wider range of responses than the previous question plus some interesting qualitative data. We subsequently coded this qualitative information, with one person responsible for coding the responses from all four countries to allow a degree of consistency. Even with the intention of minimising the number of categories, this exercise generated over 40 categories of response. Respondents were allowed to mention more than one option.

Of the 92 organisations answering this question, 28% mentioned more staff, 24% more funding, and 20% better external coordination, 15% less tied, or more flexible, funding, and 14% implementing a more strategic focus. The

Table 4.6: Most significant impediments to agency effectiveness, local government and non-local government agencies, England

	Local government			Non-local government agencies	
Rank	Impediment	% of respondents[a]	Rank	Impediment	% of respondents[a]
1	Short duration of much of the funding	73.0	1	Priorities of funders have more influence on organisation than region's needs	61.2
2	Lack of funding for core business	71.4	2	Inflexible rules and guidelines of funders	59.2
3	Inflexible rules and guidelines of funders	59.7	3	Short duration of much of the funding	55.1
4	Too much staff time spent seeking funding	52.4	4	Insufficient untied funding to use as leverage with other agencies	46.9
5	Insufficient untied funding to use as leverage with other agencies	45.3	5	Too frequent changes in priorities and objectives of funders	45.2
6	Too frequent changes in priorities and objectives of funders	40.3	6	Too much staff time spent seeking funding	38.8
7	Priorities of funders have more influence on organisation than region's needs	38.7	7	Organisation not involved in decisions about large enterprises	36.4
8	Absence of regional leadership	29.7	8	Absence of regional leadership	34.7
9	Organisation lacks capacity to undertake strategic planning	29.0	9	Lack of funding for core business	28.6
10	Involvement of local businesses in the governing body of agency	28.9	10	Involvement of local government in the governing body of agency	27.9
11	Organisation not involved in decisions about large enterprises	27.6	11	Organisation lacks capacity to undertake strategic planning	22.0
12	Staff lack appropriate skills	18.8	12	Staff lack appropriate skills	16.3
13	Involvement of local government in the governing body of agency	15.2	13	Organisation not seen as sufficiently independent of government	15.6
14	Organisation not seen as sufficiently independent of government	14.3	14	Involvement of local businesses in the governing body of agency	8.7
15	Unable to access information on best practice	12.5	15	Unable to access information on best practice	8.0
16	Organisation not seen as a legitimate representative of the region	7.4	16	Organisation not seen as a legitimate representative of the region	2.3

Note: [a] % of respondents agreeing that each represents an impediment.

attention to tied funding is a particularly striking finding relative to the other three countries. As Table 4.7 illustrates, this was a particular concern for non-local government agencies, nearly a quarter of which felt that addressing this issue would benefit them. In effect, agencies such as Local Learning and Skills Councils and Business Links were funded directly from central government, therefore they were rather less concerned about levels of funding than their local government counterparts and much more vexed by the lack of flexibility they had in using these funds to meet local needs.

For local governments, which in England lack a clear line of government funding for L&RED activities, the call for better resourcing is clearly evident, from over a third of all respondents. This reflects the fact that these agencies too were heavily dependent on central government funds, but in their case these had to be bid for competitively on a near continuous basis. Once again, the issue of the close central control over local economic development activities emerges, something which seems to be much stronger in England than elsewhere, reflecting the high proportion of regeneration funding which comes from central government and EU sources, rather than being locally raised. The problems cited were not purely external it must be emphasised – there were many problems linked to poor political support, lack of clear officer level leadership, and lack of coordination with local government.

Valuable though it is to have the summary of overall responses contained in Table 4.7, it is the written responses which provide the real flavour of the issues involved:

> More effective (not necessarily more) 'partnership' working with shared goals. (local government, South East)

Table 4.7: What would make your organisation more effective? (local government and non-local government agencies, England)

Top 5 Local government	% of respondents
1. Greater funding support	34.5
2. Additional and/or better equipped human resources	32.7
3. Better external coordination	20.0
4. Implementing strategic focus/approach	16.4
5. Less tied/more flexible funding	10.9
Top 5 Non-local government	
1. Additional and/or better equipped human resources	24.3
2. Less tied/more flexible funding	24.3
3. Better external coordination	18.9
4. Implementing strategic focus/approach	10.8
5. Improved flexibility/autonomy	10.8

More funding and less bureaucracy. Joined-up thinking by central government. (local government, London)

Increased core funding to replace time limited external funding. (local government, North West)

More funds, less tied to the rules and regulations of the funding agencies. (local government, Yorkshire and Humber)

Better internal cooperation and communication. Funding for core activities as well as 'new' projects.... Less competitive funding structures. More flexible funding guidelines to allow voluntary and community groups to participate fully. (local government, East Midlands)

Greater commitment to partnership working throughout all partner organisations. Less competition between agencies – more commitment to each other and less fighting for recognition of their individual contribution. (strategic partnership, West Midlands)

Longer-term funding. Removal of bureaucracy. Flexibility from central government. (Business Link, West Midlands)

Better regional coordination of all the alleged 'one stop shops' which have been set up. None is true to its name. All compete for funds and influence. (Local Learning and Skills Council, South East)

More flexibility to tackle local priorities. (Local Learning and Skills Council, West Midlands)

The policy effectiveness of individual activities

Which are the most effective individual activities, and why?

With a further open-ended question, we asked respondents to nominate their most and least effective economic development activity, allowing space for reasons to be given for this assessment. Again, we subsequently coded these qualitative comments in order to allow comparison, a process which created a large number of categories, so one particular form of intervention does not always automatically stand out.

For both local government and non-local government agencies business support and advice was regarded as an effective form of intervention (Table 4.8). In the case of local governments this tended to be interpreted quite widely, including, for instance, helping with premises. For non-local government agencies the emphasis was much more on advice services to small businesses.

Table 4.8: Most and least effective activities, local government and non-local government agencies, England

Most effective activities

	Local government		Non-local government	
Rank	Activity	% of respondents	Activity	% of respondents
1	Business support and advice	21.3	Training/skills/labour market interventions	29.8
2	Networking/partnerships/coordination/facilitation	19.7	Business support and advice	25.5
3	Inward investment, promotion of region (including incentives)	16.4	Can not say, too early to determine	14.9
4	Land preparation, site/premises development	14.8	Land preparation, site/premises development	8.5
5	Area-based regeneration	14.8	Inward investment, promotion of region (including incentives)	6.4

Least effective activities

	Local government		Non-local government	
Rank	Activity	% of respondents	Activity	% of respondents
1	Inward investment, promotion of region (including incentives)	34.6	Other/ambiguous	20.6
2	Other/ambiguous	13.5	Cannot say, too early to determine	20.6
3	Business support and advice	9.6	Inward investment, promotion of region (including incentives)	14.7
4	Land preparation, site/premises development	7.7	Training/skills/labour market interventions	11.8
5	Training/skills/labour market interventions	5.8	Accessing government/EU funds	5.9

These agencies tended to link effectiveness in this area to improving business competitiveness and at a more prosaic level, the ability of advisers to build good links with client businesses. While most agencies were positive about their business support activities, many also took care to praise their own tailored versions, or noted the inflexibility of the programmes they were expected to administer. Particularly striking was the respondent who felt that the least effective activity undertaken was: "Trying to stuff government programmes down the throats of small business" (Business Link, South West). Although the most vivid illustration of this theme, it was far from the only one. Indeed, much more so than dry concepts such as 'the strategic selectivity of the state' (see Chapter Two), this comment usefully captures the essence of how supposed policy devolution remains subject to continuing centralised control.

Despite being one of the most cited effective activities, business support also found its way on to the list of least effective activities for local government agencies, with the most frequent reason being that others were involved in this activity in their locality, leading to the potential for duplication.

For local governments, networking, coordination and partnership activities emerge particularly strongly, signifying the extent to which the process aspects of local economic development have started to become as important as some of the implementation activities more traditionally associated with this sector. Part of the reason for the importance of networking is undoubtedly the fact that many forms of EU and central government grants come with an expectation that local partners find 'matched funding' from other sources, building in a requirement that agencies work together. In addition, respondents frequently noted that coordination reduced duplication and helped provide better targeted responses to local issues. Two responses particularly bring out the flavour of some of the comments on this issue, one relating to partnership as a major effective activity and the other local regeneration schemes:

> Partnership achieves more than the sum of its parts – real results can be achieved on the ground due to local commitment and focused objectives. (local government, South East)

> [Of strategic planning and partnership development.] It ties together the aspirations of public, private, voluntary and community sector organisations into a prioritised, single focus action plan. (local government, West Midlands)

It is also worth noting that a minority of respondents reported the problems they faced with working in partnerships, for instance where partners were not fully committed or tended to squabble. This linked to a few comments that the most effective activities of some organisations were those not undertaken in partnership and where they had established a clear lead role.

In third and fourth place as effective activities for local government were inward investment and land and site preparation, activities which are often interrelated. When asked why site preparation was important, the most frequent response was local market failure, requiring local government to step in. Again, two quotes help add colour to a category of response which was surprisingly varied and nuanced. For a respondent citing the development of an industrial estate and business support centre:

> Intervention provided direct jobs and investment into the local economy – safeguarded jobs and allowed local businesses to develop. We had control of the project. (local government, South West)

For others, it was recovering brownfield sites for industrial redevelopment which had proven most effective since:

> They often have existing infrastructure and are closely linked to existing communities. (local government, Yorkshire and Humber)

But perhaps the most startling aspect of this finding is that both inward investment and site preparation also made their way on to the list of the five least effective forms of activity for both local government and non-local government agencies. In particular, over a third of local government respondents reported that inward investment had been their least effective activity, with many consequently seeming to maintain only a nominal level of activity in consequence. The reasons cited were usually to do with poor communications infrastructure, better placed neighbouring areas, and limited land availability making the area unattractive to mobile investors, while others mentioned the high costs and low levels of impact of marketing activity in this sphere. One organisation noted in some detail that it had switched away from inward investment to supporting existing businesses:

> While we continue to seek inward investment we realise that for our most deprived areas it is new businesses and growing our existing businesses which are more effective. (local government, West Midlands)

Another noted that sites and property development, and therefore inward investment, was not effective for them because in their county they found themselves:

> … unable to compete for inward investment with neighbouring areas, eg M1 corridor, owing to lack of incentives, poor communications and weak labour market. (local government, East Midlands)

The withdrawal from inward investment seemed particularly prominent among local areas in economically buoyant areas, where some agencies had recognised that firms were coming to their area anyway, without the need for further inducements. There was also a tendency for firms in more buoyant regional economies, particularly the South East, to regard strategic land use planning as their most or least effective policy, particularly in terms of making land available for industrial and residential usage.

Training/skills/labour market advice was the most commonly cited effective policy category for non-local government agencies, reflecting the large number of Local Learning and Skills Councils in this part of the sample. Most of the responses for choosing learning and skills tended towards the pithy but effective: "Training = competitiveness = economic and social well-being" (Local Learning and Skills Council, West Midlands); and "No learning and skills = no economic development" (Local Learning and Skills Council, South East).

Finally in this section it is worth noting that there was a large number of non-responses from non-local government agencies which probably reflect the fact that many of those in this category had been newly created, including Local Learning and Skills Councils and Business Links. Many of these were understandably reluctant to base their judgement on their experiences under the previous TEC-based system.

Conclusion

The English results stand out in several ways. First, there is the relatively large size of many of the organisations involved in L&RED. Second, there is the strong dependence of these organisations on central government and the EU for funding. This dependence is clearly associated with strong resentments against inflexible externally controlled operating frameworks. Third, there is a clear preoccupation with the local knitting together of the many different local agencies and different funding programmes. The governance of local economic development now absorbs a fairly large amount of the time and resources of those involved in local economic development, as does the bidding for resources to remain players in this highly competitive funding environment.

Lessons

The lessons which emerge from this review of L&RED organisations in England are not always clear-cut.

- Most agencies want to engage in better strategic development and partnership work, not simply more.
- There is an undercurrent of dissatisfaction with the energies that are now required for winning funding bids for local regeneration activities.
- While inward investment approaches are losing popularity, they are far from universally derided.

Perhaps surprisingly, given the growth in funding for the social economy, initiatives in this area did not merit much mention, perhaps reflecting the (psychological) distance of some of the respondents from those engaged in this form of activity and the relatively invisible nature of many of its impacts.

FIVE

Local and regional economic development in the United States

Terry Clower
University of North Texas, US

Introduction

The practice of L&RED in the US is far from monolithic. As noted in Chapter One, examining the practices and funding mechanisms of L&RED organisations in the US presents some challenges. In area, Australia and the US are similar; however, based on sheer population differences, we were forced to look at a much smaller proportion of all L&RED groups in the US survey. There are thousands of L&RED organisations working to promote employment growth, business development, and economic diversification in the US. A 2000 publication issued by the Minneapolis Federal Reserve Bank (Wirtz, 2000) reported 891 L&RED agencies operating in Minnesota, North Dakota, South Dakota, Wisconsin, and Montana – one agency for every 14,000 residents of these states. Of course, these are states with relatively low population densities, but even if this average incidence of L&RED organisations were doubled, that would suggest that more than 10,000 agencies are operating in the US.

Regional versus local in the US

As examined in earlier chapters, there are significant differences among the participating countries in this study regarding the meaning of the words 'local' and 'regional'. In Chapter One, it was noted that 'regional' in the US more often has an urban connotation, particularly regarding cooperative efforts across local governments located in a Metropolitan Statistical Area (MSA). This is, on average, correct. However, before examining L&RED organisations in any detail, especially when assessing their levels of cooperation with other agencies and groups, it is useful to take a closer look at what local and regional can mean in the US.

Practitioners and students in the US have no doubt examined economic and demographic data for an MSA. An MSA is comprised of one or more counties that the federal Office of Management and Budget (OMB) has determined meet certain size criteria and share strong economic linkages. In June 2003, the OMB revised their definitions of these areas, describing Core Based Statistical Areas (CBSAs) as regions that must contain at least one urban area of more than 10,000 population. The new designation of Micropolitan Statistical Area (McSA) applies to CBSAs with less than 50,000 population. Consistent with previous definitions, McSAs must have at least one urban area with 50,000 or more residents. Surrounding counties are included in the MSA based on one or more of several criteria, including population density, the percentage of population that is 'urban', and commuting patterns. When large central cities are in relatively close proximity, such as the case of San Francisco and Oakland, California, each city anchors a Metropolitan Division within a jointly named MSA, in this case the San Francisco–Oakland–San Jose MSA. In these urbanised areas, 'local' could mean one municipality, a grouping of smaller suburbs, or even a district within a very large municipality, whereas a region will almost invariably refer to an entire MSA or CMSA.

In practice, local economic developers in MSAs engage in regional development when there is cooperation among two or more local agencies. For example, in 2001 the Boeing Corporation took the unusual tack of conducting a very public search for a new headquarters location. The three finalists were Denver, Colorado, Dallas, Texas and Chicago, Illinois. Economic developers representing each core city combined efforts with their suburban counterparts to extol the benefits of their regions. (Chicago won.) In many MSAs, there are regional agencies supported by public and/or private funds that take on economic development tasks at the regional level while cooperating with local agencies.

In rural areas, regional and local are often practically synonymous. For many small towns the focus must be on using combined resources with neighbouring communities to actively engage in economic development activities.

In some cases, regional can mean multi-state areas. For example, the Appalachian Regional Commission focuses on economic development efforts in parts of Virginia, West Virginia, and Kentucky (Santopietro, 2002). Other organisations, such as the Tennessee Valley Authority, while having public infrastructure as their basic mission, have expanded into direct economic development programmes for their constituent regions and localities. However, our focus does not include these state and multi-state organisations.

There are potential problems when translating the findings of the US survey on local/regional contrasts and efforts to other countries, because of differences in what is understood to be 'local' or 'regional'. However, since our efforts are meant to draw broad international comparisons, we leave it up to seasoned practitioners to recognise these differences when assessing the applicability of specific approaches to economic development for their service area.

The importance of locally based economic development

More than any of the other nations studied, the US conducts its L&RED activities through local organisations. As noted in Chapter One, this is possible because the US assigns more taxing and service provision responsibilities to local government, thus allowing for local funding of economic development activities. Federalism is one reason for this structure; politics provides another. Since the early days of the nation, economic development in the US has had political undertones. And, as the saying goes, all politics are local. Wirtz (2000, p 3) expresses this particularly well: "The biggest business giveaways ever negotiated by corporate suits still end up in someone's back yard, and not in someone else's. Somebody got more tax base. Somebody got more jobs". In addition, economic development has traditionally been linked with place resources and land uses (Blakely, 2001). Land use regulations are typically controlled at the local level. So, from a very practical standpoint, local government, by virtue of zoning, controls the location of industry – to a certain extent.

Reese and Rosenfeld (2002) theorise that civil culture is a primary determinant of variations in L&RED strategies in the US. These authors posit that choices in tax abatement offerings, public support for small businesses, and business attraction marketing strategies are influenced largely by the civil culture of the municipality, not simply by fiscal, economic and demographic characteristics. For example, the southern US in the 1960s and 1970s enjoyed a massive influx of industry fleeing high taxes and production factor costs in the 'rust belt' of the upper-Midwest and eastern US. Southern political culture demanded low taxes, hence low levels of public services including education, and a bias against unions resulting in right-to-work laws. However, as non-southerners migrated to employment opportunities, their influence helped to change local cultural norms. Most notably, demands for improved public education and other public services increased the political feasibility of increasing taxes to provide these services. But there remain substantial differences in local attitudes regarding public services, taxation and economic development. Responding to these differences requires locally designed and implemented economic development strategies from the viewpoint of most US civic and political leaders.

Another reason for the dominance of local players in economic development in the US is an artefact of the growing popularity of fiscal conservatism championed by the Reagan administration. The popularity of Ronald Reagan spurred a political shift, resulting in Republicans gaining and retaining control of the majority of state governorships for more than a decade, bringing with them conservative fiscal views. In reducing the relative size of state budgets, many of the economic development activities once accomplished by state agencies have been delegated to local government – often without accompanying funding. Some of these activities have been assumed by local government; in other cases these duties have been passed on to private and public–private entities. Pushing economic development activities from state to local agencies continues a trend started in the 1930s.

Prior to the 1930s, the federal government largely controlled economic development, especially in terms of incentives for private enterprise investment.

As a way to effectively promote economic development in the depression era south, the federal government authorised the issuance of Industrial Revenue Bonds (IRBs) (Eisinger, 2002). These bonds, issued under the authority of state or local governments, allowed private enterprises to borrow money for capital investment at market rates available to government entities, which was lower than privately issued corporate bonds because the interest earned is not subject to federal income tax. The borrower retained the burden of repayment, thus the risk was assumed by bond holders and not the issuing government agency. This provided a tool for state and local governments to actively engage in the promotion of business attraction and development. IRBs became almost universally available by the 1970s; however, the Reagan administration imposed limits on the total value of tax-exempt private bonding that state and local governments may issue each year, sharply curtailing the use of these bonds (Eisinger, 2002).

The emphasis of economic development activities by local organisations in the US makes for interesting comparisons with agencies in the other nations studied. There are also interesting differences between economic development agencies located within local government and those that are organisationally separate from local government.

Describing local and regional economic development organisations

Local government and local and regional agencies

Almost one third of the US survey respondents (*n*=68, 32%) are departments or branches of local government. Regional and local development boards, organisations, and committees represent 42% (*n*=91) of the respondents. The remaining 47 respondents specifically identifying their type of organisation represented a broad cross-section of local and regional agencies, with the largest representations in Chambers of Commerce (*n*=9) and public utility firms (*n*=9). For purposes of illustrating the findings of this survey, we have segregated responding agencies between local government entities and 'other' local and regional agencies.

There are substantial differences between the legal status of organisations representing urban areas and those representing rural or mixed urban–rural areas. Respondents to the survey represent a fairly even distribution of economic regions, with about a third each being urban, rural, and mixed urban–rural regions. Slightly more than one half of all responding agencies in urban areas are a branch of local government. In contrast, only 18% of rural L&RED organisations and 22% of mixed-area agencies are housed within government. These differences likely reflect the relative fiscal capacities of local governments. As noted above, local governments in rural areas must often rely on partnerships to obtain even minimal levels of fiscal resources and human capital to operate L&RED organisations. One respondent observed: "Local rural communities often lack the budget, staff, training and equipment to engage in economic development processes on a full-time basis". This can also be true for smaller suburban communities. Therefore, individual organisational structures of L&RED agencies in these economic regions fall outside of any particular branch of local government.

The population of the regions represented by the respondents to our survey follow expectations for rural and urban agencies. The median value of the population of the service areas for rural L&RED organisations is 50,000. In comparison, the median population for urban agencies is 130,000. Interestingly, the responding organisations identifying their service areas as a mixture of rural and urban have a median population of 245,000. This seeming anomaly is based on the nature of several of the L&RED agencies operating in mixed rural and urban areas. Many of these agencies are regional in nature, serving several counties and thus inflating the number of people in their service area.

About 26% of all responding agencies were established prior to 1970, including 10 that were established in the 19th century. The oldest agency in the response set was established in 1822. However, in some cases we suspect that the reported establishment date refers to the date of incorporation of a municipality or the founding of a business organisation and not the start of economic development activities. Excluding government entities and one for-profit public utility, the 'oldest' respondent was a Chamber of Commerce established in 1884. Some 18% of the non-governmental responding organisations were established prior to the Second World War.

The decade of the 1970s began a period of comparatively rapid increases in the number of L&RED organisations that further accelerated in the 1980s as several states, particularly in the southern US, began to implement legislation allowing for broader public support of local economic development activities. Still, more than one fifth of the respondents are agencies created since 1989.

Organisation and funding of economic development organisations

L&RED organisations in the US are characterised by a small number of staff. One third of all responding agencies have two or fewer full-time equivalent paid staff, which is comparable to the Australian experience, but in sharp contrast to English organisations. Less than 10% of US agencies have more than 40 paid staff. US agencies rely on professional staff, with few utilising volunteers. This also reflects changes in the availability of funding that has occurred over the past two decades. Volunteer staff, to the extent that they exist, are more likely to work with non-government L&RED agencies.

The board of directors for L&RED agencies generally reflect their organisational basis. Government agencies, on average, are dominated by government board members; non-government organisations rely more on the private sector for their board members.

Table 5.1 shows the distribution of responses to the question regarding each organisation's annual expenditures, including salaries and benefits paid to

Table 5.1: Frequency distribution of annual expenditures by L&RED organisations, US

Range	Count	%	Cumulative %
$0-29,000	8	4.0	4.0
$30,000-59,000	10	5.0	9.0
$60,000-119,00	21	10.5	19.5
$120,000-239,000	27	13.5	33.0
$240,000-389,000	31	15.5	48.5
$390,000-569,000	25	12.5	61.0
$570,000-749,000	12	6.0	67.0
$750,000-1.13 million	16	8.0	75.0
$1.14-1.49 million	6	3.0	78.0
$1.5-2.24 million	11	5.5	83.5
$2.25-3.74 million	11	5.5	89.0
$3.75 million or more	22	11.0	100.0

employees. There appears to be little difference between funding levels for government and non-government agencies. However, rural L&RED organisations typically operate on smaller budgets. The median response for all rural agencies falls in the US$240,000-389,999 range. Urban and mixed area organisations have median annual budgets falling in the US$390,000-569,999 range.

Revenue to support these expenditures comes from a number of sources, with substantial differences between government and non-government agencies. L&RED agencies housed in local government mostly receive funding from the general revenues of their municipality. About 10% receive the majority of their funding from dedicated local taxes, with an additional 8% having a smaller percentage of the budget funded through this source. Roughly one fourth of all government L&RED groups get at least some funding from the federal government in the form of grants – both tied and not tied to specific expenditures.

Since the late 1980s, federal funding of local economic development has typically taken one of the following forms. Community Development Block Grants are largely designated for housing and public works projects; however, between 8% and 15% of these annual grants support economic development efforts including seed funding for locally administered revolving loan schemes to support business development. Since 1988, small- and medium-sized enterprises have been targeted for federally funded programmes typically providing assistance in adopting new technologies (Eisinger, 2002). Most other federally funded local economic development efforts are targeted towards distressed areas including Empowerment Zones, Enterprise Communities and other programmes (McFarlane, 1999; Brazeal and Finkle, 2001; Cohen, 2001).

Local government economic development organisations, on average, receive no, or very little, support from state government, private foundations, or 'other' sources of income. Not one local government economic development agency reported receiving funding from an international organisation.

Non-government L&RED agencies cast their funding net much farther. Reflecting the nature of Chambers of Commerce and other membership organisations that play a role in economic development, one third of all non-government agencies rely, in part, on membership dues as a source of revenue. This includes public–private organisations that require annual subscriptions from their member municipalities and corporations. Approximately 55% are partially funded from municipal general revenues. Other significant sources include grants from state and federal government agencies and the sale of services. Similar to government L&RED organisations in the US, only 2% of non-government agencies report any funding from international sources, drawing a sharp contrast with agencies in Northern Ireland. Case studies 5.1, 5.2 and 5.3 illustrate the variety of these organisations in the US.

Effectiveness of local and regional economic development organisations

As shown in Figure 5.1, L&RED organisations in the US give themselves very satisfactory marks in accomplishing their agencies' goals. Over 75% of both

---

Case study 5.1: San Diego Regional Economic Development Corporation

The San Diego Regional Economic Development Corporation (SDRED) is the lead regional agency for San Diego County in southern California. With a staff of 19 and an annual operating budget of US$3.5 million, SDRED is a well-funded, sophisticated coordinator of economic development activities. Approximately one half of operating funds come from the public sector, while the remainder is based on membership fees and sponsorships from regional corporate 'investors'. The management board, made up mostly of private sector chief executives, has focused the agency's core objectives on being a catalyst for investment in the San Diego region, retaining high-value jobs, and assisting existing area businesses with expansion. Around this core mission, SDRED takes on special projects including infrastructure development, workforce development, education, and general quality of life issues. SDRED's development strategy is targeted on wireless telecommunications and biotechnology industries. This strategy includes being actively engaged with international organisations from Pacific-rim nations as well as German and Swedish biotech groups. When asked to describe their operating relationship with state development agencies, William Carnet (interview, 8 October 2002) of SDRED responded: "Our relationship works this way. We try maintaining a regional distribution structure so that leads normally come to us first. They [local agencies] rely on us to distribute and coordinate the local resources. We play the local facilitator on behalf of the state".

Author: Guy Brown

Figure 5.1: Respondent assessment of effectiveness, local government and non-local government agencies, US

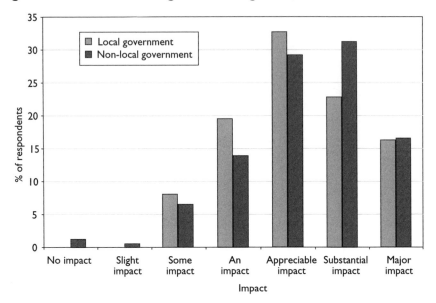

Note: Bars show percentage by group (government/non-government), not percentage of total respondents.

local government and non-government agencies rate themselves as having an appreciable, substantial, or major impact on their local economies. Of course, being positive about your region is a necessary, if not sufficient, condition to being successful in encouraging local business investment, whether homegrown or through business attraction. Moreover, it is the nature of the economic development profession in the US to be self-promoting, at least to some extent. So, is this seemingly strong result braggadocio, or is there substance to these claims?

In addition to asking the respondents to rate their agency's performance, open-ended questions asking for the basis of their self-ratings were presented. Over the past few years, L&RED agencies in the US have made efforts to track performance. Some of these efforts focus on anecdotal and qualitative evidence gathered through informal monitoring. However, many organisations have specific performance measures that are monitored and reported on an on-going basis.

Formal approaches to self-evaluating L&RED agency performance include monitoring programme outcomes, comparing outputs against strategic plans, budgetary revenues and expenditures, benchmarking, annual reports, and other measures. Specific data gathered for these measures include local economic and demographic indicators such as population, unemployment rates, wages, building permits, property vacancy rates, business start-ups, changes in local industrial structure, loans made and repaid, number of visitors/conferences, and solicited feedback from the organisation's stakeholders (Weinstein et al, 1994; Hatry et al, 1990; Poole et al, 1999).

Unfortunately, only about one half of all respondents to the US survey provided the basis for their effectiveness rating. However, we can pick up trends in performance evaluation within L&RED agencies, even if we are cautious about generalisations. About one quarter of all respondents engage in formal monitoring and performance evaluation. The most popular measures include: the number of business start-ups, survivals, expansions and retentions supported; number of jobs created or retained; amount of investment secured; other results-oriented quantitative measures; and changes in local economic and demographic measures. Some interesting responses, both positive and negative, include:

We have 90-95% retention by our clients and our revenue base has grown each year.

Relatively few defaults on loans (5 of 31).

Benchmark ratings are very good as well as feedback from stakeholders.

Feedback from local businesses.

There are now 13 diversified businesses in our industrial park.

Quantity and quality of recent successes that mirror our strategic business plan and the tremendous amount of positive international, national, and local media attention that our efforts have [gained].

Annual reports detailing organisation's results.

Praise from peers.

Lack of local implementation of regional recommendations.

Creation of jobs and the effect those businesses have had on the tax base.

We play at best an ancillary role in bringing about the major changes taking place in our service area.

Interestingly, no respondents to the US survey reported using measures such as the number of tourists or visitors attracted to the area or the number of inquiries or referrals fielded by the agency. This shows important progress over older measures that tracked activity, such as contacts, number of mailings, and quantity of trade shows attended, rather than measuring outcomes.

Even with a low response rate to the question regarding evidence for judgements of organisational effectiveness, we are drawn to the conclusion that formalised performance measurement may not be as prevalent as anticipated. Undoubtedly, L&RED agencies in the US perceive themselves as effective; however, there appear to be opportunities for these agencies to implement programmes of formal performance measurement to support these assertions. In an era of tightening government budgets and lower membership of business organisations, being able to clearly justify the resources committed to L&RED becomes increasingly important.

In the following sections we examine dimensions of agency effectiveness, specifically looking at measures illustrating the scope of activities undertaken by L&RED organisations, the degree to which partnerships with other agencies are formed, and the presence of significant obstacles to meeting goals and objectives.

Objectives and activities of local and regional economic development organisations

Objectives

Consideration of a self-reported measure of effectiveness and the criteria used to make that assessment leads to obvious questions: what are the objectives of L&RED organisations, and what activities are undertaken to achieve these objectives?

Respondents to the survey were asked to choose among a broad list of core objectives for their organisations. Realising that many L&RED agencies will have special projects, such as supporting a convention, or that they may engage in recurring minor activities, such as fundraising for local charitable campaigns, we asked respondents to focus on their core objectives. The question was formatted as a 'check all that apply' so that we could assess not only the type of objectives but also the total number of objectives each organisation assumes. Table 5.2 presents a ranking of the core objectives of L&RED agencies in the US.

Government-based agencies and non-government organisations adopt core objectives in about equal measure. However, there are a few differences among urban, rural, and mixed urban–rural agencies. Urban agencies are less likely to see local capacity building as a core objective than rural and mixed economy organisations, reflecting the presence of existing services and physical infrastructure in urban areas. Alternatively, this may reflect the presence of other organisations or departments of local government in urban areas that specifically address capacity building, including infrastructure development, job training, housing, and other issues, so freeing economic development groups to focus on other core objectives. In rural areas one organisation, as noted earlier, may handle a broad range of tasks. This hypothesis is supported by another difference in objectives among economic areas. Only 13% of urban

Table 5.2: Core objectives for L&RED organisations, US

Rank	Description	% of agencies	Rank	Description	% of agencies
1	Promote economic growth	93	11	Protect/increase local tax base	46
2	Promote employment growth	75	12	Stimulate involvement in local development	39
3	Attract/recruit new businesses to the area	75	13	Promote area nationally, internationally	39
4	Develop local businesses (new, expansion, retention)	71	14	Improve jobs/income of disadvantaged groups	35
5	Improve quality of life	67	15	Promote property development	34
6	Diversify the regional/local economy	63	16	Promote environmentally sustainable development	32
7	Partnerships among public/ private sector, community	56	17	Provide/facilitate labour market training	28
8	Regenerate/revitalize local economy	55	18	Retain, increase local population	27
9	Build capacity for development	54	19	Lobby government on behalf of region	26
10	Increase local incomes	51	20	Provide job placement services	7

L&RED agencies report having job training as a core objective compared to 28% in rural organisations and 39% in mixed market groups.

One difference in objectives between urban and rural agencies is clearly related to the proportion of L&RED organisations housed in local government. While almost two thirds of urban organisations report that protecting or increasing the revenue base of local government is a core objective, only one third of rural organisations include this objective.

Activities of local and regional economic development agencies

In this section we examine the activities that L&RED organisations undertake in order to reach their objectives. We have classified these activities into two categories. The first are business development activities designed to attract firms or to assist existing businesses. The second category includes activities that are not targeted at specific businesses, but rather work to enhance the development capacity of the region and its population. In either case, we asked respondents to limit their selections to those activities in which their organisation has been actively engaged in the past two years.

Table 5.3 lists business development activities in rank order. Marketing and being an information resource dominates the list of development activities. Other popular services include coordinating public sector activities, labour training and recruitment, assisting with large special events, and tourism promotion. In 1989, Levy (1990) asked economic development practitioners to identify the activities that occupied the majority of their time. By far, the two activities requiring the most time were public relations, advertising, provision

Table 5.3: Business development activities by L&RED organisations, US

Rank	Description	% of agencies	Rank	Description	% of agencies
1	Marketing the region to prospects	86	13	Marketing assistance within nation	40
2	Provide programme information	81	14	Assist access to venture capital	37
3	Assistance in accessing government funds	72	15	Assist with technology transfer/innovation	35
4	Coordinating public sector activities	69	16	Assist development of industry clusters	33
5	Assist with labour training and recruitment	58	17	Offering tax incentives (government only)	32
6	Assisting with major special events	58	18	Operating industrial/science parks	29
7	Tourism promotion	57	19	Streamlined permitting (government only)	27
8	Commercial district development[a]	54	20	Marketing assistance internationally	20
9	Provide SME support programmes	53	21	Operating a business incubator	18
10	Entrepreneur assistance programmes	52	22	Subsidising business relocation costs	18
11	Providing land or buildings not including industrial parks	45	23	Assist firms in meeting quality standards (ISO)	15
12	'Other' local jobs programmes	45	24	Promoting supply chain associations	7

Note:[a] Such as Main Street programmes.

Case study 5.2: Economic Development Division, Metro-Atlanta Chamber of Commerce

The Metro-Atlanta Chamber of Commerce's Economic Development Division (MACCED) serves 20 counties in the Atlanta, Georgia region, covering more than 5,000 square miles with a population of 4.2 million. The Chamber was incorporated in the 1860s and has been directly involved in economic development since the 1920s. MACCED relies solely on private funding through membership dues and donations. In the latest round of fundraising, US\$4.2 million in supplemental funding was generated to support marketing and economic development activities for a five-year period. City and county governments are not members of the Chamber, although they are partners in economic development efforts. John Gilman, Director of Prospect Services, describes MACCED's mission: "The main work we are doing is business recruitment. We are trying to attract facilities of companies either through expansion or relocation, with a main bottom line purpose of creating quality jobs.... We work an awful lot on brand identity through media relations and media coverage – nationally and internationally.... We do a lot of work when it relates to maintaining a relationship with site selection consultants. We do no cold calling" (interview, 8 October 2002). The division also employs a talent development director who works through college placement offices: "We are not only attempting to recruit companies, we are aiming to recruit talent". When a prospect is identified, MACCED almost always maintains a lead role in assisting the prospect to connect with local government and development agencies. MACCED does experience competition from organisations at different levels of government. State economic development officials promote economic development in Georgia's rural areas, sometimes competing with MACCED. However, Gilman says the competition is very professional: "Each party's agenda is well known to the other". Gilman continues: "Competition also occurs locally. County A and County B may vie for the same project that we are leading. There is no harm in that. They [the counties] will put their best business deal on the table. The prospect will look for the best deal and ultimately make a decision. We are a facilitator. We are not adversarial with anyone in the 20-county region".

Author: Guy Brown

of data, and responses to inquiries (consolidated as one class of activity); and outreach to existing firms. It appears that the activities engaged in most frequently by practitioners have remained relatively constant over the past 12 years.

Three of the more frequently occurring activities deserve further clarification. Slightly more than one half of responding L&RED organisations reported engaging in urban business/commercial district development. These activities include downtown redevelopment programmes, Main Street programmes, and other development activities targeted to specific areas within a community. Small- and medium-sized enterprise assistance programmes offer technical, marketing, and sometimes financial assistance to help them grow to the next level of business activity. In contrast, entrepreneur and self-employment programmes are typically designed to help people establish their own small business.

There is only one notable difference in business development activities between government and non-government L&RED agencies, aside from the obvious role of local government in granting tax incentives and streamlining permitting processes. Some 58% of local government economic development departments provide land and/or buildings to businesses that are not associated with industrial or technology parks. In contrast, less than 40% of non-government and public–private organisations offer these services. However, there are several notable differences in the business development activities among L&RED groups in rural, urban, and mixed areas.

Table 5.4 shows the participation rate of economic development organisations in business development activities by economic area. Urban government-based L&RED organisations apparently rely more on tax abatement, fee waiver, and other incentive programmes in their arsenal of business attraction tools. Given that rural government entities often tax at lower rates, there is less need for using abatements as recruitment tools. Moreover, if tax abatements are little more than redistributing the tax burden from one firm to another, as suggested by some researchers (Wirtz, 2000; Woodward et al, 2000), there are fewer firms in rural communities to whom to redistribute the tax burden. Also, since many labour market and cost factors are relatively constant within a given region, urban areas, with higher numbers of competing municipalities, rely more on taxes and fees for competitive differentiation (Mark et al, 2000).

Rural respondents less often report streamlined permitting and approval processes as an economic development activity. This is probably due to the size of municipal government in rural areas where one department, and perhaps one individual, has the permitting responsibilities that are shared across several departments in larger government entities. The size of the economy is also the most likely explanation for why urban L&RED organisations place more emphasis on industry clustering. However, the biggest surprise is the degree to which urban-based agencies do not offer technical assistance to firms wishing

Table 5.4: Selected business development activities of L&RED organisations, by economic area, US

Activity	% of agencies		
	Rural	Urban	Rural–urban
Government offering incentives	25	48	28
Streamlined permitting and approval	17	48	17
Assistance with quality standards (ISO, customer-based)	23	8	13
Assistance developing industry clusters	22	41	36
Commercial district programmes (Main Street, downtown)	39	74	54

Table 5.5: Capacity building activities by L&RED organisations, US

Rank	Description	% of agencies	Rank	Description	% of agencies
I	Improving strategic planning and implementation	81	8	Improve telecommunications infrastructure	50
2	Improve physical infrastructure	79	9	Influence land use regulations/planning	49
3	Development/planning for business sites	73	10	Advocate/lobbyist for area to government	46
4	Analysis of regional/local economy	67	11	Education and training general, not targeted	42
5	Developing networks among firms/agencies	62	12	Improve local services (education, health)	36
6	Coordinating government programmes	61	13	Education and training for youth, not targeted	32
7	Identifying business gaps and opportunities	51	14	Education and training for minorities, not targeted	22

to adopt quality standards. Only 8% of responding urban organisations offer this service.

Table 5.5 shows a listing of capacity building activities for L&RED agencies in the US. The good news for economic development consultants is that 81% of all L&RED organisations engage in activities designed to improve regional or local economic development strategic planning and implementation capacity.

Just as important as strategic planning, economic development agencies are actively engaged in promoting the quality and quantity of their area's physical infrastructure including roads, utilities, and, potentially, railways. The recent site location choice for a new Toyota light truck assembly plant reinforces the importance of railway infrastructure to industrial development in the US. One of the necessary conditions of Toyota's site location decision was competitive access to at least two major rail carriers. The selected site in San Antonio, Texas, qualified only after receiving state and local support for the construction of a new rail spur providing the required access to a second railroad. Interestingly, San Antonio offered the lowest level of tax and other incentives of the site finalists. Moreover, the company reportedly turned down tax incentives offered by the local school district. This supports claims that proximity to markets, labour force characteristics, and the availability of desired physical infrastructure are still primary components of business location decisions (Gabe and Kraybill, 2002; Strozniak, 2002). Emphasising the physical infrastructure element of capacity building is well justified.

However, actively working to enhance local telecommunications infrastructure is only performed by 50% of responding agencies – an interesting finding when put into context with the emphasis placed on economic development in the cyberspace age (Blakely, 2001). A smaller emphasis on telecommunications infrastructure may be an artefact of substantial overcapacity in telecommunications infrastructure that has been building over the past few years in the US. It is estimated that as much as 95% of existing telecommunications fibre optic network capacity is unused (Gain and Dunn, 2001).

Other leading capacity building activities include planning and developing business sites, developing cooperative networks among firms and agencies, and coordinating government programmes. Having the capacity to analyse local economic conditions and trends is important to two thirds of all responding L&RED agencies.

Interestingly, only about one third of the respondents engage in education and training that is not targeted to a specific business. Adult training and remedial education services are often offered by civic, charitable, and community development organisations, but the largest efforts are administered through federal government agencies and programmes. As noted by one respondent, however, training should include basic business skills for entrepreneurs and e-commerce awareness programmes because: "e-commerce awareness catapults regional business into a global proposition".

When segregated by government and non-government agencies, a striking difference is revealed in education-related activities. About 80% of government L&RED programmes include general education services that are not targeted to specific businesses or to youth or minority cohorts. Just over 50% of non-governmental economic development entities engage in similar activities. As might be expected, a slightly higher percentage of government agencies (88%) include physical infrastructure development activities versus non-government organisations (74%).

Correlation analysis reveals only the slightest suggestion that increasing the number of activities adopted at L&RED organisations positively impacts on performance ratings. More importantly, we can investigate the relationship between patterns of activities and agency performance as a first step in suggesting a series of best practices for L&RED organisations.

Table 5.6 presents the Spearman correlation coefficients examining the relationship between engaging in specific activities and being at least moderately effective. While the coefficients are small, they do allow us to suggest which business development activities are potentially the most effective. Based on these correlations, the development activities associated with higher effectiveness ratings include the development of industry clusters; labour force recruitment and training; national and international marketing assistance; facilitating access to venture capital; industrial and technology parks; and assistance in accessing government funding and programmes. Several of these activities are considered third wave economic development as noted in previous chapters. Given that less than half of responding firms engage in these activities, with the exception of labour recruitment, there appears to be opportunity for many agencies to consider adopting these activities and perhaps increase their effectiveness.

Interestingly, engaging in tourism promotion is negatively related to the effectiveness ratings, meaning that organisations undertaking this task, on average, have lower self-ratings of agency effectiveness. This could be the result of

Table 5.6: Correlation between business development activities and effectiveness ratings for L&RED organisations, US

Activity	Spearman *rho* correlation coefficient	Significance
Assisting with the development of industry clusters	0.24	$p<0.001$
Assisting with the recruitment and/or training of labour	0.20	$p<0.01$
Assistance, financial or advisory with marketing with the nation	0.19	$p<0.01$
Assisting firms to access venture capital	0.18	$p<0.01$
Assistance, financial or advisory with marketing internationally	0.16	$p=0.02$
Operating industrial or science parks	0.15	$p=0.03$
Assistance in accessing funding and support services from government	0.13	$p<0.01$
Tourism promotion	−0.15	$p=0.03$

agency specialisation, particularly in urban areas, which often have an independent convention and visitors' bureau.

The number of capacity building activities an L&RED organisation undertakes does not have a clear relationship to that agency's effectiveness rating. Similarly, there are few individual capacity building activities related to higher organisation effectiveness. Working to improve local telecommunications infrastructure and developing networks among and between firms and government organisations have a small positive relationship with higher effectiveness ratings. Of note, engaging in coordinating government programmes as a capacity building activity is associated with lower effectiveness ratings.

Partnerships of local and regional economic development organisations

Economic development organisations often work with a wide variety of partners in pursuit of their objectives. We asked the responding agencies to rate the level of importance of several different types of partners. The top three most important partners represent different levels of government including state agencies, local agencies, and individual local politicians. This finding is supported by the work of Olberding (2002) who found that needs and a willingness to cooperate are driving some municipalities to take a regional approach to economic development. Only slightly behind these government agencies in importance are business associations and other L&RED agencies in the respondent's area. The second tier of partners, generally rated as being moderately important, include industry representatives from banking, manufacturing, public utilities, retailers, and property developers. Groups that are considered less than mildly important partners to L&RED agencies in the US include

Case study 5.3: Cedar Valley Economic Development Corporation

The Cedar Valley Economic Development Corporation (CVEDC) serves Blackhawk County, Iowa. The Corporation is the lead economic development agency for all county municipalities, which includes Waterloo (population 68,000), Cedar Falls (population 35,000), and other smaller communities. The total county population is 128,000. CVEDC employs four people, with a US$385,000 budget, to accomplish its primary mission of facilitating job creation and capital investment. About 22% of the Corporation's funds come from public sources, including funding from local municipalities, a state university, a community college, and some public school districts. Local public utility companies provide major funding. About 10% of CVEDC's budget and 35% of staff time are spent on marketing. The remaining budget is targeted towards specific projects and business retention. Because of a lack of resources, the Corporation relies on state-level programmes for media advertising. Coordination with the state economic development agency is also emphasised in broad strategies such as clustering, according to Carl Adrian, CVEDC's president: "We have piggybacked on a group of state targets [for industry clusters]" (interview, 8 October 2002). Mr Adrian believes that the CVEDC does a pretty good job. When asked how the organisation's performance is evaluated, Adrian responds that new jobs are tallied along with new wages and capital investment: "We are embarking on a new effort that will try to benchmark our community and [identify] some broader indicators ... not just jobs created, but in terms of personal income growth [in the region]".

Author: Guy Brown

environmental groups, associations representing indigenous peoples, trades unions, and international organisations.

Only one group of partners shows differential levels of importance between government and non-government economic development agencies. Property developers and/or retailers are judged to be more important partners to government L&RED agencies compared to non-government agencies. Developers and retailers are also more highly valued by urban economic development practitioners. Rural L&RED organisations place more importance on partnering with federal agencies than their counterparts in urban or mixed areas.

Problems and challenges of local and regional economic development organisations

Problems and challenges faced by L&RED organisations are addressed in two ways. For the first approach, we presented a question that included several challenges and problems cited by economic development practitioners in previous studies as impediments to meeting their agency's objectives (Beer et al, 2003). Respondents were asked to use a scale of 1 to 7 to rate each problem, where a score of 1 represents 'not a problem' and 7 is 'a major problem'. These problems included issues of conflict and competition with non-L&RED government agencies, different and uncoordinated L&RED efforts in the same area, competition among L&RED organisations in the same region, and lack of a lead agency to engage in strategic planning for the region. None of these problems were rated higher than 'minor' problems with all mean ratings falling between 2.5 and 3.3. There are no statistically significant differences in the rating of these problems between government and non-government agencies, or among rural, urban and mixed region L&RED organisations.

The second approach included a question with several statements indicating various challenges faced by L&RED organisations. Using a modified Likert-type scale, respondents indicated their agreement or disagreement with each statement identifying a potential problem area. Table 5.7 presents the percentage of respondents rating each area as a problem for their organisation. Given that US L&RED organisations rate their effectiveness highly, we expect there to be few major problems. As with agencies in other countries, funding is the number one challenge according to these findings. Even so, over half of the respondents indicate that funding is either no problem or only a minor problem. Influence by funders presents problems for some organisations, while restrictions on funding, both duration and limitations on the use of funds, is a problem for about one third of respondents. Access to information regarding good development practices is the issue with the fewest reported problems.

The duration of the funding cycle is less of a problem for government agencies compared to non-government organisations. Some 21% of government-based L&RED agencies report that funding duration is a problem compared with 38% of non-government entities. About one fifth of government organisations

Table 5.7: Percentage of L&RED organisations rating each issue as a problem, US

Issue	%	Issue	%
Lack of funding	44	Agency lacks capacity for strategic planning	16
Short duration of funding	33	Unable to access information on good development practices	7
Insufficient untied funding to use as leverage with other agencies	36	Staff lack appropriate skills	11
Too much staff time spent seeking funding	25	Lack of effective leadership in the area	22
Rules or guidelines of funders restrict agency flexibility	27	Agency not seen as legitimate representative of the region	16
Priorities of funders have more influence on activities than needs of the region	26	Agency not seen as sufficiently independent of government	17
Too frequent changes in priorities and objectives by funders	11	Agency not involved in negotiations or decisions about large firms or projects	23

Table 5.8: L&RED organisations' problem issues, by type of economy, US

| Issue | % of respondents rating issue as a problem | | | |
	Rural	Urban	Mixed	Significance p=
Lack of funding	56	31	43	0.01
Too much staff time spent seeking funding	35	16	20	0.02
Rules of funders restrict agency flexibility	32	15	30	0.04
Staff lack appropriate skills	16	3	12	0.04
Agency not seen as independent of government	25	16	9	0.04

report that staff skills are a problem versus only 8% of non-governmental bodies reporting the same problem. There are, however, several differences in problems among rural, urban, and mixed area agencies. Table 5.8 shows problem issues by economic area based on statistically significant Chi-square tests.

The three major funding issues are a bigger problem for rural economic development agencies. As one respondent observes:"[We could be more effective if we had] a dedicated source of revenues and a 50% increase in our budget". Overall, more than half of all responding rural organisations report that access to funding is a problem. Rural agencies also have increased challenges based on restrictions placed on funds and an increased perception that they are not sufficiently independent of government. The availability of qualified staff is a much smaller problem for urban agencies, most likely due to labour market size and diversity.

Overall, the average number of issues that are reported as a problem by all responding L&RED organisations is 3.1. Government agencies report fewer average numbers of problems (2.6) compared to non-government entities (3.4). As suggested above, rural L&RED agencies find more of these issues a problem (mean = 3.9) than either urban (2.6) or mixed areas (2.9).

As noted earlier, based on the comparatively high effectiveness self-ratings of L&RED organisations in the US, we would expect relatively few problems. Are the problems noted above correlated with effectiveness scores? Table 5.9 presents the Spearman correlation coefficients between the degree to which an issue is a problem and the agency's self-reported effectiveness score. Since we expect the presence of a problem to negatively impact on the effectiveness score, all significance tests are performed as 1-tail tests. Interestingly, there is little correlation between identifying issues as problems and effectiveness ratings for government L&RED agencies. Only two issues, lack of funding and lack of local leadership, are statistically related to agency effectiveness. Two of several possible explanations seem appropriate. Either the potential problem issues included in the survey instrument are not the problems faced by government L&RED organisations, or their self-evaluation is based on criteria not affected by these problems.

Table 5.9: Spearman rank order correlation coefficients between problem issues and effectiveness ratings of L&RED organisations, government and non-government agencies, US

Issues (% reporting problem: government/ non-government)	Spearman correlation	
	Government	Non-government
Lack of funding (39/46)	−0.24[a]	−0.23[b]
Short duration of funding (21/38)	0.05	−0.20[b]
Insufficient untied funding to use as leverage with other agencies (32/38)	0.13	−0.20[b]
Too much staff time spent seeking funding (17/28)	−0.01	−0.17[a]
Rules or guidelines of funders restrict agency flexibility (21/29)	−0.06	−0.13
Priorities of funders influence activities more than region needs (20/29)	−0.20	−0.19[a]
Too frequent changes in priorities and objectives by funders (11/11)	−0.05	−0.21[b]
Agency lacks capacity for strategic planning (15/16)	−0.06	−0.17[a]
Unable to access information on good development practices (6/7)	−0.01	−0.26[b]
Staff lack appropriate skills (18/8)	−0.11	−0.15[a]
Lack of effective leadership in the area (18/25)	−0.27[a]	−0.20[a]
Agency not seen as legitimate representative of the region (9/19)	−0.02	−0.34[b]
Agency not seen as sufficiently independent of government (11/21)	0.01	−0.16[a]
Agency not involved in decisions about large firms or projects (21/25)	−0.08	−0.31[b]

Notes: [a] Significant at 5% level (1-tail).

[b] Significant at 1% level (1-tail).

In contrast with government L&RED entities, non-government organisations' problems *are* correlated with their effectiveness ratings. Only one issue regarding the lack of agency flexibility due to funding restrictions is not significantly correlated with effectiveness, and this coefficient would be significant if we relaxed our standards to the 90% level ($p=0.10$). Therefore, with some level of confidence, we can assert that the issues identified as potential problems for non-government L&RED organisations can be thought of as impacting on their ability to meet their goals and objectives.

Improving effectiveness

The natural extension of identifying problem areas is to ask respondents to identify ways to make their L&RED organisation more effective. Similar to the responses for identifying the methodology used to assess effectiveness, roughly half of our respondents answered this open-ended question. About one third of these stated that greater levels of funding would lead to enhanced effectiveness, corresponding nicely with the percentage of respondents reporting this issue as being a problem.

Just over 31% of the respondents tied improved effectiveness to either additional personnel or better equipped human resources. Given the small staff size of most of the respondents to this survey, this seems obvious. Less obvious is the connection to better-equipped personnel. Since only 11% of the respondents noted problems with staff skill levels, this response may indicate the need for capital resources, such as computers and other equipment, for use by agency personnel. This is supported by respondents calling for additional funds to "get more training on software usage" and training to achieve "better use of available technologies in the office".

Strategic issues such as devising and implementing strategic plans or identifying specific projects are identified as ways to improve effectiveness by 18% of the respondents. If combined with better information gathering, as noted by about 3% of the respondents, the need to develop strategic plans that are better tuned to local needs becomes evident. As suggested by Cox et al (2000), this could also include formally incorporating community preferences in local economic development strategies. The remaining sources of improvement are scattered widely, including interaction with local government, broadening and/or stabilising funding sources, and enhanced coordination with local leaders and organisations.

Conclusion

The findings of the US survey of L&RED organisations allow us to draw several conclusions. These agencies are characterised by a small staff and rely largely on paid professionals to run their operations. While about one third of these agencies suggest that they could improve their effectiveness if they were given access to additional funds, they appear to be relatively well-funded, especially compared to L&RED groups in other countries included in this study.

The most frequently cited core objectives of US L&RED organisations remain in traditional areas of economic growth through business development and attraction. However, a substantial number of agencies report focusing on economic diversification, revitalisation, and capacity building. One third also identifies environmentally sustainable development as a core objective, although very few consider environmental groups as even mildly important partners. Benchmarking these findings for future studies will help identify trends in how L&RED organisations are adapting their roles in economic development to meet new challenges and civic norms.

Economic development agencies in the US rate themselves as being 'effective' to 'very effective' in meeting their goals and objectives. However, much of this self-assessment appears to be based on anecdotal and qualitative evidence. While this does not mean that these ratings are inaccurate, adopting a set of validated performance measures would lend credibility to these claims of success. Moreover, it would enhance agency management's ability to better identify areas of strength and areas that need improvement.

Our effort to assess the problems faced by L&RED organisations in the US is a qualified success. Based on correlations with effectiveness ratings, a lack of funding and leadership gaps in regional economic development efforts are the only meaningful problems faced by local government-based agencies. However, that is hard to believe. Either the survey instrument did not identify other important problem areas, or government agencies rate their effectiveness using criteria largely unaffected by the problems listed. In contrast, non-government agencies show identifiable relationships between problem areas and their performance ratings. Most notably, non-government agencies, in addition to funding issues, see problems in establishing their own legitimacy for engaging in economic development activities.

Lessons

Based on correlations between L&RED organisation activities and effectiveness ratings, a preliminary set of potential best practices in the US can be listed:

- Work to develop industry clusters, especially in urban areas.
- Increase involvement in labour recruitment and training.
- Give agency staff members the training and tools to maximise small staff effectiveness.
- Help local companies promote their products to national *and* international markets.
- Assist local entrepreneurs in their pursuit of venture capital.
- Improve telecommunications infrastructure, as even with current network overcapacity this remains an activity worth pursuing.
- Develop and support networks between firms and government, and among firms.
- Work to establish the relationships necessary to be seen as a legitimate participant in local economic development activities (for non-government agencies).
- Consider leaving the coordination of government programmes to other entities.
- Examine the role of tourism promotion in L&RED efforts.
- Continue to seek ways to enhance the strategic planning process for L&RED efforts.

Several of these suggested best practices should come as no surprise. They are the activities that economic development practitioners have sought to perfect for many years. But there apparently remains room for improvement. In the accompanying chapters, readers can examine the findings of surveys of L&RED organisations in Australia, England, and Northern Ireland to assess, edit, and improve this list of best practices.

Local and regional economic development organisations in Australia

Alaric Maude

The organisations

A very diverse range of organisations undertake the tasks of L&RED in Australia. This diversity reflects the federal structure of Australian government, in that development organisations have been sponsored by all three levels of government, as well as the process of institutional accretion, in which new programmes and new agencies are created by new governments and ministers while some of the old agencies continue to survive despite the withdrawal of their original support. Diversity is also a product of the way in which local and regional development organisations can be created from above and from below: by governments as part of a regional development programme, and by communities responding to specific needs and issues. The first process leads to a common set of organisations within a jurisdiction, while the second produces considerable variety.

In Australia the questionnaire was sent to all local governments and to all identifiable RDAs, as outlined in Chapter One. Table 6.1 shows the distribution of the responding organisations by state or territory, and demonstrates that local government dominates the L&RED scene in Australia, at least in terms of the number of organisations. With 505 useable questionnaires for Australian organisations it is possible to further divide those that are not local government into three groups. The first are termed agencies, and their common features are that they are not a branch of one of the three levels of government, are managed by boards or committees consisting of members of the region, and undertake a wide range of regional development activities. They include ACCs established by the Commonwealth government, the Development Commissions of Western Australia, the Regional Development Boards of SA and NSW, the various RDOs of Queensland, Voluntary Regional Associations of Councils, and a variety of community-based RDOs. The second type are business enterprise or support centres (BECs) which are similar to the first group but have a narrower range of functions, serve smaller regions, and essentially focus on small business advice and support. They may be sponsored by a state government, a Chamber of Commerce or some other business association. The third type covers the rest, a diverse group ranging from urban commercial district development bodies (typically called Main Street organisations in Australia) to Aboriginal and other community development organisations and a few utilities. This diversity makes it hard to generalise about them. The 'other' group is also largely missing from the surveys in the other countries in this study, which makes cross-national comparison of non-local government organisations somewhat risky. For these reasons the 'other' category will not be separately analysed in this chapter, but it is still included in the totals for non-local government organisations.

Based on the distribution of respondents, L&RED organisations in Australia are more common in rural or mixed rural and urban areas than in the urban areas. About 40% of respondents reported that the economy of their region is predominantly rural, another 40% reported mixed rural and urban, and only 20% reported predominantly urban. This contrasts strongly with the distribution of the Australian population, as about 65% of the national population live in the six state capital cities. That so few of the responding agencies are located in predominantly urban areas is a reflection of the way that regional problems in Australia have been constructed as non-metropolitan problems by both national and state governments, as discussed in Chapter One.

Most organisations are relatively young, a consequence of the newness of local and regional involvement in economic development, and the high mortality rate of the non-local government organisations (Beer and Maude, 2002). For example, the NSW Regional Development Boards were established in the late 1970s, the South Australian Regional Development Boards in the late 1980s, the Western Australian Development Commissions in the late 1980s and early 1990s, and the ACCs in the mid-1990s. About 80% of agencies and BECs are therefore less than 12 years old. It is difficult to obtain a comparable figure for the age of local government organisations, as many local government respondents

Table 6.1: Type of organisation by state/territory, Australia

| State/territory | Local government | Non-local government | | | | Total |
		Total	Agency	BEC	Others	
NSW	77	64	30	31	3	141
Victoria	52	25	17	6	2	77
Queensland	51	19	16	3	0	70
SA	39	42	24	6	12	81
Western Australia	64	27	10	17	0	91
Tasmania	15	10	1	8	1	25
Australian Capital Territory	0	2	1	1	0	2
Northern Territory	4	14	1	0	13	18
Australia	302	203	100	72	31	505

appear to have given the year of establishment of their authority rather than the year of establishment of its economic development function.

The only agencies that are uniformly spread across the country are the 56 ACCs supported by the national government (also known as the federal or Commonwealth government). They were originally established within the national government department responsible for employment and labour market programmes, with the task of advising on and generating support for the Commonwealth government's employment and training programmes, and facilitating employment growth within their region. They have recently been moved to the department responsible for regional development, and given a wider role. At the state level Western Australia, SA and NSW each have a uniform network of state government supported RDAs, but these only cover the non-metropolitan areas. In the rest of Australia the institutional landscape for L&RED is more varied. In Queensland, for example, the agencies are a very diverse group of organisations, and do not conform to any one model. This reflects the fact that they are the survivors of several decades of 'bottom-up' local development activity, and the absence of direct state government involvement in their establishment and management. As a consequence of this institutional architecture, most regions of Australia have several organisations devoted to L&RED. All regions have an ACC, many have a local government involved in economic development, most areas outside the capital cities have an agency (and sometimes more than one) and most urban areas (large and small) have a BEC. Some of these organisations, such as agencies and BECs, operate at different scales, serve different clients and are complementary rather than competitive, but some overlap and create a need for coordination, such as between the agencies and the ACCs.

Explaining regional development organisations

The RDOs outlined above are the product of a complex set of processes that have influenced regional policy in Australia. These policies reflect the changing ways that governments have responded to the imperative to support economic growth in an ever changing world economy, the different ideologies of the two main political parties, their attempts to respond to regional political pressures, and the overlapping roles of the three levels of government in a federal structure. Since the 1980s Australian governments, led by the national government, have pursued neoliberal or market rationalist policies, in an endeavour to make the Australian economy more internationally competitive. Government direct intervention in the economy has been greatly reduced, as has government investment in both physical and social infrastructure. As a result, the funds to pay for major programmes in regional development, and the ideology that could support such expenditure, are both absent, regardless of which of the two major political parties is in power. These policies have supported over a decade of sustained national economic growth (Dawkins and Kelly, 2003) but have also led to reduced service provision, loss of employment, and greater competitive and adjustment pressures in many regions, particularly in some non-metropolitan areas.

Governments are obviously not responsible for all the economic and social problems that have emerged in Australia's regions since the 1970s. Declining commodity prices, increased competition from other producers, and the investment decisions of multinational corporations, for example, have forced the restructuring of a number of regional economies. The concentration of 'new economy' jobs in Sydney and Melbourne has also increased the inequalities between dynamic and marginalised regions. However, the political outcome of the combined impacts of economic restructuring and government reforms at both national and state levels has been a loss of support for the two major political parties and an increase in the number of independents and minor party representatives elected to represent non-metropolitan areas (McManus and Pritchard, 2000). Political pressures have therefore forced governments at both state and federal levels to at least appear to be doing something to stimulate local and regional development, but they are constrained by their perceived need to continue with policies of market rationalism, reduced government intervention, and international competitiveness (Stilwell, 2000) and by a discourse that condemns policies that look like 'picking winners' and instead advocates 'a level playing field'. The result is that Australia does not have a strong national policy on regional development, or strong industry policies (apart from a few exceptions such as the motor vehicle industry) which could support the activities of L&RED organisations.

The current federal (national) government maintains that regional problems will be mainly solved by focusing on national economic growth through a continuation of market rationalist policies (Tonts, 1999). Yet the persistence of these problems, and the electoral pressures noted above, have pushed it to provide funding for regional organisations and community groups, and to expand the functions of its own ACCs. The specifically regional programmes of the national government now have a larger budget than the regional development programme of the previous Labor government, which was terminated by the present government in 1996 on the grounds that the Commonwealth had no constitutional role in regional development (Beer et al, 2003), and the Commonwealth's ACCs now have functions and a departmental home similar to those of the RDOs which were also abandoned by the current government in 1996.

The states have also developed modest regional development programmes, again in response to political pressures. Probably the clearest example of an RDO created for political reasons is the South West Development Authority in Western Australia (now the South West Development Commission), established in 1983 to fulfil an electoral promise of the winning Labor Party, and to demonstrate to non-metropolitan voters that a Labor government could bring them development (Pradzynski and Yiftachel, 1991; Barker, 1992). Political considerations also led to the extension of the RDA concept to other non-metropolitan regions, culminating in the present nine Regional Development Commissions which cover the states outside the Perth metropolitan area.

We could therefore interpret the growth of RDOs in Australia as a product of government attempts to address regional problems within the framework of market rationalist policies, that is, without establishing new bureaucracies or spending large amounts of money or intervening in the economy. We could also interpret it as an attempt to shift the responsibility (and the blame) for regional development to regions and communities. Taylor, for example, suggests that the regional development programme of the national government in the mid-1990s "made adjustment to the problems of internationalization a local community problem" (Taylor, 2000, p 120). The current national government sees its role as supporting "local ideas and aspirations, so that communities can lead their own development and realise their own future" (Anderson and Tuckey, 2002, p 1) while the Western Australian Development Commissions are also based on the ideology that "economic development initiatives must come from the local communities and, in large part, from local resources" (Tonts, 1999, p 584).

These interpretations ignore the bottom-up processes that have created and sustained many RDOs. Those established by local governments, communities and business associations are a result of the interest of local people in their own economy and its future. Their protagonists may be business people seeking to increase their local market, community members wanting to create employment opportunities for their children, or local governments responding to community concerns about declining services or the impacts of economic restructuring, and they are essentially grass-roots responses to regional issues. In Queensland such organisations have flourished for several decades without direct support from state and national governments. This is because local government in that state has wider powers and responsibilities than in other jurisdictions, and therefore has had a greater ability to take the initiative in the formation of RDOs, and has not had to depend on state government programmes as elsewhere in Australia. Queensland also seems to have been more influenced by the local government and community-based development organisations of the US than the rest of Australia. Such grass-roots organisations will no doubt continue to emerge around Australia wherever local people perceive a need, and they could be interpreted as the rise of a new form of governance that fills a gap created by the partial withdrawal of higher levels of government from services, programmes and policies that affect localities and regions (Allison and Kwitko, 1998).

To understand the existence of RDOs we therefore need to combine the top-down and bottom-up processes by which they have been created. However, the two processes are related in that the policies of state and national governments have partly created the gap which local agencies attempt to fill (Allison and Kwitko, 1998). Furthermore, the bottom-up initiatives do not challenge the dominant ideology of market rationalism, as local government and communities have neither the resources nor the constitutional powers to be more interventionist in the economy.

Resources

The resources available to L&RED organisations were measured in the questionnaire by data on annual expenditure (which can also be used as a surrogate measure of income), staff numbers, and sources and types of income. As explained in Chapter One, much of the data on expenditure is inaccurate, because many local governments reported the total expenditure of their council rather than the amount devoted to economic development activities. To get around this problem all organisations reporting an annual expenditure of AUS$5 million or more were deleted from the analysis for this chapter, but even with this adjustment some of the organisations in the AUS$2-4.99 million class probably reported their expenditure incorrectly. Table 6.2 shows that BECs have the lowest levels of expenditure, with over half spending less than AUS$150,000, the equivalent of less than four average annual salaries. Expenditure is higher for agencies, while local government organisations reported the highest levels. On the other hand, a breakdown by type of economy shows little difference, with urban areas having only a slightly higher median expenditure compared with rural and mixed urban and rural areas.

Data on the number of full-time equivalent paid staff employed by L&RED organisations mirror these levels of expenditure. They also have the same deficiencies, as many local government organisations appear to have responded with the total number employed by the organisation rather than the number specifically employed on economic development activities. Even so, two thirds of non-local government organisations employ four or fewer staff, and 8%

Table 6.2: Annual expenditure by type of organisation, Australia (%)

| Annual expenditure (AUS$) | Local government | Non-local government | | | |
		Total	Agency	BEC	Total
$0-39,999 (less than 1 average salary)	7.5	9.9	8.4	5.7	8.8
$40,000-149,999 (from 1 to less than 4 average salaries)	16.9	26.6	12.6	50.0	22.2
$150,000-299,999 (from 4 to less than 8 average salaries)	10.0	28.1	35.8	24.3	19.9
$300,000-749,999 (from 8 to less than 20 average salaries)	16.3	17.7	25.3	12.9	17.0
$750,000-1.99m (from 20 to less than 50 average salaries)	21.3	10.4	12.6	4.3	15.3
$2-4.99m (50 to less than 125 average salaries)	28.1	7.3	5.3	2.9	16.8
All organisations	100	100	100	100	100
n	160	192	95	70	352

have no full-time paid staff. As with the pattern for expenditure, agencies employ more staff than BECs, with median staff numbers of 3-4 compared with 1-2 in BECs.

The ability of L&RED organisations to engage in effective economic development activities depends not only on their resources of money and staff, but also on the sources of their income and the conditions attached to this income. Table 6.3 divides the income of organisations into government and non-government sources, and into tied and untied income. Tied income is income which is granted for a specific purpose or project, and high levels of tied income may restrict the ability of an organisation to determine its own priorities or to fund basic activities such as research into the local economy or strategic planning (Monks, 1994). Local government organisations have greater freedom of action, because nearly two thirds of their funding comes from their own revenue and only 35% is tied, while non-local government organisations are dependent on national and state governments for over two thirds of their income, and much of this comes tied to specific projects.

Combined, the data on expenditure, staff and sources of income show that Australian non-local government L&RED organisations are generally small and modestly resourced units. They also serve relatively small populations. Agencies serve a median population of 70,000, followed by BECs with a median population of 44,600, local government organisations with a median of 12,500 people (reflecting the very small size of much of local government in Australia) and the 'others' with a median of 1,500. They have a large proportion of their income tied to specific projects, through funding from state and national government agencies. Although we do not have accurate data for local government development organisations, it is very likely that their levels of expenditure and staffing are similar to those of the agencies, but their proportion of untied income is much greater. Consequently, the majority of L&RED

Table 6.3: Mean percentage of tied and untied income by type of organisation and source of income, Australia

| Type of income | Local government | Non-local government | | | Total |
		Total	Agency	BEC	
Grants from government tied to specific projects	23.3	46.0	47.9	43.7	32.7
Grants from government not tied to specific projects	21.3	27.2	32.2	24.8	23.8
Other income tied to specific projects	12.2	8.0	3.3	14.6	10.4
Other income not tied to specific projects	42.3	20.0	17.3	22.5	32.8
Total income from governments	44.6	73.2	80.1	68.5	56.5
Total tied income	35.5	54.0	51.2	58.3	43.1
n	255	188	95	66	443

organisations in Australia lack the financial and staff resources to have a major direct impact on regional development, and instead rely heavily on influencing public sector agencies with greater resources, or on influencing the decisions of the private sector. Furthermore, while some of the rhetoric of L&RED emphasises community responsibility for local and regional development, the fact that non-local government organisations are dependent on the three levels of government for nearly 80% of their income (and agencies are dependent for nearly 90%) must limit their ability to act autonomously. Even local government, despite its greater ability to fund itself, is subordinate to state governments (Munro, 1997).

Objectives, activities and partnerships

Objectives

The questionnaire presented organisations with a list of 20 objectives or goals, and asked them to select those that best described the core objectives of their organisation. Of the objectives that represent outcomes rather than the means to achieve these outcomes, the most common are to promote economic and employment growth, and to improve the quality of life (Table 6.4). Environmental protection is also important, but social goals rank much lower, with only a quarter stating that improving the employment, incomes and welfare of disadvantaged groups is an objective. Local governments are also involved in trying to regenerate or revitalise their regional economy, retain or increase their populations, increase their revenue base, and diversify their economy. Organisations in rural areas, and in mixed rural and urban areas, had on average one to two more objectives than those in urban areas. They were more likely than those in urban areas to be involved in promoting economic growth, regenerating and diversifying the local economy, retaining or increasing the local population, building capacity for development, lobbying governments on behalf of their region, and promoting their area. These differences reflect the particular economic difficulties of many rural areas and the rural–urban fringe of the cities, and a common feeling that these issues are not being addressed by state or national governments.

Objectives that are relatively unimportant for Australian L&RED organisations, but may be more common in other countries, include the promotion of property development, providing or facilitating labour market training, and providing a job placement service. Even among local government organisations only 28% stated that property development was an objective, reflecting the fact that in Australia this is very much seen as a private sector activity. The lack of involvement in labour market programmes, on the other hand, is because these are largely provided through the Commonwealth government's Job Network programme.

Table 6.4: Objectives by type of organisation, Australia

| Objective | Local government | Non-local government | | | Total |
		Total	Agency	BEC	
Promote economic growth	82.5	77.8	84.0	80.6	80.6
Improve quality of life	81.5	47.3	64.0	19.4	67.7
Promote employment growth	62.9	68.5	80.0	65.3	65.1
Attract/recruit new businesses to the area	69.2	49.8	54.0	54.2	61.4
Partnerships among public–private sector, community	65.2	54.2	67.0	40.3	60.8
Lobby government on behalf of region	62.3	48.3	67.0	27.8	56.6
Develop local businesses (new, expansion, retention)	49.0	61.6	49.0	94.4	54.1
Regenerate/revitalise local economy	57.9	46.8	57.0	43.1	53.5
Build capacity for development	57.9	44.8	63.0	29.2	52.7
Promote environmentally sustainable development	62.6	37.4	48.0	30.6	52.5
Stimulate involvement in local development	50.7	49.3	51.0	52.8	50.1
Diversify the regional/local economy	50.7	43.8	54.0	43.1	47.9
Retain/increase local population	54.3	28.6	35.0	20.8	44.0
Promote area nationally, internationally	45.4	29.6	42.0	12.5	39.0
Protect/increase local tax base	51.3	11.8	14.0	6.9	35.4
Improve jobs/income of disadvantaged groups	25.8	28.1	33.0	19.4	26.7
Increase local incomes	25.2	26.6	24.0	31.9	25.7
Promote property development	28.1	5.4	8.0	1.4	19.0
Provide/facilitate labour market training	13.2	22.7	22.0	22.2	17.0
Provide job placement services	3.0	5.9	3.0	9.7	4.2

Activities

To achieve these objectives L&RED organisations in Australia undertake a number of activities. The most common can be grouped into four categories. The first involves marketing, promotion and advocacy for the region. This includes assisting with major or special events, marketing the attractions of the region to prospective businesses, tourism promotion, Main Street programmes, and acting as an advocate or lobbyist for the region with governments. This is mainly an information or publicity function and does not involve direct subsidies or other financial assistance to businesses. Local government organisations are an exception, with about one third of them offering reduced rates, taxes or charges to attract or retain businesses.

Business development activities are a second category. They include linking regional businesses to appropriate support services; developing cooperation and networking between business firms in the region, and between firms and public and private sector agencies; and employment creation programmes. A third category is regional strategic planning, which includes analysis of the regional economy, identifying business gaps and opportunities for new industries, and strategic planning for the region. The fourth category can be described as regional capacity building. This focuses on the improvement of regional physical infrastructure, including telecommunications (the quality of the telecommunications network in some parts of non-metropolitan Australia is a major political issue). Much less common are activities to improve the quality of the workforce negotiate education and training, but a number of organisations are involved in improving regional service provision, such as general education and health services.

The majority of local government organisations are also involved in the development or provision of business sites and premises, and in assisting businesses negotiate the permit and approval processes. The majority of agencies and BECs provide a range of services to assist small- and medium-sized enterprises, while a small majority of BECs provide general education and training programmes, and assist firms to market nationally or to access venture capital. The case studies of the Wheatbelt Development Commission (Case Study 6.1) and the City of Onkaparinga Economic Development Unit (Case Study 6.2) included in this chapter illustrate the range and combination of activities undertaken by Australian organisations.

The common element in all these activities is that of facilitation and information. Organisations do not have the financial and staff resources to provide many services themselves, or to subsidise business firms in order to attract them to or retain them in the region. Most are not directly involved in industrial recruitment, unlike the US organisations. Only a minority of local government respondents offered reduced rates, taxes or charges to attract or retain businesses, and even fewer subsidised the relocation costs of businesses prepared to move to the region. One of the main roles of L&RED organisations is therefore to link local businesses to those agencies that can provide these

Case Study 6.1: The Wheatbelt Development Commission

The Commission is one of nine Regional Development Commissions in Western Australia established under the 1993 Regional Development Commissions Act. It serves a population of about 72,000 people in a region of over 150,000 km^2 to the north and east of the state capital of Perth. The economy is based on agriculture and horticulture, with some mining in the east and fishing industries along the coast on the west. The Commission is a statutory authority of the Western Australian government, managed by a board consisting of three members selected from the community, three from local government, and three selected by the Minister of the State Government responsible for the region, plus the Director of the Commission as an ex officio member. The Commission has 15 staff spread over four sub-regional offices.

The broad role of the Commission is to facilitate the economic and social development of the Wheatbelt region, and the inclusion of social development gives it a wider role than most other L&RED organisations. Under the 1993 Regional Development Commissions Act the role of the Commission is to:

- maximise job creation and improve career opportunities in the region;
- develop and broaden the economic base of the region;
- identify infrastructure services to promote business development within the region;
- provide information and advice to promote business development within the region;
- seek to ensure that the general standard of government services and access to those services in the region is comparable to that which applies in the metropolitan area; and
- generally take steps to encourage, promote, facilitate and monitor the economic development of the region.

In 2001 the Commission's revenue from the Western Australian Government was AUS$1.5 million. Another $83,000 was received in grants and $55,000 in other income. The main areas of expenditure were on staff ($757,000) administration and accommodation expenses ($391,000) and grants and subsidies ($156,000). In 2002 it was ruled that the Commission did not have the power to pay grants, and these have ceased. The Commission is therefore essentially a provider of services, not financial assistance.

The Commission's recent industry projects include: an examination of the potential of the olive industry; support for a group developing alternative agricultural and horticultural industries; commissioning of a report on inland saline aquaculture; assistance to a network of farmers developing a new tree crop; financial support for research into the commercial value of salt lake biota; information and facilitation services for a variety of tourism projects, and commissioning a study of groundwater resources. Service provision projects include collation of information on energy infrastructure and gaps in energy provision; assistance for a project to improve mobile phone coverage; and lobbying for highway development. Social welfare projects include: assistance in the planning of aged care services, and assistance to a Wheatbelt Youth Network. The Commission is also involved in work on: several sub-regional strategic plans; assisting in the development of natural resource management plans; provision of advice and information to community groups and local government authorities (of which there are 44 in the region) that are developing regional economic development projects or applying for funding; and administration of a scheme to fund economic and social projects within the region.

Source: Wheatbelt Development Commission (2002)

services, and to coordinate these services so that they better meet local needs. This is a useful function because many small and medium firms do not have the resources or the time to track down the services that might help them, or to work their way through the application procedures (see Case Study 6.2). In addition, Australian L&RED organisations attempt to identify regional infrastructure and service needs and lobby other agencies to meet these needs, and to assist (but not financially) any activity that will generate local employment. Local government and agencies have the largest variety of activities, while BECs are more specialised, focusing on support programmes for small- and medium-sized enterprises rather than on regional capacity building. Organisations in rural and mixed rural and urban areas averaged one-and-a-half to nearly three more activities respectively than those in urban areas, demonstrating again the greater diversity of the non-urban organisations.

What these organisations *do not do* is also of interest, in that several of the newer strategies of regional and local business development are relatively uncommon activities among the Australian organisations. Assisting the development of industry clusters was an activity for only 35% of organisations, and was most common among the agencies. Even fewer organisations assisted with technology transfer, helped firms access venture capital, promoted supply chain associations, assisted with marketing internationally, operated a business incubator, or assisted firms to meet quality standards. Yet these are widely advocated techniques of business development, both in Australia as well as internationally. The reasons for their low uptake may be a lack of capacity, slowness in adopting new ideas, or the role of private sector, state and national government agencies in their provision. In SA, for example, the largest cluster building programme is sponsored by a peak business association.

Partnerships

In undertaking these activities organisations work with a variety of partners. The questionnaire presented respondents with a list of 20 possible partners, and asked for their importance to be scored on a scale from 0 (not a partner) to 3 (a very important partner). The mean of these scores is used to evaluate the strength of each partnership. Table 6.5 groups partnerships into three types – public sector, private (business) sector and other – and shows that, overall, the

Case Study 6.2: City of Onkaparinga Economic Development Unit

The City of Onkaparinga spreads from the southern suburbs of Adelaide, the capital city of SA, into the rural–urban fringe of the metropolitan area. It contains a growing population of about 150,000 people, making it the largest local government authority in SA. The economy is based on services for the residential population, significant areas of manufacturing in the north, recreation along the coastline, and intensive grape production, wine making and other agricultural industries in the south. Economic development is the responsibility of the Economic Development Unit of the City Development Department, with a professional staff of four officers.

The Council describes its role in local economic development as follows:

> Rather than have an economic development strategy, the Council has a 'strategy for involvement in economic development', the semantics of which recognise that the economic development challenge is shared by all levels of governments. Whereas federal and state governments work at the macroeconomic and microeconomic policy levels with attention to general industry strategies, local government has a genuine role to play in economic development at the enterprise level. The Council is best placed to understand the needs of local business; not just at a general industry level but for individual enterprises.

Assistance to local business is provided through partial financial support for a local export enhancement programme and a BEC. These provide a link between local businesses and federal and state government programmes designed to assist them, but which many find difficult to access without more direct support. The Department also provides support for several Main Street programmes, designed to improve the attractiveness and marketing of older retailing areas, and for the activities of local business associations. The latter is intended to help these associations improve the skills of their members, through formal training programmes and informal advice and mentoring, as well as to provide channels for communication between business and the Council. Another channel of communication is a quarterly Economic Development Forum. The Council also sponsors, and provides partial funding for, a range of employment programmes, some its own but most developed by state and federal government agencies. These particularly target groups with specific employment difficulties. Finally, the Council assists the tourist industry by providing funding for the regional tourism boards, a visitor centre, special events such as the Tour Down Under road cycle race, and tourism signage.

In working to improve the local economy the Council has adopted the following principles:

- to be strategic – plan for the long term and in a way which achieves social and environmental objectives;

> - to be international – recognise that integration into the global community is a source of opportunity if planned for appropriately; and
> - to retain strong partnerships – with the business sector and other levels of government.
>
> *Source*: City of Onkaparinga (2003) and personal communication

most important partnerships are with the public sector. Business partnerships rank second, but within this category only partnerships with business groups (such as Chambers of Commerce) and private businesses have mean scores indicating moderate importance, and the lack of strong relationships with private sector suppliers of finance (mean score of 0.95 for venture capital providers and 0.92 for banks and other financial institutions) could be considered a weakness. In an increasingly knowledge-based economy the low rating of partnerships with universities (mean score of 1.29) and research and development organisations (mean score of 1.26) is also a possible weakness, although it could reflect the largely metropolitan location of these institutions in Australia rather than any lack of interest on the part of development organisations. Within the 'other' category, community groups are moderately important partners, but indigenous and environmental groups and trades unions are only mildly important. The current discourse of L&RED in Australia often portrays the latter groups as problems rather than partners in local development.

This outline of the objectives, activities and partnerships of Australian L&RED organisations shows that they are essentially *economic* development organisations, with only limited involvement in community development or social equity programmes. Their main functions are to promote economic and employment growth, and to strengthen, diversify or regenerate their economy. Only a minority have the objective of improving the jobs and income of disadvantaged groups. Almost all depend on other agencies to actually implement and fund development activities, so their impact on regional development depends on their ability to undertake sound strategic planning, to mobilise local support and to influence the decisions of other agencies. The next section examines

Table 6.5: Mean importance of partners by type of organisation, Australia

Partner	Local government	Non-local government			Total
		Total	Agency	BEC	
Public sector organisations	2.02	1.97	2.18	1.82	2.00
Business sector	1.54	1.23	1.31	1.29	1.41
Other	1.18	1.07	1.30	0.75	1.13
Mean	1.64	1.48	1.65	1.37	1.76
n	291	195	100	69	486

Scale: 0 = Not a partner, 1 = Mildly important, 2 = Moderately important, 3 = Very important.

the evidence from the questionnaires on what the organisations thought about their effectiveness and the factors that aided or reduced their ability to have an impact.

Effective activities

The questionnaire asked respondents to nominate their most and least effective economic development activity, and some nominated more than one in each category. Table 6.6 lists all activities that more than 5% of respondents nominated as a most or least effective activity, divided between local government and non-local government organisations. The most effective activities are listed first in rank order for local government, then any remaining activities for non-local government, followed by any least effective activities nominated by more than 5% of respondents not already included, again in rank order. Not surprisingly, some activities ranked highly as both most and least effective, reflecting the varying experiences and situations of organisations, but the difference between the two percentages provides an overall measure of respondents' evaluations of the utility of each activity. On these measures the traditional business recruitment activities of promoting the region, attracting inward investment and streamlining approvals processes are rated poorly by respondents, while land preparation and site or premises development gets a mixed assessment from local government. On the other hand, business support and advice (such as training, advice, mentoring, and business retention and expansion services), provision of infrastructure and services, and facilitating networking, partnerships and cooperation, are all more likely to be rated as most effective rather than as least effective. These latter activities, which involve working with existing firms and local entrepreneurs to create development from within the region ('endogenous' development) have long been advocated as more effective ways of developing a region's economy than trying to recruit new firms from outside the region ('exogenous' development). The promotion of tourism and special events is also rated as effective, probably because the strategy of bringing customers to the region through tourism is one of the better tactics available to many non-metropolitan regions in Australia (Beer et al, 2003, chapter 6).

Effective organisations

To find answers to the question of what factors influence the effectiveness of organisations, respondents were asked to indicate their agreement or disagreement with a number of statements about situations or conditions that might reduce or increase their effectiveness. Agreement with a statement was measured by a score of 5, 6 or 7 and a 7-point scale in which 1 represented 'strongly disagree' and 7 represented 'strongly agree'.

Table 6.6: Most and least effective economic development activities, Australia

Activity	% nominating as most effective		% nominating as least effective	
	Local government	Non-local government	Local government	Non-local government
Infrastructure development, provision of services	19.3	8.1	5.0	3.7
Business support and advice	13.6	31.8	10.6	9.3
Networking/partnerships/coordination/ facilitation	13.2	15.0	2.8	3.7
Tourism promotion and special events	12.8	5.2	3.3	0.0
Land preparation, site/premises development	11.5	0.0	8.9	0.9
Sector planning and development initiatives, including exports and import replacement	9.5	11.6	7.8	4.7
Inward investment, promotion of region	8.6	8.7	18.9	5.6
Influencing/advocacy/developing policy/profile building	5.3	4.6	2.2	3.7
Developing/implementing a strategic plan	5.3	1.7	2.2	0.9
Working with community sector, social economy	4.9	9.2	1.7	2.8
Provision of Rural Assistance Programme funding	0.0	5.8	0.0	0.0
Managed workspaces, incubators, enterprise centres	1.2	3.5	1.1	5.6
Accessing government funds for the organisation	1.6	2.3	2.8	5.6
Training, skills, and supply side labour market interventions	0.4	0.6	5.6	4.7

Funding

The top six constraints to effectiveness, as measured by the percentage of respondents agreeing that they were a constraint, all relate to funding issues. Sixty per cent of respondents agreed that a lack of sufficient untied funding to use as leverage with other agencies was a problem. This is because funding that is not tied allows an organisation to attempt to influence the decisions of other agencies by offering partial funding for a project that the organisation wants implemented, or by undertaking studies that support the benefits of a proposed project. An equally important issue, also agreed to by 60% of respondents, is a lack of funding to support the core management, research and planning functions of the organisation. Another issue is the short duration of funding (53% agreement) which makes it difficult to develop the long-term projects which may produce the best results, and uses up staff time in repeatedly applying for the renewal of funding. Yet another issue is that the priorities of the funders have more influence on the organisation's activities than the needs of the region/local area (47% agreement). Organisations whose activities are determined by the programme funding offered by state and national government departments may be unable to undertake activities that meet the specific needs of their region or locality, as found by Allison and Kwitko (1998) in their study of local authorities in South East Queensland.

A similar picture of funding problems emerged from the answers to the question: 'What would make your organisation more effective?'. Respondents could write down as many factors as they liked, and 60% of their answers relate to funding issues. Typical answers included:

> Sufficient funding to just get on and do the job rather than half doing and half seeking additional funding. (BEC, NSW)

> Access to untied funding to use as leverage to seed fund projects and initiatives to meet the needs of the region. (agency, SA)

> Funding programmes that allow us to achieve our objectives, not what the state or federal government wants. (local government, SA)

> More and consistent funding. When we do receive good staff they have no guarantee of jobs beyond three years (often only two months). Because of inconsistency of funding we probably operate at about 70% of our potential. (agency, NSW)

A common theme was a call for greater local autonomy:

> More flexibility and decision making at the local and state level. (agency, SA)

> More independence from the federal government in assessment of projects. (agency, Tasmania)

> Local determination of priorities and solutions. (local government,Victoria)

These responses reflect the lack of empowerment of many L&RED organisations in Australia, including those belonging to local government, and their dependence on funding programmes closely controlled by state and national governments.

Regional competition and lack of coordination

A second set of issues relate to a lack of coordination and cooperation in regional development at the local level. These include the lack of a lead agency in strategic planning in the region, the existence of several different and uncoordinated economic development plans, competition and/or conflict between agencies belonging to different levels of government, as well as to the same level of government, a lack of effective regional leadership, competition and/or conflict between L&RED organisations in a region, and a lack of coordination between the government programmes delivered by these organisations. These problems result from the multiplicity of L&RED organisations in Australia and the failure of the three levels of government to cooperate effectively. That from 20% to nearly 40% of respondents agreed that these were problems influencing the effectiveness of their organisations suggests a serious deficiency in the management of local and regional development in Australia.

Once again, a similar picture emerged from the responses to the question: 'What would make your organisation more effective?'. Eleven per cent of answers were about coordination and cooperation issues, and typical comments were:

> A more coordinated (state/local) approach to economic development – local cooperation and reduction of local competition. (local government, SA)

> A better governance framework across the region to avoid duplication. All agencies working from the one regional strategic plan and focused on our core strategies. (agency, SA)

> Much of the ineffectiveness is a result of the conflicting objectives of the many organisations involved in development. (local government, NSW)

> Rationalisation of the number of entities trying to carry out a developmental role. (BEC, NSW)

Respondents also wanted:

A greater willingness on the part of Commonwealth agencies to embrace (rather than duplicate) state government delivery agencies and mechanisms. (agency, Western Australia)

Coordinated infrastructure planning for regions across all state agencies. (agency, SA)

State and federal governments to actually develop a coherent, united and flexible regional development policy. (agency, SA)

Organisational roles and capacities

A third set of issues relate to the roles and capacities of the organisations themselves. Over a third of respondents agreed that the effectiveness of their organisation was reduced because it was not involved in negotiations or decisions about large enterprises or large projects in its region. Many L&RED organisations are confined to working with small- and medium-sized enterprises, and large developments (with greater political significance) are managed by state government agencies. In addition, a quarter of organisations agreed that their effectiveness was reduced because they lacked the capacity to undertake strategic planning for their region (see also Allison and Kwitko, 1998).

The answers to the question about what would make your organisation more effective reinforce these results, with a quarter of respondents nominating a response that fits this category. Some typical responses were:

We don't have a sound strategic approach − until we have a properly based strategy any additional resources will be as ineffective as in the past. (local government, Victoria)

We need to focus well on fewer more strategic issues. (local government, Queensland)

Staff with more ability, willing to spend longer in the job − the average term of employment is 12 months. (agency, Queensland)

Respondents also identified a number of additional issues to the ones asked about in the questionnaire. Some felt that their effectiveness was reduced because of a lack of understanding in the community of what creates economic development and of the role of the organisation, or because of the limited involvement by local business in its activities, or because of political interference from all levels of government. A number of responses concerned the very limited powers and status of L&RED organisations. They expressed the view that their organisations should have greater autonomy, and be consulted more by state and federal governments on the development of their region. There were calls for:

> A greater level of decision making and authority to make regional planning and policy decisions that impact on the region. (agency, SA)

> A higher profile and early inclusion in major resource and other development projects. (agency, Western Australia)

Another theme was a plea for a greater understanding by governments of the needs of regional communities. To quote one response:

> I might sound biased, but I get fed up with city based bureaucrats trying to make decisions for local communities. (local government, Western Australia)

These issues of role and capacity relate partly to the funding problems of the organisations, which affect their ability to employ skilled staff, undertake strategic planning and deal with large firms, but they also relate to whether they are constituted and empowered to have a central or only a marginal role in the economic development of their region.

The most important impediments to effectiveness, according to the organisations, are therefore funding, followed by deficiencies in the roles, powers, and capacities of the organisations, and the lack of a framework for cooperative regional development planning and implementation. The strength of these problems, however, varies between the types of organisations. Responses to items in the questionnaire indicate that the 'other' group of non-local government organisations felt the most underfunded, the most threatened by a lack of regional coordination and cooperation, and the most lacking in capacity. The agencies, on the other hand, were less concerned about their funding and their capacity, and more positive about their role in local and regional development. For example, most of the Commonwealth government's ACCs, the Western Australian Development Commissions, and the larger agencies in other states disagreed that they were excluded from decisions about large projects. They also strongly disagreed that they lacked the capacity to undertake strategic planning, or lacked skilled staff. However, over half of the agencies and half the local government organisations still agreed with most of the funding problems.

Evaluating these responses

These are the opinions of the respondents in the survey of Australian L&RED organisations, but can they be validated? Most organisations will say they need more funding, and effective organisations are well aware of what useful extra activities they could undertake with extra money. For example, six of the eight responding Western Australian Development Commissions, the best funded

Figure 6.1: Respondent assessment of effectiveness of the organisation in meeting its objectives, Australia

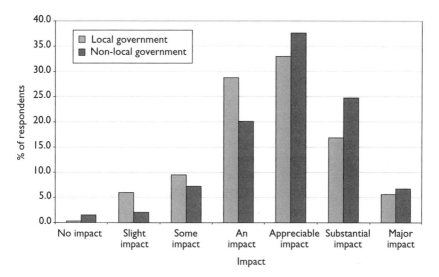

agencies in the nation, nominated funding issues in answer to the question: 'What would make your organisation more effective?'. The questionnaire enables us to probe these opinions, although not in a fully rigorous way, through the answers to the question: 'How would you rate the effectiveness of your organisation in achieving its objectives?'. The results of this self-assessment, based on a scale from 1 (no impact) to 7 (major impact) are set out in Figure 6.1. Few organisations claimed to have no impact or a major impact, but there was a fair spread of assessments in between. Exactly what this self-assessment of effectiveness represents cannot be determined. It could reflect the personality of the respondent, the pressure to be seen to perform, confidence or its absence, or an informed assessment of the organisation's impact. The answers to the next question, 'What evidence do you use to make this rating?', show that many respondents did in fact have legitimate ways of evaluating the performance of their organisation, and that their assessments might therefore be accepted as valid. Whatever its real meaning, the analysis below shows that its use leads to some interesting conclusions. It can also be noted that since the 1996 survey of a similar but not identical sample of organisations there has been a small upward shift in the rating of effectiveness, suggesting a maturing of the industry over this period.

Correlation analysis was used to find relationships between the self-assessment of effectiveness and the factors that might influence effectiveness discussed in the previous section. This analysis does not demonstrate a strong relationship with funding (Table 6.7). There is a moderate and statistically significant correlation between expenditure and the rating of effectiveness, but only for agencies and BECs, using Spearman's *rho* as the measure of correlation. As

Table 6.7: Correlation between rating of effectiveness of organisation and selected explanatory variables, Australia

Spearman correlation of rating of effectiveness with:	Local government	Agencies	BECs
Expenditure class	−0.05	0.29**	0.33**
Average scores on funding statements	−0.07	−0.11	−0.02
Average scores on coordination statements	−0.12	−0.12	−0.07
Average scores on capacity statements	−0.35**	−0.25**	−0.23*
Number of activities	0.37**	0.36**	0.40**

Spearman correlation of rating of effectiveness with:	Rural	Urban	Mixed urban and rural
Expenditure class	−0.03	0.15	0.03
Average scores on funding statements	0.00	−0.21	−0.12
Average scores on coordination statements	−0.09	−0.11	−0.20*
Average scores on capacity statements	−0.27**	−0.33**	−0.40**
Number of activities	0.43**	0.19*	0.27**

Notes: * = statistically significant at 0.05 level (one-tailed); ** = statistically significant at 0.01 level (one-tailed).

before, all organisations reporting an annual expenditure of AUS\$5 million or more were deleted from this analysis, in order to reduce the problem of local governments reporting the total expenditure of the authority rather than the expenditure on economic development, but even then there is no statistical relationship between expenditure and effectiveness among the remaining local government organisations.

We might also expect that if funding issues are a major constraint to effectiveness, then there will be a relationship between an organisation's rating of its effectiveness and its rating of the effect of the various funding problems discussed earlier on that effectiveness. For example, it might be expected that, on average, the more a respondent agrees with the statement that 'The effectiveness of this organisation is reduced by the short duration of much of its funding', the lower they will rate the organisation's effectiveness. However, Table 6.7 shows that there is no statistical relationship between an organisation's rating of its effectiveness and its average score on the funding statements. In a reverse of the expected relationship, further analysis shows that the higher the percentage of income that is tied, the higher the organisation rated its effectiveness, despite the fact that 60% of respondents agreed that a lack of untied funding to use as leverage with other agencies reduced their effectiveness. This can probably be explained by arguing that effective organisations are active organisations with a number of projects, and because projects generally involve tied funding, these active organisations will therefore have relatively high levels of tied funding.

Similarly, there is no statistical relationship between an organisation's rating of its effectiveness and the average scores on its responses to the statements that evaluate regional coordination and cooperation. On the other hand, the responses that evaluate the role and capacity of the organisation do have a moderate and statistically significant correlation with the rating of effectiveness for all the categories in Table 6.7. They suggest that organisations which rate their effectiveness as high are likely to consider that they have the capacity to undertake strategic planning, that they are involved in negotiations or decisions about large enterprises or large projects, that they have the capacity to undertake strategic planning, that they are able to access information on good regional or local development practice, and that their staff have appropriate skills. They also believe that they are seen as a legitimate representative of the region, and as sufficiently independent of government. On the other hand, organisations that rated themselves low in effectiveness were likely to think the opposite.

These are measures of respondents' judgements of the capacity of their organisation to undertake regional development activities, and of acceptance of its role within the region by other agencies and the community. Another proxy measure of capacity is the number of activities that an organisation undertakes, with organisations with more activities having a wider range of ways of influencing the economy. Table 6.7 shows that the statistical association between an organisation's rating of its effectiveness and the number of activities it was engaged in is the highest of all the correlations reported in the table for all but one category, and provides further support for a relationship between capacity and effectiveness[1].

The results presented above suggest that the Australian organisations' perception of their effectiveness is related not only to their funding but also to their staff skills, their access to information, and their relationships with other agencies with an involvement in economic development. Table 6.7 shows that, for all types of organisations, those that rated their effectiveness highly are more likely to be in a higher expenditure class, to disagree that the conditions of their funding reduce their effectiveness, to engage in a wide variety of business development and capacity building activities, and to disagree that their organisation lacks capacity and influence. This conclusion also holds if the same relationships are analysed by the type of economy. Table 6.7 shows that the relationship with expenditure disappears, but this may be because local government (whose expenditure data is suspect) is now included in all categories rather than being kept separate. On the other hand, a moderate and statistically significant relationship with the measures for coordination emerges in mixed urban and rural areas. This hints at problems in this type of regional economy, possibly because of its greater complexity, or because organisations in the mixed urban and rural areas have a slightly larger number of partners than those elsewhere, or because they are, on average, younger and possibly less experienced at networking than those in the predominantly rural or urban areas.

Other factors that might influence the effectiveness of an organisation are the type of organisation, its partnerships, and the composition of the board of management. For example, local government organisations rate themselves lower in effectiveness than non-local government organisations, especially the agencies and the BECs. This result suggests that specialised organisations are more effective, or are more confident about their effectiveness. Organisations managed by boards comprised of a variety of interest groups, with no one group dominant, give themselves a higher rating for effectiveness (70.1% in the 'high' category) than those dominated by the private sector (61.5%) followed by those dominated by the government sector (55.0%) and those dominated by the voluntary sector (46.9%). This is an interesting result, given the debates over whether regional development should be driven by organisations representing local business, or by a partnership of the public and private sectors and the community. The latter type was advocated by the McKinsey Report, an influential 1994 study on regional development strategies for Australia, and was the model for the national Labor government's RDOs in the mid-1990s (McKinsey & Co, 1994). The former is supported by some who argue that only business creates economic growth and jobs, and that the representation of other interests can produce an ineffective body unable to act and unable to get business sector involvement. The importance of business representation is shown in the positive correlation between respondents' agreement with the statement that 'the involvement of local business in the management of the governing body of this agency increases its effectiveness', and their rating of their organisation's effectiveness. However, when disaggregated, local government organisations were more likely to disagree with this statement, while agencies were more likely to agree, and the responses to open-ended questions revealed some frustration on the part of local government organisations at the lack of involvement of local business in their activities. Finally, on the role of partnerships, there was a weak but statistically significant positive relationship between an organisation's rating of its effectiveness and the average importance of its public and private partnerships – the higher an organisation rated the importance of its partners, the higher it rated its effectiveness – and this relationship was slightly stronger for private partnerships. This reinforces the arguments for the importance of developing partnerships with the business sector, as well as the arguments for the importance of partnerships in general.

The results reported above are based on the separate relationships of each explanatory variable with the assessment of effectiveness. In the second stage of the statistical analysis the explanatory variables were incorporated into a multivariate logistic regression analysis that assessed the effect of each variable when acting in combination with the others. Organisations were grouped into 'high' effectiveness (a rating of 6 or 7 in the questionnaire) or 'low' effectiveness (a rating of 1 to 4). Organisations that gave themselves a score of 5 were ignored, and the 'other' group of organisations was also excluded from the analysis. Logistic analysis identifies which of the explanatory or predictor variables are best able to classify cases into their correct effectiveness class. The results of this analysis indicate that three explanatory variables correctly predict 77.6% of high and low rated organisations. Organisations that rate themselves as having a 'high effectiveness' have, other factors being equal, a larger number of activities than those that rate themselves as having a 'low effectiveness', they are more likely to disagree that they lack capacity, and they are more likely to be an agency or BEC than a local government organisation. The next most strongly associated variable was that for a mixed board of management comprising a variety of interest groups, but this association was not quite significant at the conventional 5% level. None of the other explanatory variables – the measures of funding and coordination problems, expenditure class, or the average importance of partnerships – had a statistically significant relationship with the rating of effectiveness.

Several conclusions can be drawn from these results. One is that the greater the variety of economic development activities that an organisation undertakes, the higher it rates its effectiveness. This could be explained by arguing that organisations that have a lot of activities think they are doing a lot and therefore *must* be having a significant impact. An equally plausible explanation is revealed in Table 6.8. This shows the percentage of organisations undertaking development activities that match the ones nominated by the questionnaire respondents as their most effective (as listed in Table 6.6), cross-tabulated with the number of activities undertaken in the last two years. The table demonstrates that organisations that undertake a large number of development activities are, not surprisingly, much more likely than organisations that undertake fewer activities to be engaged in those activities that respondents say are effective in increasing economic activity and employment. A second conclusion is that local government tends to see itself as less effective in L&RED than agencies and BECs. On the basis of some of the written responses in the questionnaire we can suggest, but not prove, that this is because some local government economic development units are not as well staffed and experienced as the agencies and BECs, which are specialist organisations. A third conclusion is that the results support the view outlined earlier that boards with a mixed membership have advantages over boards dominated by either the government or the private sector.

Conclusion

This chapter has analysed the views of Australian L&RED organisations on what constrains their effectiveness, and what would improve it. It has also used their ratings of their effectiveness to evaluate these views. Because we cannot be sure whether this rating is measuring the ambition or confidence of the respondent, or the real impact of the organisation, the results of the statistical analysis should be interpreted with caution. However, these results are backed up by the answers of respondents to other types of questions. The conclusions outlined above on the factors associated with a high effectiveness rating, and the responses of respondents to the question of what would improve their effectiveness, suggest that it would be possible to improve their effectiveness in several ways. In the first place, most organisations could do more with more money (and a number seem desperately underfunded for what they are expected to do) so better funding, and longer-term and more stable funding would all

Table 6.8: Percentage of organisations (local government, agencies and BECs) undertaking selected development activities by number of activities, Australia

Activity	% of organisations undertaking the activity in last 2 years, by number of activities			
	0-13 activities	14-21 activities	22 or more activities	
Improvement of regional/local physical infrastructure (roads, railways, utilities, etc)	60.1	75.1	85.5	
Improvement of regional/local service provision (such as education or medical services)	29.4	48.6	71.5	
Improvement of regional/local telecommunications infrastructure	31.9	52.6	81.8	
Providing general small- and medium-sized enterprise business support programmes	23.1	39.9	74.5	
Programmes to help people establish their own small business (self-employment programmes)	23.8	39.9	69.1	
Developing cooperation and networking between firms, and/or between firms and relevant public and private sector agencies and institutions	23.9	63.0	87.9	
Tourism promotion	52.5	79.8	87.3	
Assisting with major or special events in the region/local area	58.8	88.4	97.6	
Development of or planning for business sites and premises	20.2	53.8	77.6	
Analysis of the regional/local economy	26.4	64.7	93.3	
Identification of business opportunities or gaps in the regional/local economy and implementation of strategies to fill them	15.4	57.2	90.9	
Assistance, either financial or advisory, in marketing internationally	4.4	13.3	45.5	
Acting as advocate or lobbyist for the region/local area with governments	45.4	71.7	92.7	
Improving regional/local economic development strategic planning and implementation capacity	40.5	79.8	93.9	

improve effectiveness. Respondents also proposed reducing application and reporting requirements, in order to free time for development activities, and increasing the autonomy of organisations to make decisions, which could lead to more appropriate decisions being made by people closer to the problems, as well as raise the profile of the organisations within their regions. An OECD LEED programme recommendation is that national or state agencies should give L&RED organisations an incentive to innovate and develop programmes tailored to their own needs (OECD, 2001), a proposal that seems well worth trying in Australia.

However, actions to address the 'coordination' and 'capacity' constraints discussed earlier would also help, and may be a prerequisite for the effective use of better funding. These relate to the need for a framework for effective cooperation between organisations within each region, and to the need to strengthen the roles and capacities of the organisations. One strategy to improve coordination would be to ensure that there is a stable and recognised L&RED organisation in each region with the ability to lead on strategy development. This is another 'best practice' recommendation of the LEED programme (OECD, 2001) but was also one of the proposals to come out of the 1999 Regional Australia Summit. The Summit recommended that all levels of government "accept joint responsibility to ensure that there is only one recognised regional forum for each regional community and that the body used is the best existing body serving its region" (Regional Australia Summit, 1999).

A second strategy to improve regional coordination would be to develop a more effective framework for cooperation between organisations belonging to the different levels of government, including whole of government approaches that incorporate all three levels. There are already examples of how this might be achieved, such as the Upper Spencer Gulf Common Purpose Group in SA, which links together three local governments and three regional development boards (Beer, 2000b). Third, rationalisation of the number of organisations operating in some regions could help effectiveness. If organisations with the capacity to undertake more activities are in fact more effective, then consolidating current funding in a smaller number of organisations could increase effectiveness at no cost.

Capacity problems could be addressed by assisting organisations to improve their regional development skills, particularly in the area of strategic planning, and the LEED programme recommends that national or state agencies should provide technical support structures to assist local agencies to learn about good practices (OECD, 2001). Particular attention needs to be given to those organisations, especially in local government, who agreed that their effectiveness was constrained by capacity problems. The statistical findings also suggest that some organisations could consider whether widening the membership of their board of management could increase their effectiveness. Finally, state governments could ensure that L&RED organisations are involved in all significant projects within their region. This will enable them to attempt to maximise the benefits of major new projects to their regional economy, as well as enhance their profile within their communities.

This chapter has argued that the impact of L&RED organisations on regional development in Australia depends not only on their size and funding, but also on their ability to undertake good strategic planning, make sound choices on their priorities, mobilise local support, and influence the decisions of other agencies. Improving their capacity to undertake these tasks, as well as addressing the issues of coordination and cooperation identified by some organisations, will increase their ability to promote the economic development of their regions. A wider issue raised by some of the respondents, but beyond the scope of the analysis, is whether the effectiveness of these organisations also depends on the adoption of stronger state and national regional development and industry policies.

Note

[1] Because respondents were asked to rate their effectiveness in relation to their objectives, their assessment should be independent of their range of activities.

Lessons

The analysis above suggests that while funding is a constraint on the ability of Australian L&RED organisations to contribute to regional economic development, their impact could also be enhanced by:

- Improving the stability and duration of their funding.
- Giving them more opportunity to decide on priorities and programmes that suit their needs, rather than being dependent on the priorities of their funders.
- Improving the structure of coordination between organisations in each region, and ensuring that there is a recognised lead agency.
- Providing training and information programmes to improve the capacity of organisations to undertake their role, and establishing best practice recommendations on their governance and structure.

SEVEN

Local and regional economic development in a 'post-conflict' society: lessons from Northern Ireland

Rachel Naylor and Terry Robson
University of Ulster

Introduction

Northern Ireland is well known for 30 years of 'The Troubles'. It is also becoming notorious for a 'peace process' punctuated by localised instances of violent sectarianism and characterised by such severe political disagreements at the Northern Ireland Assembly that there is constant switching between government from this institution of devolved power and direct rule from Westminster.

Less well known, however, are both the nature of Northern Ireland's economic decline and the complex of L&RED initiatives in this region. These cannot be understood outside the socio-political context although equally their influence on 'The Troubles' and subsequent political events is important. While industrial decline may have contributed to the years of violence, many contemporary L&RED programmes and projects have been developed to address social divisions as well as to reverse the economic problems. In Northern Ireland, perhaps more than other jurisdictions then, the conjoining of the economic and socio-political objectives of contemporary L&RED is the norm. However, we believe that lessons learned from the Northern Ireland L&RED experience do have wider relevance, and not just to jurisdictions where ethnic conflict is significant. This is not least because, given the region's multiple problems, there has been considerable national and EU funding and encouragement of innovatory L&RED work. These funding and political opportunities have led to an interesting complex of L&RED initiatives. We argue that there is much to learn from these although, given the nature of the micro- and macro-political economic spaces in which they operate, issues relating to the endogeneity and sustainability of initiatives are of key importance.

Northern Ireland's economy and the 'national' context

Northern Ireland is a constituent country of the UK with a population of just 1.7 million. Northern Ireland was once part of the 'core' of UK industrial manufacturing, specialising in shipbuilding and linen. Since the 1920s, however, when Northern Ireland was created by the partition of Ireland, the key industries have been in decline and unemployment on the rise. On the UK's accession to the European Economic Community in the 1970s, Northern Ireland completed a transformation from a core area of the Empire to a peripheral region of Europe (see, for example, O'Dowd, 1995). In the 1960s the policy response to industrial decline was to attract new foreign direct investment into the region. This worked for a time, attracting in textile and other firms and addressing unemployment to some degree, although mainly through low-waged jobs. The 1970s saw the start of 'The Troubles' and the linked decline in multinational investment. Mass unemployment returned and, in the view of many scholars, the higher rates of unemployment experienced by the Catholic community contributed to the conflict (Gallagher, 1991). The introduction of the UK welfare state in the 1950s did provide some assistance as well as greater public sector employment. Security-related employment opportunities also vastly increased. Subsequent post-Fordist restructuring and forces of globalisation began to take further toll on the economy which started to see the relocation of manufacturing (particularly textiles) to even lower-waged economies overseas.

Government in the 1970s and the 1980s sought to boost the regional economy and mitigate the negative effects of political violence through the generous provision of subsidies to business. This makes Northern Ireland unique in the context of the UK, where the Thatcher government implemented neoliberal approaches to L&RED. Because of 'The Troubles', Northern Ireland operated in a different politico-economic space to the rest of the UK and was therefore somewhat insulated from structural adjustment. However, these subsidies reduced competitiveness, supported low productivity (which stood at approximately 75% of UK productivity during this period) and produced grant dependence. In the 1990s these subsidies continued, although official rhetoric toed the neoliberal line in arguing that subsidies would be reduced and competitiveness promoted. Again, Northern Ireland was insulated from the effects of the mini-recession in the early 1990s because of the extent of government support for business. The 1990s did see drops in unemployment and in other indicators of deprivation, although statistics indicate that Northern Ireland is still peripheral within the context of the UK and the EU. Unemployment data using International Labour Organization criteria indicate a current unemployment rate of 6.3% as compared to the UK average of 5.2% (National Statistics, 2002).

The 1998 Belfast Agreement led to the devolution of power to Stormont and laid the foundations of wide-ranging governance changes in Northern Ireland. The Belfast Agreement made reference to the development of new economic policy. After consultation, *Strategy 2010* was duly released in 1999, and this forms the basis for current regional economic initiatives. The policy's aims were bold, seeking to increase productivity from the 1999 figure of 80% of the UK average to 90% in 2010. The policy itself has been much criticised by observers (Bradley and Hamilton, 1999; NIEC, 1999) but it is probably too early to assess how it is working out in practice. For example, one of its key objectives, the amalgamation of most key regional government agencies promoting L&RED into *Invest Northern Ireland* within the new Department for Trade, Enterprise and Industry, only took place in March 2002. Prior to this, and forming the backdrop to this survey, the then Department of Economic Development had responsibility for five regional development agencies: the Industrial Development Board, the Industrial Research and Technology Unit, the Northern Ireland Tourist Board, the Training and Employment Agency, and the Local Economic Development Unit. Rural development continues to be treated separately in Northern Ireland, falling under the auspices of the Department for Agriculture and Rural Development. However, the rural development programme is managed in conjunction with the Rural Development Council (a regional independent body set up by government) and the Rural Community Network (an umbrella organisation for rural community groups).

Post-1998, Northern Ireland citizens continue to have entitlement to the benefits of the UK welfare state. Given this, plus ongoing government support to business and encouragement to multinational investors and the massive provision of 'security', the annual UK subvention to the region is running at approximately £4 billion per annum, and approximately 33% of the workforce is employed by the state (the figure is approximately 22% for the rest of the UK). This has led to continuing characterisations of the Northern Ireland economy as a 'dependent' economy, Northern Ireland being dependent on aid and foreign direct investment, both of which reduce the nation's capacity to develop independently (see, for example, O'Dowd, 1995). Northern Ireland's economy has also been termed a 'workhouse economy', in which most people are engaged in servicing or controlling each other through employment in the civil service and policing or the military (Teague and Wilson, 1995).

The typical supply- and demand-side factors relating to the condition of a peripheral industrialised economy have been identified by analysts in the case of Northern Ireland, ranging from low educational attainment to poor transport and communications infrastructure. However, one is particularly worthy of note, the issue of institutional thickness. Under the 'new regionalism', it is acknowledged that the boosting of institutional thickness is significant for economic growth because it can help stimulate endogenous growth (as well as help embed foreign direct investment) and reduce dependence. One factor which might impede institutional thickness is sectarianism (Morrissey and Gaffikin, 2001).

Given Northern Ireland's predicament, its extreme economic dependency and its continuing sectarian divisions, hopes have become even more strongly pinned on L&RED to provide a way forward. This is, of course, a tall if not impossible order. L&RED has been given the task of reducing dependency through fostering endogenous entrepreneurship. As if this were not enough, many L&RED initiatives stemming from supranational actors also have the objective of attempting to build institutional thickness across the sectarian divide. It is to this supranational context that we now turn.

Local and regional economic development and the supranational context

The Northern Ireland economy and L&RED initiatives cannot be understood without the supranational context. As a peripheral region of the EU, Northern Ireland has qualified for considerable help from EU structural funds. Most structural funds are administered through a single, integrated programme (known as the Northern Ireland Community Support Framework for the 2000-06 funding round). Some funds are also made available under Community Initiative programmes. This adds another layer of complexity to the economic picture, not least because, as Hodgett and Johnson (2001) argue, some EU policy has been based on contradictory principles to those of the UK (broadly, regulatory capitalism rather than neoliberalism, although of course Northern Ireland has been somewhat insulated from the full force of neoliberalism, as we argued above).

Partnership working and integrated area-based approaches are the new orthodoxies for EU-funded L&RED in Northern Ireland. Although partnership working owes much to the EU for its prevalence, it is also endorsed under the neoliberal agenda. The two operational programmes of the Support Framework are the Building Sustainable Prosperity (BSP) programme, worth £575 million, and the PEACE programme, worth £274 million. The BSP programme aims to promote economic growth and competitiveness, employment, urban and social renewal, agriculture and a sustainable environment, complementing government efforts. PEACE aims to promote peace and reconciliation through economic *and* social development. In this case, partnership working has been realised through the creation of partnerships to administer funds in each of Northern Ireland's district council areas. The main Community Initiative programmes impacting on economic development in Northern Ireland include URBAN II and LEADER+. LEADER is a French acronym translated as Links Between Actions for the Development of the Rural Economy, which focuses on innovative economic development, again implemented through partnerships.

A final aspect of the supranational context is the important role of the International Fund for Ireland (IFI). This is a unique fund set up by the British and Irish governments as part of the 1985 Anglo-Irish Agreement, and it has received financial support from the EU, the US, Canada, Australia and New Zealand, totalling some £383 million to date. In some ways similar to the PEACE programmes, the aim of the IFI is to promote reconciliation through economic and other forms of development.

The local context: local authorities and the community sector

Up until this point we have said little about the role of local authorities. While local authorities have played an interesting political role in Northern Ireland society and have been the only democratic fora for most of the period since the 1970s, they were stripped of most of their key roles in 1972, including most functions to do with economic development (Birrell and Hayes, 1999). Local authorities were also hampered in being small (with average populations under 65,000, reducing economies of scale), limited in terms of abilities to raise funding for economic development (only in 1992 were councils allowed to spend up to the product of a 2p rate on this work, equivalent to a possible total of £3.45 million for the entire region), and divided in terms of sectarian issues. However, there has been a resurgence of local authority economic development activity. Under the 1995-99 EU funding round, local councils were able to access resources to draw up local economic development strategies and implement projects under the Local Economic Development Measure. This also empowered them to lobby to secure an increase in the 2p limit permitted for economic development spending (White et al, 2000).

Local authorities have also been able to increase their influence over economic development with the growth of partnership working, such as within the PEACE and LEADER programmes (partnerships generally include local authority representatives). Currently, the local government structure is under review with the aim of increasing efficiency through the reduction of numbers of authorities. Although there is some informal cooperation across local authorities the problem of the lack of economies of scale continues.

Finally, the important role of grass-roots organisations involved in community economic development cannot be ignored in any analysis. Northern Ireland is well known for a vibrant community sector that in part developed due to the democratic deficit, and also because of local perceptions that state-led development initiatives were historically biased towards one community. Important overarching umbrella groups are the Northern Ireland Council for Voluntary Action and the Rural Community Network. However, the long-term viability of many community economic development initiatives is questionable, given funding dependencies, as we will go on to show.

Characteristics of agencies responding to the survey

The types of agency responding to the survey and the proportions of these types in the survey reinforce the accuracy of the overall picture presented in the literature. The survey results do indeed suggest a complex regional and local development scene, with strong representation of the community and social economy sector. Local government constituted 11.4% of respondents and non-local government 88.6%. The latter are further broken down into regional government agencies and non-departmental public bodies such as

LEDU and the Rural Development Council (4.9%); community and social economy organisations such as community economic fora and the Social Economy Agency (52.8%); business organisations, which included local Enterprise Agencies and Chambers of Commerce (14.6%); partnerships such as District Partnerships and LEADER groups (13.0%); and others (3.3%). The strong representation of the community and social economy sector contrasts with the picture in Australia, the US and England.

Figure 7.1 presents the years in which agencies were established. These findings are interesting, showing large increases in establishment in the early years of the 1995-99 structural funds. These increases are largely accounted for by the formation of community agencies and partnerships. In terms of the community/social economy sector, *some* of these organisations are associated with the long tradition of community development in Northern Ireland described above (in our survey one organisation was founded as far back as 1938 and others between the 1960s and 1980s). Significantly, however, our findings indicate that many are also quite new, being created during the boom times of grant availability (at the beginnings of the 1995-99 structural funds period), and therefore reflecting the dependent nature of local, apparently endogenous, development in Northern Ireland and the way in which the EU plays an important part in shaping this sector. Partnerships are also entirely dependent on EU funding.

The rural–urban dimension is also an important one to document, not least because of the traditional urban bias to economic development in Northern Ireland (Murray and Greer, 1993). In fact the largest proportion of agencies (39%) served predominantly rural areas, while 22% were predominantly urban and 36.6% worked in mixed rural and urban areas. This disparity is accounted for largely by the fact that 56.5% of community agencies served rural areas as opposed to 22.6% serving predominantly urban areas. This is not surprising

Figure 7.1: Years in which agencies were established, Northern Ireland

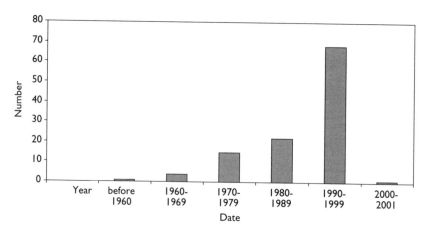

given that the majority of Northern Ireland's population lives in rural areas and community agencies generally serve one locality. However, larger proportions of all other types of agencies (except partnerships) work predominantly in urban rather than predominantly rural areas. This is not indicative of urban bias, however, because 61.9% of all agencies, other than community agencies and partnerships, worked in both urban *and* rural areas. This is encouraging given that much current literature advocates integrated town/hinterland development strategies for larger agencies.

Findings relating to the size of agencies are revealing. One way that size was assessed was by looking at staff numbers. Table 7.1 indicates the numbers of full-time paid staff at the agencies. It might be expected that regional government agencies are likely to employ the most staff, and indeed they did, employing staff in numbers out of all proportion to the other agencies, with an average of 104.7 staff members. However, the findings for community organisations are striking. These employed more staff on average than all other types of agencies except the regionals, with a mean of 6.3 staff members. This finding belies the stereotypical picture of community organisations as voluntary organisations, lacking in professionalism and having a minimal impact (see Case Study 7.1). In comparison, local government economic development departments and partnerships are very small, with an average of 2.6 paid staff, although it is acknowledged that local governments as political actors are likely to have a greater impact on economic development than the size of their development departments suggests. Some local authorities also commit other staff resources to cross-cutting sustainable development programmes (see Case Study 7.2). Table 7.1 also shows that voluntarism is not dead in the community sector in Northern Ireland, and on average 3.7 voluntary staff swell the size of each community/social economy organisation, potentially increasing impact. Regional agencies have on average six unpaid staff, while partnerships and local governments do not increase their impact this way. The questions of impact and effectiveness are returned to below.

The expenditure levels of agencies varied immensely. Again, regional government agencies were in a different league from the others, with a median expenditure of £20-29.9 million per annum compared with medians of £50,000-99,000 for local government and community agencies, £100,000-199,000 for business agencies, and £400,000-599,000 for partnerships. There were quite large variations between the median and mean in the case of local government and community agencies, reflecting the diversity of sizes of

Table 7.1: Average number of staff, Northern Ireland

Full-time equivalent staff	Local government	Regional government	Community	Business	Partnership
Paid	2.6	104.7	6.3	5.2	3.4
Voluntary	0.1	6.0	3.7	2.3	0.1

Case Study 7.1: Example of a community economic development agency in Derry/Londonderry

Derry City Council's constituency comprising 30 electoral wards is situated at the edge of the border with Donegal in the Republic of Ireland, and is an urban area straddling the river Foyle. Recognised as the regional city of the North West of Ireland, Derry is the second largest urban settlement in Northern Ireland. Its hinterland includes the neighbouring towns of Strabane, Limavady and parts of Donegal and the population of this wider north western region is approximately 300,000.

The council is one of the largest of the 26 district councils in Northern Ireland, serving a population of 95,371, of which an estimated 85,000 live within the urban area, making the city the largest centre of urban population outside Belfast. A high proportion of the population (28.1%) is aged between 0-14 with those aged between 15-29 amounting to 23.4%. Those between 30-49 represent 24% with the remaining 50+ years coming to 23.5%. Of the total, 58% are described as 'economically active' with the remainder, 42%, described as 'economically inactive'.

One local response to the problem of the 'economically inactive' – the unemployed – in the area, has its origins within the Social Economy Agency (SEA), a non-governmental, not-for-profit local development organisation with a Northern Ireland wide remit and an emphasis on a cooperativist approach to local economic development. The Ráth Mór Business and Community Enterprise Limited (CEL) – one 'flagship' example of an SEA initiative – is a community enterprise and a company limited by guarantee established in 1991 with an annual turnover of £320,000 and managed by a voluntary board of directors from the local community. At present it is directly responsible for the employment of 13 people. It is a community-based company with assets in excess of £3,000,000. The enterprise consists of three elements: the Ráth Mór centre, community service units and an enterprise park. In total the enterprise is responsible for the management and administration of 80,000 ft^2 of working space and has recorded customer use in excess of 3 million per annum since its formation.

The initiative has been responsible for the establishment of several community enterprise initiatives, including a catering company, computer manufacturing, retail and training unit; a number of other retail and manufacturing units including a supermarket, community printing and publishing company and other projects awaiting the completion of industrial units.

The Ráth Mór centre was established at an initial cost of £3.2 million. A total of 165 new jobs have been created in the various enterprises and projects now located at Ráth Mór, with an estimated £900,000 per annum in wages being paid, spent and circulated within the locality. The company secured £350,000 for the development of a Neighbourhood Partnership, Creggan Neighbourhood Partnership (CNP) to facilitate and support local community activity, and has contributed £70,000 to assist community-based initiatives within the area. The CEL and CNP played a crucial role in the EU funded URBAN programme in the city between 1994-99. CEL built new community service units during this period costing £340,000 and financed by the IFI, the European URBAN programme and the local community through CEL. More recently it has created an indigenous enterprise park at a cost of £800,000 (see also www.rathmor.com).

Case Study 7.2: Example of a local authority economic development agency: Cookstown District Council Development Department

Cookstown District is a largely rural district situated in mid-Northern Ireland on the Western shores of Lough Neagh. It has a population of 32,000 and covers some 235 m². Manufacturing accounts for 24% of employment while agriculture is also an important sector, employing 2,600 on 1,434 farms.

The Development Department has £1.08 million at its disposal for local economic development, sourced from council funds and EU structural funding. The Department describes as its main task the design, development, implementation and monitoring of an Economic Development Strategy. The objectives of the Local Economic Development Strategy (2001-06) are to "drive forward economic change and stimulate further economic development", "contribute to improved infrastructure" and "enhance long-term economic prospects for the area". Investment is focused on:

- *Business Start Programme* (a Northern Ireland-wide programme delivered in each district council area; in Cookstown it is implemented by Cookstown Enterprise Centre and the aim is to start 207 businesses).
- *Enterprise/Business Development Programme* (for small, medium and large businesses; the support is delivered by a range of partners).
- *Marketing/ICT Development Programme* (to promote marketing of the district and increased commercial use of ICT).
- *Physical Regeneration Programme* (its aim, as identified within a recent participatory Community Plan, is to "enable and empower communities to undertake sustainable regeneration projects, which improve the physical infrastructure and aesthetic appearance of their areas").
- *Town Centre Regeneration Programme*.

Cookstown District Council also promotes a programme of sustainable development through its Environmental Health Department (see also www.cookstown.gov.uk).

organisation in these sectors. For example, for local government agencies the mean was in the bracket £200,000-399,000 whereas the median was much lower, within the range £50,000-99,000. This portrays a picture of a small number of large, urban-based councils spending in the millions on economic development and a larger number of smaller counterparts, serving smaller and/or rural areas with less significant purses.

Agencies also varied according to their sources of income and this produced some interesting results (Table 7.2). Local government, community/social economy organisations and business organisations had relatively broad revenue bases. Unsurprisingly, regional government agencies were run on the basis of regional government funding with some EU funding in addition. Partnerships were almost completely dependent on EU funding, leaving open the question as to whether they could become more independent, genuinely endogenous organisations (the median figure is 81-100% dependency on this form of income). While community/social economy agencies have a wider resource base, they are also shown to be highly dependent on EU funding in these figures. However, they do illustrate the potential to develop other avenues for sustainability. Business agencies illustrate the lowest level of dependence on grant funding, using the sale or lease of property to generate much of their income.

What is the extent of EU funding dependency across the board? Of all the agencies surveyed, 59.3% received income from the EU. The two major programmes represented were PEACE (from which 37% of agencies received funding) and LEADER (which funded 10.6% of agencies). Many other programmes were represented (from INTERREG to Leonardo) but each funded only a small proportion of the agencies in the survey.

Finally, given the extent of grant dependency, it is also useful to explore how free the agencies were to pursue their own strategies with the funding they have. Table 7.3 gives a flavour of this, showing the proportions of each type of agency enjoying untied funding. Only a small percentage of the agencies had

Table 7.2: Sources of agency income, Northern Ireland (%)

| Mean % of income from | Local and regional agencies | | | | |
	Local government	Regional government	Comm-unity	Business	Partnership
Charges and services	<20	0	<20	<20	<20
Sale/lease of property	<20	0	<20	21-40	0
Sale of services	0	0	<20	<20	0
Membership fees	0	0	<20	<20	0
Voluntary fundraising	0	0	<20	<20	<20
Regional government	<20	21-40	<20	<20	<20
Local government	21-40	0	<20	<20	<20
Non-EU foreign aid	0	0	<20	<20	<20
EU	<20	<20	21-40	<20	61-80

Table 7.3: Percentage of untied funding, Northern Ireland

% of untied funding	Local government	Regional government	Local and regional agencies		
			Community	Business	Partnership
0	40	100	38.2	33.3	71.4
1-20	0	0	36.4	16.7	21.4
21-40	0	0	5.5	16.7	7.1
41-60	20	0	12.8	11.1	0
61-80	30	0	1.8	16.7	0
81-100	10	0	5.5	5.6	0
Total	100	100	100	100	100

81-100% untied funding (a tenth of local government agencies and very small proportions of community and business organisations). On the other hand, large proportions of all the organisations had no untied funding (including 100% of regional government organisations and 71.4% of partnerships). Only local government agencies had more untied than tied funding, but about a fifth of both the community/social economy and business organisations had over 40% untied funding and hence some room for acting independently, without guidelines and reporting regimes implemented by grant awarding institutions.

Objectives of the agencies

The objectives of the agencies span many areas of economic development activity. The top objectives are ranked in Table 7.4. Overall, improving the quality of life was listed as a key objective by most respondents, paralleling the findings for England and contrasting with the US and Australia.

The emphasis on building local partnerships, developing local business and attracting new business on the part of local government agencies indicates that these agencies concentrate on betterment of the economic picture of their

Table 7.4: Top ranked agency objectives, Northern Ireland

	Local government			Local and regional agencies	
Rank	Objective	% of respondents	Rank	Objective	% of respondents
1	Improve quality of life	85.7	1	Improve quality of life	78.5
1	Build local partnerships	85.7	2	Improve incomes of disadvantaged	68.2
3	Promote economic growth	78.6	3	Stimulate entrepreneurship	67.3
4	Stimulate entrepreneurship	71.4	4	Build local partnerships	66.4
4	Develop local business	71.4	5	Promote economic growth	62.6
4	Attract/recruit new business	71.4	6	Regenerate the economy	61.7

Note: Objectives nominated by over 60% of respondents.

own locales (as per their mandate). On the other hand, objectives relating to reducing the social exclusion of the disadvantaged (such as improving the incomes of the disadvantaged, and regeneration of the local economy) rank more highly among local and regional agency objectives. While improving incomes of the disadvantaged is ranked number two and economic regeneration six, the comparable rankings for local authority agencies are seven and eight, listed by just over half of respondents. This reflects the strong influence on local and regional agencies of the PEACE agenda in particular and EU structural fund programmes in general, as well as the agencies' own commitments.

Looking at disaggregated figures (Table 7.5), these issues can be further explored. While economic growth is a principal concern of large proportions of all the agencies in the survey, this was an objective of only just over half of community/social economy organisations. Rather than a lack of commitment to economic development, we would argue that this reflects thinking, represented in the community sector more than most, in which the link between economic growth and development is contested. A concern for development, but with equity, is indicated in the fact that 73% of community economic development organisations have as a main objective the improvement of incomes and employment opportunities of the disadvantaged. This is a large proportion relative to the other agencies, bar partnerships that are constituted to promote this as part of the PEACE agenda. Beyond the scope of Table 7.5, because it does not rate highly in the overall figures, is evidence of a relatively strong concern for environmentally sustainable economic development among community/social economy agencies. This is a main objective of 47.6% of these respondents as opposed to only 16.7% of regional government respondents and 27.8% of business agency respondents. This finding also attests to the broader developmental thinking in this sector. However, environmentally sustainable development is also an objective of 57.1% of local government agencies and 50% of partnerships, probably reflecting the influence of Local Agenda 21 discourse on local government in Northern Ireland.

Table 7.5 shows that improving the quality of life, the number one ranked objective for agencies overall, was an objective of large proportions of community/social economy agencies and partnerships and correspondingly

Table 7.5: Objectives of L&RED organisations, Northern Ireland

		% of respondents			
Rank	Objective	Regional government	Comm-unity	Business	Partner-ship
1	Improve quality of life	33.3	88.9	50.0	93.8
2	Improve incomes of disadvantaged	50.0	73.0	38.9	87.5
3	Stimulate entrepreneurship	50.0	60.3	83.3	81.3
4	Build local partnerships	83.3	65.1	55.6	81.3
5	Promote economic growth	66.7	52.4	88.9	75.0
6	Regenerate the economy	66.7	57.1	66.7	68.8

small proportions of regional and business agencies. For the community sector, this emphasis can also be construed as being part of the broader development agenda. For partnerships, the objectives of economic and social development are also fused in a sector where improving the quality of life through removing the conditions which lead to violent sectarianism is its raison d'être. Similar to local government agencies, community/social economy agencies also identified promoting local development, stimulating entrepreneurship, building local partnerships and local regeneration as prominent objectives. This reflects the locally based nature of many of these agencies, as well as the commitment to socially driven economic and participatory development which this 'joined-up' approach can facilitate.

Among the agencies where promotion of economic growth per se was more important, major objectives also included attracting new business and developing local business. There were also strong commitments to developing the partnership approach in this sector. Employment growth was an objective of over two thirds of business and partnership agencies but of only half of regional government agencies. Regeneration was an objective of over two thirds of regional government, business and partnership agencies.

In some ways, the objectives that turned out to be uncommon provide just as interesting a profile of L&RED in Northern Ireland. Increasing local incomes and employment is not an objective of most agencies. Neither is diversification, often claimed to be crucial for regions dependent on a narrow and declining industrial and agricultural base, such as Northern Ireland. The lack of prioritisation accorded to safeguarding or growing the local government revenue base (which, as noted, is extremely small in Northern Ireland) also implies that continued external grant dependence will be the norm, with implications for the direction and nature of L&RED as we will explain below. Although Northern Ireland no longer experiences net population loss through emigration, it is often argued that a 'brain drain' of talent impacts negatively on L&RED. It is perhaps surprising then that more L&RED agencies do not count skilled population retention among their main objectives. Property development, labour market training and job placement are also not major objectives for most L&RED agencies. However, job placement, provided by the Training and Employment Agency in Northern Ireland, is a service available in every town. Lobbying for and promotion of the region also do not figure prominently in the data.

Finally, it is interesting to note the numbers of objectives of agencies in the findings. Regional government had the greatest average number of objectives, followed by community agencies, local government, partnerships, and business agencies. This range in the number of objectives illustrates the differences between organisations with a broad range of functions and those that are more narrowly focused.

Activities of the agencies

So much for aspirations – what about activities? In the questionnaire, activities were divided into business development and capacity building.

Business development

In terms of business development, the main activities of local government and local and regional agencies contrast (see Table 7.6). When the local and regional agency category is disaggregated the most notable feature is the contrast between the activities of community/social economy agencies and those of other organisations.

Capacity building

Capacity building activities are ranked in Table 7.7. There are large variations between the main activities conducted by local government agencies and the other agencies surveyed and there is less of a convergence of activities in the local and regional agencies sector. Only education and training activities (of youth and of the general population) were carried out by over half of local and regional agencies. Of these, non-targeted education and training was also carried out by over half of local government agencies, but this stood at number seven in the rank order. Ranked number one for local government was the identification and implementation of strategies to fill gaps in the local economy. This is consistent with this sector's objectives as are the other high ranked objectives: improving local economic development strategic planning and implementation capacity, providing an analysis of the local economy, acting as an advocate for the local area, and developing cooperation and networking for local development. The latter, of course, is also in tune with the need to increase 'institutional thickness' in Northern Ireland. It is also interesting to note that the attempt to influence land use regulations and planning decisions impacting on businesses ranks as a joint fifth activity for local government agencies. This relates to a long-running battle local authorities have to increase their influence in the area of planning, which is currently very weak because such decision making rests with regional government and is centralised in Belfast (contrasting with the situation in the rest of the UK). Decisions are often perceived to be undemocratic and insufficiently in tune with local needs.

Disaggregation of the local and regional agency category shows that education and training is a particularly important activity for partnerships, whereas improving strategic planning, networking, and analysis of the regional economy are particularly important as activities for regional government organisations and quite important for business agencies. These do not rank highly in the overall figures because of the preponderance of community/social economy agency respondents in the survey. Community agencies show lower involvement in these activities but have a stronger involvement in education/training work.

Table 7.6: Business development activities, Northern Ireland

Business development activity	Rank	Local government	Rank	Total	Regional government	Community	Business	Partnership
				% of agencies undertaking the activity — Local and regional agencies				
Tourism promotion	1	92.9	8	39.6	0.0	38.7	33.3	75.0
Assisting major events	2	92.9	2	59.4	83.3	56.5	66.7	62.5
Small- and medium-sized enterprise business support	3	85.7	7	42.5	83.3	17.7	88.9	68.8
Programmes to support small business creation	4	85.7	5	48.1	83.3	35.5	72.2	62.5
Marketing the region to prospective businesses	5	78.6	6	45.3	66.7	33.9	66.7	56.3
Providing information on government programmes	6	78.6	4	54.7	100.0	45.2	66.7	68.8
Assistance with access to funding for businesses	7	71.4	1	61.3	50.0	67.7	66.7	31.3
Local employment creation	8	71.4	3	58.5	66.7	48.4	77.8	81.3

Note: All eight activities identified by over 60% of local government respondents, and the top eight activities of local and regional agencies.

Table 7.7: Capacity building activities, Northern Ireland

| Business development activity | Rank | Local government | % of agencies undertaking the activity | | | | | |
| | | | Local and regional agencies | | | | | |
			Rank	Total	Regional government	Community	Business	Partnership
Developing strategies to fill business opportunities	1	78.6	6	39.8	66.7	28.6	72.2	43.8
Improving economic development strategic planning	2	71.4	3	51.5	100.0	42.9	61.1	56.3
Analysis of the regional/local economy	2	71.4	5	43.7	83.3.	36.5	61.1	50.0
Acting as advocate or lobbyist for the region/local area	2	71.4	6	39.8	50.0	44.4	27.8	31.3
Developing cooperation and networking	5	64.3	4	45.6	83.3	34.9	61.1	56.3
Attempting to influence land use regulations and planning	5	64.3	13	12.6	16.7	9.5	22.2	18.8
Education and training, general	7	57.1	2	57.3	50.0	55.6	38.9	75.0
Education and training for youth	9	42.9	1	60.2	50.0	61.9	50.0	75.0

Note: The table combines all six activities listed by over 60% of local government respondents and the top six activities of local and regional agencies.

Once more, these differences mirror differentials in agency objectives that reflect somewhat different visions of L&RED.

When business development and capacity building activities are combined, regional government is again shown to engage in the largest number of activities, with a mean of 14.4 activities, followed by partnerships with 14.2, community agencies with 13.4, local government with 11.4 and business agencies with 9.4 activities.

Partners

Given the current 'partnership' orthodoxy in L&RED discourse, it is insightful to document survey responses to the question of partners. What stands out is the large numbers of partners per local government agency. Over half of local government agencies had 16 or in excess of 16 partners and none had five or less. Case Study 7.2 illustrates the extent of partnership working in the case of Cookstown, for example. This contrasts with the local and regional agencies where only 30.3% had 16 or more partners and 15.6% had 5 partners or under. Disaggregation indicates that half of business agencies have 16 or more partners but that large numbers of partners are not generally characteristic of the other types of agencies.

It is revealing to look also at the types of partners reported by respondents (see Table 7.8). Given the current political discourse, advocating public–private partnerships, the relatively small number in the survey findings is quite striking.

Disaggregation of local and regional agencies informs us that regional government agencies are less likely to have larger numbers of partners in any of the three categories (none had over six partners from any one category). Also, 16.7% had no partner in the 'other organisations' category. Community/social economy agencies, on the other hand, were likely to have fewer or no private sector partners, which contrasts with the norm for local and regional agencies. Perhaps unsurprisingly, business agencies' modal number of private sector category partners was by contrast 5-6, but they also averaged high numbers of partners in the other two categories. The profile of partnerships did not differ significantly from the average across regional and local agencies.

Table 7.8: Partners of agencies by sector, Northern Ireland

Number of partners	Partners of local government agencies (%)			Partners of local and regional agencies (%)		
	Private sector	Public sector	Other organisations	Private sector	Public sector	Other organisations
0	7.1	0.0	0.0	26.6	4.6	7.3
1-2	28.6	14.3	7.1	33.0	13.8	8.3
3-4	35.7	14.3	14.3	16.5	22.9	22.0
5-6	28.6	71.4	14.3	23.9	58.7	21.1
7-8	0.0	0.0	64.3	0.0	0.0	41.3
Total	100	100	100	100	100	100

These results show that agencies of all hues have teamed up with partners in all three sectors. The findings reveal a high level of partnership with 'other' organisations, that is, 'social partners'. In addition, there are also high levels of partnering with public sector partners. However, our key finding here is that across L&RED agencies, there is on average less partnership with the private sector than with the other sectors. Of course, these findings cannot tell us about the experience of partnership working. We will return to this later in our discussion of the qualitative data.

Effectiveness and impact of the agencies

All the factors described so far are likely to be related to the impact and effectiveness of L&RED agencies. However, it is important to gauge practitioners' perspectives of both levels of effectiveness and the issues that influence effectiveness, as well as to cross-reference these with quantitative data such as on numbers of activities and partners. How effective were the organisations according to the practitioners? How were the issues influencing effectiveness perceived by those surveyed? Finally, how do the quantitative findings presented so far relate to perceived impact?

Perceptions of effectiveness

Figure 7.2 shows respondents' perceptions of organisational effectiveness. Local and regional agency respondents tended to be more reticent about the impact of their agencies. A small proportion claimed 'some', 'slight' or even 'no impact'! On the other hand, a larger proportion of these respondents also claimed their agencies had a 'major impact' than did respondents from the local government sector. All local government agency respondents perceived their agencies to have at least 'an impact', which was the modal response given by over 40% of respondents. The modal response for local and regional agencies was 'appreciable impact' but this was given by just over 30% of respondents as there was a broader spread of responses from these respondents.

The disaggregated chart in Figure 7.2 reveals that the negative impression of impact is associated with the community and business agencies, although there were respondents from all five agencies who regarded their organisation as having a 'major impact'. The level of confidence about effectiveness was highest in the regional government agencies where impact was seen as 'appreciable' (the modal category) or more so. Confidence levels were also high among partnerships where all respondents reported at least 'an impact' and the modal category is also 'appreciable impact'.

Factors influencing the effectiveness of agencies according to practitioners

How then did respondents perceive what influenced their agencies' effectiveness? First we look at quantifiable responses from a 'closed' question in the survey.

Figure 7.2: Respondent assessment of agency effectiveness, Northern Ireland

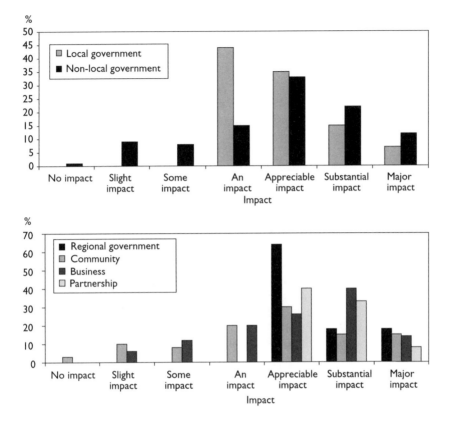

We look at two sets of factors, a general set and a set relating to regional coordination problems, starting with the general set.

General factors

Table 7.9 ranks impediments to agencies' effectiveness for local government and local and regional agencies. Of the top six impediments, five relate to the issue of funding. As explained above, local authorities in Northern Ireland find it difficult to finance their economic development activity since their ability to raise revenue from local taxes is minimal and they must rely on relatively few alternative sources of funding (mainly EU funding). Thus it is not surprising that they encounter problems with the inflexibility of the funding they can access, where the development agenda is set outside the locality yet they are the only site of local representative democracy where alternative ideas about appropriate local economic development can be debated. It is also not unexpected that local government agencies report short-term funding frames as an impediment, since they are in local economic development for the long haul and yet cannot fund it beyond the short terms of EU structural funds, except, in small measure, from local taxes. The sixth impediment, the fact that local government is not involved in decisions about large-scale enterprises, indicates a lack of joint planning between local and regional level economic development agencies. Given the impact that larger-scale business can have on the economic development locality, this flags up an important issue for policy makers.

The picture for local and regional agencies is more complex. Table 7.10 gives the disaggregated picture. Again, most of the top impediments relate to funding. However, government agencies do not experience significant funding impediments (presumably because their core funding is governmental). Indeed regional government agency respondents did not report any significant impediment to their effectiveness.

Community/social economy, business and partnership organisations report more significant impediments. Funding is a key concern in the community sector with 87.9% of respondents indicating that searching for funding used up too much of staff time, and as many noting the short duration of funding to be a major impediment. The lack of funding for core business was also a constraint on a large percentage of community agencies. This reflects the extreme dependency of this sector on extra-local funding (principally EU) and raises important questions about the sustainability of these organisations. It also suggests that the raison d'être of these agencies might become survival with important implications for quality of service. Community agencies also

Table 7.9: Most significant impediments to agency effectiveness, Northern Ireland

Local government			Local and regional agencies		
Rank	Impediment	% of respondents	Rank	Impediment	% of respondents
1	Inflexible rules and guidelines of funders	66.7	1	Short duration of much of the funding	83.5
1	Priorities of funders have more influence on organisation than needs	66.7	2	Lack of funding for core business	73.7
3	Short duration of much of the funding	58.3	3	Too much staff time spent seeking funding	73.6
3	Too frequent changes in priorities of funders	58.3	4	Inflexible rules and guidelines of funders	68.0
5	Insufficient untied funding to use as leverage with other agencies	50.0	5	Insufficient untied funding to use as leverage with other agencies	67.8
6	Organisation not involved in decisions about large enterprises	42.9	6	Involvement of local government in governing body of agency	66.1

Note: Responses given by over 60% of local and regional agency respondents and the top six responses from local government agency respondents.

Table 7.10: Most significant impediments to agency effectiveness by type of agency, Northern Ireland

		% of respondents			
Rank	Impediment	Regional government	Comm-unity	Business	Partner-ship
1	Short duration of much of the funding	25.0	87.9	87.5	80.0
2	Lack of funding for core business	0	83.9	72.2	50.0
3	Too much staff time spent seeking funding	0	87.9	68.8	36.4
4	Inflexible rules and guidelines of funders	0	74.1	75.0	68.8
5	Insufficient untied funding to use as leverage with other agencies	0	75.9	66.7	61.5
6	Involvement of local government in governing body of agency	57.1	66.7	72.3	61.1

rated as impediments the inflexible rules and guidelines of funders, the dominance of funders' priorities in their work and insufficient untied funding.

The least significant impediments reported are also instructive (see Table 7.11). For local government agencies, 90% of respondents thought that the least significant impediment to effectiveness was that the organisation was not seen as a legitimate representative of the area. They might well state this, given that local councils are currently the only democratic fora in Northern Ireland! An endorsement of the valuable role local government plays for these agencies is also reflected in the findings that two thirds of respondents thought that the involvement of local government in agency governance was not an impediment. In contrast to the negative views about local/regional leadership expressed by the business agencies, 69.2% of local government agency respondents did not think an absence of local leadership detracted from their work. Local government agencies also did not see the involvement of local business in agency governance as an impediment; indeed this was ranked as the second least impediment. Finally, problems with staffing were not a major issue, 75% said that a skills shortage was not a problem and 63.6% that the search for funding did not take up too much staff time.

Disaggregation of the local and regional agencies category highlights further issues related to these questions of agency governance and capacity. It is evident that there is less confidence in the business sector that business agencies are not seen as sufficiently independent of government or as legitimate representatives of the area, as opposed to the feelings of respondents in the regional government agencies. However, the greatest diversity was shown on the issue of the involvement of local government in the governing body of agencies. Here only large proportions of partnerships view this involvement as a least impediment. Returning to the issue of an absence of regional and local leadership (seen as an impediment by the majority of business agencies, as we noted above), it is interesting that it was mainly regional government agency and partnership respondents who saw this issue as unproblematic for their

Table 7.11: Least significant impediments to agency effectiveness, Northern Ireland

Local government			Local and regional agencies		
Rank	Impediment	% of respondents	Rank	Impediment	% of respondents
1	Organisation not seen as a legitimate representative of the region/locality	90.0	1	Organisation not seen as sufficiently independent of government	86.5
2	Involvement of local businesses in governing body of agency	81.8	2	Staff lack appropriate skills	82.7
3	Staff lack appropriate skills	75.0	2	Organisation not seen as a legitimate representative of the region/locality	82.7
4	Absence of regional/local leadership	69.2	4	The organisation lacks the capacity to plan strategically	77.9
5	Involvement of local government in governing body of agency	66.7	5	Unable to access information on best practice	76.0
6	Too much staff time spent seeking funding	63.6	6	Involvement of local government in the governing body of agency	64.4
7	Unable to access information on best practice	58.3	7	Absence of regional/local leadership	61.5

Note: Responses given by over 60% of local and regional agency respondents and the top seven responses from local government agency respondents.

work. Moving on to the issue of agency capacity, community and business agencies showed less confidence than regional government agencies over their abilities to plan strategically. Finally, there were some differences over the issue of accessing best practice. While no regional government agencies saw this as an impediment, at the opposite end of the spectrum only two thirds of partnership respondents did not see this as an obstacle. The skilling and information richness associated with regional government agencies reflects resourcing and training.

Regional coordination factors

Aside from the set of impediments already discussed, survey participants were also asked to comment on a set of regional coordination issues. The disparities between responses from different agency sectors are quite revealing. Table 7.12 ranks the responses. On average, local government respondents did not get unduly exercised by any of the issues. Over half of regional and local agency respondents saw as problematic the fact that no one organisation is recognised as a lead agency in strategic planning terms and that there are several different and uncoordinated plans for the region.

The disaggregation of these figures discloses stronger concerns in some sectors, however. This diversity of experience itself suggests that there are significant

Table 7.12: Regional coordination problems affecting agencies, Northern Ireland

	Local government			Local and regional agencies	
Rank	Regional coordination impediment	% of respondents	Rank	Regional coordination impediment	% of respondents
I	No development organisation recognised as the lead agency	42.8	I	No development organisation is recognised as lead agency	51.4
I	Competition between agencies at different tiers of government	42.8	2	Different and uncoordinated development plans for region	50.5
I	Programmes uncoordinated	42.8	3	Competition and conflict between development agencies	42.0

Note: The top three responses from the agencies.

coordination problems in the L&RED sector in Northern Ireland. The most significant regional coordination problem, the lack of a recognised lead agency in strategic planning for the region, was regarded by the business and partnership sectors as especially problematic for the effectiveness of their work. The same two sets of respondents saw the existence of several different and uncoordinated development plans for Northern Ireland as detrimental to their operations and indicated some problems stemming from competition between agencies.

Effectiveness and improving effectiveness: the qualitative evidence

Correlation analysis shows no relationship between the self-rating of effectiveness and numbers of objectives, numbers of activities, numbers of partners, or the mean importance of these partners. Much more can be learned from a qualitative exploration of effective activities and the ways that effectiveness can be improved from the viewpoint of practitioners.

Effectiveness and effective development activities

Respondents were asked to comment qualitatively on what constituted effectiveness for them. Reasons given for citing L&RED work as effective commonly referred to monitoring and evaluation, often specifically to that conducted by external agencies. Where monitoring was not referred to, quantitative indicators of success were often presented. For example, business start-ups were sometimes described as the most effective activity because of the 'rate' of creation of new businesses. Similarly, numbers trained and levels of job creation were named as indicators of success. However, there were numerous responses that referred to numbers *and* qualitative indicators or purely qualitative indicators. For example, on support for community economic development initiatives, one respondent wrote that this aspect of the agency's work was the most effective because community economic development initiatives were being changed "from a grant-led and grant-chasing culture ... to one of independent community activity that is sustainable and need/user led ... ie not just short term development initiatives". Similarly, a local government agency described its effectiveness in the following terms:

> People are now less dependent on, or expectant of, advice from 'experts in Belfast'. A greater confidence of doing things in our District for/by people in [our] District is evident.

In other words, reducing dependency was what made for effectiveness (although the notion of the virtues of working less with RDAs is a controversial one, as we shall see). Another respondent, citing their agency's most effective activity as provision of workspace, wrote:

> It has enabled individual creative enterprises to come out of isolation and use shared resources to improve production, marketing and sales opportunities.... Enables business to survive the ups and downs of the economy.

Thus, long-term economic sustainability, through providing a space for 'clustering', was the reason given for effectiveness here.

Respondents were also requested to comment qualitatively on what their most effective development activity was. Responses were coded and quantified and the top six most effective activities are presented in Table 7.13.

Ineffectiveness and ways forward

There was less convergence among agencies regarding the activity seen as least effective. In addition, many respondents chose to cite more than one activity as part of fairly long responses. Table 7.13 indicates the frequency of the top six 'least effective' activities according to the first response given by respondents. Practitioners were asked to give reasons for the ineffectiveness of these activities and we provide an analysis of this here. The issues are overlapping, but we divide them as follows for the sake of clarity. One set of issues was related to governance. Quantitative analysis disaggregated by agency types indicated that governance issues might be an underlying problem influencing effectiveness; here some of the reasons for this are given. A second set of issues relate generally to the current political context. A third set relate to the contested nature of community economic development, and ultimately to debates about how a balance can be struck between social and economic development objectives (the EU and social economy agenda) and which institutions are best placed to

Table 7.13: Most and least effective development activities, Northern Ireland

Most effective development activity	% of respondents
Business start-up and small- and medium-sized enterprise support	25.8
Support for social economy/community economic development projects	17.2
Workspace provision	16.1
Training for the general population	15.1
Partnership building	8.6
Job creation	6.5
Others	10.8
Total	100 (*n*=93)

Least effective development activity	% of respondents
Problems with partnership and building cooperation between public and private sector agencies	15.4
Community economic development	11.5
Training for the population	9.6
Promoting tourism	5.8
Building agency's own sustainability	5.8
Attracting inward investment	5.8
Others	46.1
Total	100 (*n*=52)

work in development. Fourth, issues relating to tied funding and short-termism in funding were tackled in detail by respondents. Again, we put further flesh on the bones of our quantitative analysis of these issues and highlight some of the ways forward to tackle these problems as suggested by the practitioners.

Governance issues: problems with partnerships and the coordination and 'division of labour' in the local and regional economic development sector

Problems associated with governance issues figured most prominently and were discussed at some length by numerous respondents. The qualitative reflections on partnerships proved insightful, refining the notion suggested by the apparent relationship between large numbers of partners and high degrees of effectiveness that 'more is always more'. There was a plethora of comments relating to the difficulties of partnership work and the views expressed assumed a much stronger note of criticism of partnership working than those put forward in Australia, the US and England. One respondent wrote, "[It is] very difficult to achieve consensus/agreed strategic priorities – [rather, it is a case of] every man for himself". Shared visioning, never mind shared working, was described as difficult because of the inevitable power struggles. Respondents singled out regional government agencies as difficult to work with, although this may well reflect the fact that it is easier for the community and local government sector to be seen to be critiquing these agencies than vice versa, within the Northern Ireland political context. One respondent referred to the 'Direct Rule' culture permeating regional government agencies which meant, in their view, that *some* regional government agencies acted in a 'top-down', non-consultative manner. Another respondent wrote of the "reluctance of public sector agencies to engage in a meaningful way with the private sector, that is [they are] fearful about protecting their patch". Perhaps the pithiest comment about partnership problems came from the respondent who stated: "Not being dentists – we don't get paid for pulling teeth!". However, this respondent went on to write that the "sustainability of subsequent work is dependent on how well this baseline [partnership-building] work is done". This comment reflects the general endorsement of the potentials of partnership among respondents, despite the pitfalls. Given this data, we need to revise our conclusions on the ideal numbers of partners, to suggest that more and better quality partnerships make for greater effectiveness. We also need to stress that partnership building can take up disproportionate amounts of agency time and energy; in other words, it is not necessarily without costs. These findings reinforce the challenge in the literature to the notion of partnerships as unproblematically good (see, for example, Greer, 2001; Hodgett and Johnson, 2001).

Data on the issue of governance pertain to a related issue – that of the coordination and indeed the division of labour and responsibilities in the L&RED sector as a whole in Northern Ireland. Conscious that within a metropolitan area of similar population size, all economic development activity might be described as 'local', it is fair to say that the testimonials relating to the lack of coordination of effort and the quasi-territorial struggles between agencies lead to the conclusion that there needs to be greater and more democratic coordination of economic development work.

One way in which many organisations would like to improve their effectiveness is through change in regional level policy and decision making so that the process becomes more transparent and participatory. As one respondent said: "Often decisions are made which may affect the local community and what are very important issues are not even discussed at local community level". Respondents suggested that inputting into policy and decision making would increase their effectiveness greatly. One respondent (from a community agency) said that what would make their organisation more successful would be: "to be able to input more effectively to strategic policy decisions that affect local development". Similarly, a LEADER partnership respondent wrote simply that the efficacy of the partnership would be improved through the "Ability to influence government policy". These are representative of many similar views expressed.

Some agencies suggested that there was a need to reduce the complexity of the L&RED sector to make it more manageable. One regional government agency respondent stated:

> [The agency] could increase effectiveness in achieving/contributing to other regional development activities if there was less competition and increased cooperation between the plethora of local/regional development organisations in Northern Ireland.... Increasing complementarity and reduced duplication would contribute to increased effectiveness on the ground by all of these agencies.

However, some agencies went further in wanting to see an increase in their own formal power and authority as a solution to the coordination of the L&RED sector. One regional government agency asked for: "More authority to take the lead in local economic development". Some local government agencies also wanted to see an increase in their own development powers vis-à-vis the region. There is obvious potential for future disagreements here.

Political issues: problems with community economic development and tourism development

Other explanations for ineffectiveness given were related more directly to the Northern Ireland political context. Some of the problems with promoting community economic development were related to social divisions along politico-religious community lines. This brought about a lack of community cooperation. The reason for the ineffectiveness of tourism development activities was always explained as related to tourist perceptions of an unsettled local political context. However, such political issues were not mentioned in relation to more 'mainstream' economic initiatives such as training. How far this may be due to the lack of acknowledgement of problems here is uncertain.

Issues relating to the debates about 'development' and the fate of community economic development initiatives

Suggestions for the improvement of community economic development/social economy work included many calls for greater official 'recognition' of the potential of this sector. This was a viewpoint not expressed in Australia, the US and England. One respondent called for "recognition that the social economy has a key role to play in economic and social regeneration". Another, putting it more bluntly, wanted "recognition by economic development agencies as opposed to patronising platitudes". However, respondents from partnerships suggested that the difficulty was more fundamental, that realising simultaneous economic *and* social development goals is problematic. A practical example given was: "Difficulty to match 'needs' of business community with those of disadvantaged group [because the] skills gap and expectations gap is significant".

Of course, while incorporating social goals is part of a new EU development orthodoxy, the debate about the incompatibility of social and economic development is an old chestnut in the literature. Practical suggestions from other respondents included a call for retraining of community development workers in *economic* development work and a new agency at regional level to provide specialist support for community economic development.

Problems associated with tied and short-term funding

The problems associated with funders 'calling the shots' and 'setting out the hurdles' are fleshed out in the responses of many agencies. The particularly negative experience of one respondent is worth mentioning as it is not unique. The respondent's agency rated their training programme as ineffective, stating that it did not meet 'real' needs. This was because the training provided was 'as the funder wanted it'. A pre-project ritual of participative planning had been undertaken, but the process and plans were neither believed in nor adhered to by either the community or the funder.

> ... [here] people have got to accept the training that is available. It is rarely customised to the precise needs of the group to be trained, never mind the individual. Technical assistance as in feasibilities, needs, audits and action plans are not genuine: they are created because they are demanded but they are not 'bought into'.

Another community agency respondent expressed anger at what they perceived as money-wasting formalities, necessary to funded L&RED.

Inevitably, respondents described the impact of current funding regimes on their work, as they did in the other nations in this study. Northern Ireland respondents described the funding regimes as impacting on their ability to innovate as opposed to slavishly following funding guidelines, to be proactive rather than reactive and dependent, to retain skilled staff and to offer a consistent, quality service. One respondent noted the relationship between short-termism in funding and the number of objectives and activities within their organisation and argued that the organisation would be more effective with:

> ... more certainty/long-term stability within revenue funding to enable organisation to focus on fewer/longer-term objectives and programmes. Because of funding constraints we often tend to be forced to focus on the short-term.

This suggests that the link between high agency effectiveness and large numbers of objectives and activities is not a clear-cut one either. Rather, unsurprisingly, effectiveness can be even greater where an agency has the opportunity to concentrate strategically on an optimum number of objectives and activities.

Local government agencies also referred to their relative financial powerlessness:

Faced with this situation of having to spread out resources, it is not always possible to make a substantial and much-needed impact in certain geographical areas or on certain sectors of economic activity.

Illustrating the problem vividly, another respondent said:

We are [one of the smallest councils in the UK] with very limited funding. What can we raise on rates in an area of sparse population and no industry?

Another less usual but important development activity, which had limited effectiveness, was the attempt by some community agencies to persuade cross-border black economy businesses to formalise. Accusing the relevant entrepreneurs of reticence, these respondents were also reticent about the main reasons behind the project failures. However, it is worth noting in passing that cross-border fuel smuggling (estimated to supply a third of Northern Ireland's fuel usage) is credited with a significant negative impact on Northern Ireland's economy and is often linked to paramilitary activity (*Guardian*, 2002). While this example is conspicuous, notable by its absence is the lack of discussion of cross-border issues in the responses generally, given the importance of the Republic of Ireland's economy to the North.

Conclusion

There is clearly a wealth of L&RED activity taking place in Northern Ireland. This is indicated in the sheer number and variety of L&RED organisations that we unearthed in our sample frame of about 400. It is also evident in the large number and diverse range of objectives and activities which practitioners report. Many of these organisations are doing innovative, effective work. Sampling the views of practitioners has also given us some insightful critical assessment of the inadequacies of the L&RED sector and ways forward. Few of our conclusions are entirely new, but confirm that earlier findings about the sector still hold (see especially NIEC, 2000). We begin by pointing out key contradictions in the L&RED sector in Northern Ireland.

First, high hopes are placed on the ability of the L&RED sector not only to bring about economic prosperity but to also help bed in a peace process. Yet more emphasis has been placed on subsidy and attracting inward investment than on endogenous initiatives. Subsidies and investment incentives may sometimes even stifle local development initiatives where uncompetitive firms are sustained through official support.

Second, the Northern Ireland L&RED sector is multilayered and very complex. Yet the sector serves a region of only 1.7 million people. We have demonstrated the complexity of the sector throughout this chapter. There are 26 local authorities and enterprise agencies, at least six different government agencies prior to March 2002, and many agencies with over 16 objectives, activities and even partners.

There are crucial governance and coordination issues here. We would argue that there is some need for rationalisation in the sector, to avoid replication of effort and energy and resource sapping competition, to improve coordination, to build in more economies of scale without sacrificing 'spatial equity' and to enable specialisation. While greater coordination is needed, coordination should facilitate rather than stifle innovation. Participatory planning can be used to help bring about such coordination.

Third, the L&RED sector is encouraged to be innovatory yet extreme dependency militates against creativity. If the L&RED sector is to meet halfway the demands made on it, it needs to be able to innovate and to sustain, scale up and mainstream successful initiatives. The apparent diverse fragmentation in the sector is explained not so much by the creative forces of entrepreneurship (although this is not entirely absent of course) but by the succession of funding streams laying down their own sediments of funding opportunities. New, long-term L&RED work can be suppressed because organisations must conform to funding guidelines, expend time looking for funding and in negotiating over bureaucratised applications, reporting and so on.

Fourth, a partnership can work but sometimes a partnership is like forced marriage in a jurisdiction without divorce! The data show a high degree of partnership working and much support for it. It has the potential to build up institutional thickness. Yet much of this partnership working follows development orthodoxy and new funding requirements. The costs of partnership are not being counted.

Fifth, mainstream funding looks for economic development with social development/ peace building, yet some respondents argue that the 'social economy' sector is not 'recognised'. The problem of framing the L&RED sector, stating what is within the picture and what is outside, was explored earlier in this book. Setting boundaries, of course, is a political act and this can produce reactions such as 'we are not recognised' when an agency feels some of its work is defined as beyond the frame. A small sub-sector of the agencies we have bracketed as 'community/ social economy' regard themselves as part of the 'social economy'. The 'social economy' has a considerable intellectual history and its proponents put forward a powerful critique of the mainstream economy. A full exploration of the 'social economy' sector is beyond the scope of this chapter, yet what it may have to offer for L&RED practice merits further exploration.

More broadly, much of the work of L&RED agencies in Northern Ireland is funded on the basis of its contribution to peace. We question how far there are trade-offs between peace building and economic development, which may, in the end, have implications for the sustainability of both. For example, competitiveness between agencies for scarce resources (from funding to tourists and inward investment) can promote rather than reduce tensions.

Within the global context, the Northern Ireland economy remains peripheral. Yet we believe that the L&RED sector can make a major contribution to the economy and ultimately to the quality of life in Northern Ireland, which was the number one objective of the agencies in the survey. Our recommendations for policy change would therefore refer to improving funding, governance, coordination and partnership working, as well as to increasing activities which our data show are rarely engaged in within the Northern Ireland L&RED sector but which could improve the development of the region.

Lessons

- More attention should be given to endogenous development, and less to subsidies to attract inward investment.
- Rationalisation of the complex L&RED sector in Northern Ireland would improve its effectiveness by reducing competition and increasing economies of scale.
- The dependence on external funding, and the lack of flexibility in this funding, stifles innovation and reduces effectiveness.
- The costs as well as the benefits of partnerships need to be considered.
- Despite the strength of the social economy sector in Northern Ireland compared to the other countries in this study, there is considerable scope to increase its contribution to L&RED.

EIGHT

Local and regional economic development: improving our understanding and advancing our policy frameworks

Andrew Beer, Graham Haughton and Alaric Maude

The aim of this book was to map the similarities and differences in the practice of L&RED across England, Australia, the US and Northern Ireland. We found that while organisations from different nations often share objectives, strategies and types of partner, it is possible to identify distinctive institutional architectures in each. The emphasis given to the needs of businesses, partnership building, technology transfer and the relationship with governments, varies appreciably. One of the achievements of this book has been its capacity to quantify this difference through the use of measures of an organisation's behaviour, values and perceptions. We have been able to use a common set of indicators to assess what is important in each nation, why it is important and how L&RED organisations relate to other agencies.

Understanding differences in local and regional economic development

Through this book we have been able to show that there is considerable commonality across the four nations in the number of types of partners L&RED agencies work with, as well as convergence in the number of objectives, capacity building and business service activities undertaken by these bodies (Table 8.1). To a certain degree this convergence was anticipated: organisations were selected for inclusion in the survey because their engagement with their local economy was perceived to conform to current understandings of L&RED. However, our definition of an L&RED organisation is a little broader than those of other studies. Halkier and Danson (1998, p 27), for example, suggest that it is possible to identify three broad criteria that denote an RDA: organisationally it is in a semi-autonomous position with respect to its political sponsors; strategically it supports endogenous growth through 'soft' policy instruments; and these agencies implement L&RED through the integrated application of a range of policy instruments. Many of our respondent organisations conform to these criteria, but the US respondents were perhaps more concerned with industrial recruitment and infrastructure provision, and less focused on endogenous development, than Halkier and Danson (1998) would allow. The main difference between our organisations and those in some other studies, however, is the inclusion of the economic development activities of local government in all four countries, as well as the inclusion of a number of organisations that are structurally independent of all three levels of government. This enables us to examine and compare a multiplicity of organisations, all of whom play a role in L&RED, and to gain an appreciation of the benefits and pitfalls of this aspect of 'institutional thickness'.

To a certain degree, we found greater commonality across the nations covered in this study in the ideology and practice of L&RED and more acute divergence in their institutional architectures. We can see in Table 8.1 that the importance afforded partners varied little across the four nations; that the median number of capacity building development activities reported by respondents was very similar, especially in the three larger nations; and that the median number of objectives reported for our four case studies was limited to a range of 9 to 11. By contrast, there was a much more substantial variation in the number of paid staff and the percentage of untied income (Table 8.1). These outcomes emphasise the important role of governmental structures, and wider debates on the function of the public sector within the economy, in mediating the implementation of L&RED policy, with subsequent impacts on implementation.

Table 8.1: Summary indicators of organisation performance

	Australia	England	Northern Ireland	US
Number of full-time paid staff (median)	7.0	70.0	4.0	4.0
% of untied income (median)	63.0	11.5	12.0	75.0
Number of objectives (median)	9.0	11.0	10.0	9.0
Number of business development activities (median)	10.0	12.0	6.0	10.0
Number of capacity development activities (median)	7.0	8.0	5.0	7.0
Average importance of partners (median)[a]	1.3	1.6	1.5	1.6
Average score on funding constraints (median)[b]	4.4	4.5	5.4	3.2
Average score on coordination constraints (median)[b]	3.3	3.3	4.6	2.9
Average score on capacity constraints (median)[b]	3.3	3.1	3.4	3.0
How effective is your organisation? (mean)[c]	4.7	5.0	4.9	5.3

Notes:

[a] Scale: 0 = Not a partner, 1 = Mildly important, 2 = Moderately important, 3 = Very important.

[b] Scale: 1 = Strongly disagree that the constraint is a problem to 7 = Strongly agree that the constraint is a problem.

[c] Scale: 1 = No impact to 7 = Major impact.

Differences between L&RED organisations across nations arise for a number of reasons. A society's understanding of the nature and intent of L&RED is one of the most powerful influences, and Northern Ireland's experience bears witness to the impact of these varying discourses. As Chapter Seven showed, L&RED in Northern Ireland is linked to peace building processes, directly affecting the nature and level of funding available; the types of organisation encouraged to participate in L&RED; the relationship with governments; and the types of activities undertaken. Respondents to the survey from Northern Ireland tend to be closely involved with their communities, focused on improving the well-being of their regions – rather than simply seeking economic growth – and working in partnership with others. In the US, by contrast, and to a lesser extent Australia, L&RED is tightly focused on economic growth, employment growth and the generation of wealth. There is an unequivocal concern with meeting the needs of businesses, and securing economic growth. L&RED organisations in the US, for example, are far more likely than comparable organisations in the other three countries to offer tax abatements to attract a firm to their region. In both Northern Ireland and England there is a far broader ideology surrounding L&RED, embracing community development, inequality and broader measures of well-being. This contrast has a profound influence because it affects the objectives of individual agencies, which in turn shape the types of partnerships that are established, the activities undertaken and the mindset used to judge how well organisations perform.

L&RED is also affected by governance structures operating at a range of scales. The European Commission and its regional development programmes have exerted a very considerable impact on the nature and direction of locality focused economic efforts in both Northern Ireland and England. European Commission funding has added depth to the L&RED effort of UK-based agencies, and added a dimension to their work absent in Australia and the US.

Governance or techniques: what contributes to effective regional programmes?

Differences in the goals of development are not the only substantial divergence between nations. Funding regimes exert a significant influence on how L&RED agencies intervene within their local or regional economy, as well as how they evaluate themselves. For the respondents participating in the survey it was possible to identify a range of outcomes by nation, ranging from apparently well-funded organisations in England through to small bodies with limited resources in Northern Ireland. But differences in resource levels do not determine whether individual agencies or the network of organisations across a nation are effective or ineffective in promoting L&RED. Factors such as the source or sources of funding, governance, and local legitimacy are equally, if not more, important, in determining whether organisations are effective in meeting their goals. The responses from Australia illustrate this point: Australian L&RED agencies reported a broadly comparable range of objectives and strategies to their counterparts in the US. However, the Australian respondents were more likely to provide negative self-assessments of effectiveness than US respondents, and there were far fewer assessments at the top of the scale. This difference was a product of the more complex funding of L&RED organisations in Australia compared with the US (Table 8.1). As a group, Australian respondents drew funding from all three tiers of government while US agencies were more likely to draw their funding from a single tier of government or raise income from private sources. Some US organisations were funded via dedicated local taxes. For Australian respondents, success in L&RED was the ability to win funding from one of the tiers of government, while US respondents drew upon both anecdotal information and formal evaluation instruments to estimate their impact.

The complex relationships between governance, funding and how organisations rate their effectiveness are also evident when we consider England and Northern Ireland. By any rational measure English respondents to the survey should have had the most positive assessment of their effectiveness: they were the largest and best funded organisations across the four nations, as a group they applied the most sophisticated approaches to encouraging development, and they had the benefit of a stable national policy framework that awards priority to L&RED. The English respondents, however, were the most cautious in their self-assessments of effectiveness. There are a number of possible explanations for this apparent contradiction between how English organisations would be expected to see themselves, and the judgements they provided through the questionnaire. We believe that their relatively pessimistic assessments were a product of governance issues, and, in particular, the highly centralised system of funding and regulating L&RED in England. 'Target and audit' culture may reassure politicians and senior public servants that public monies are being well spent, but such strategies make it difficult for L&RED organisations to achieve their broad objective of promoting economic development.

Kevin Morgan (1997) has written on this theme, arguing that L&RED bodies need to operate as a 'regional animateur', building trust, partnership and capacity within their jurisdiction. The Welsh Development Agency, the focus of Kevin Morgan's analysis, was least effective when subject to a greater level of central control. It lost its capacity to be innovative and surrendered its legitimacy within its community. The dead hand of political and bureaucratic guidance is anathema to the building of social capital and encouraging innovation at the regional level, particularly when there is conflict between national and local political cultures. The problems generated by apparently excessive central government control were evident in the qualitative comments reported in Chapter Four. Respondents called for a freeing up of processes and procedures, and while the English respondents were not alone in expressing this sentiment, it was the dominant theme among their comments. Hughes (1998) has also commented on the difficulty of developing regulatory frameworks for the supervision of L&RED agencies that do not render these organisations ineffective.

We would argue that the imposition of external control is an appreciable problem for L&RED organisations in England. We should recall that when asked to nominate factors that impeded their effectiveness, the level of funding available for L&RED in England was not considered to be a problem, but the tight time frames and strict funding guidelines of funding departments were seen to generate substantial difficulties. The need to maintain the local legitimacy of L&RED organisations is an important concern within the institutional architectures of all nations. While few respondents from any nation reported that they were not seen as legitimate representatives of their local community, the grass-roots relevance of 'top-down' programmes or organisations is open to challenge (Beer and Maude, 1997).

Governance factors also help us to understand why L&RED agencies in Northern Ireland assessed their own performance so positively. Northern Ireland's respondents came from the smallest organisations within the four nations studied, and reported multiple problems. However, our analysis suggests that the grounding of the L&RED sector within the broader community provides a resilience and local legitimacy that overcomes many challenges. Community-based models of L&RED would therefore appear to have much to commend them. Following this logic we can also see that the apparent success of L&RED agencies in the US is as much a function of their independence from central government influence and close ties to their local community, as of the nature of their funding regime or business sector focus.

Suarez-Villa (2002) has suggested that the rise of the US Sunbelt states can be attributed to the diffuse set of local, state and community-based actors seeking to stimulate growth through business attraction, infrastructure provision and the further development of human capital. From Suarez-Villa's perspective, it was the independence of local and state development efforts that enabled the Sunbelt states to bridge the substantial economic gap with the wealthier Mid-western and North Eastern states. The rise of the Sunbelt states to pre-eminence within the US national economy marks a remarkable reversal of regional fortunes, and as Suarez-Villa notes, one that has not been reproduced to an equivalent degree by the centralised planning of the European Commission or individual European nations.

On the basis of our analysis we would argue that when comparing across nations governance factors are *the* critical determinant of an organisation's effectiveness, at least as measured via self-assessment. Ensuring legitimacy and accountability to the local community, and constructing an appropriate relationship with stakeholders and governments appears to be a more important determinant of success than funding levels or central government support. It follows from this that much of the L&RED literature that emphasises the development and application of new and better strategies for encouraging development – such as business clusters or new analytical techniques – is misplaced. Strategies alone do not determine success any more than governance structures do. But contrary to much conventional wisdom, our findings seem to suggest that it is governance structures which are the more powerful influence in determining whether an agency feels its actions are making a positive impact. Many of the problems confronting L&RED organisations are best addressed by reordering their priorities and relationships, rather than attempting to introduce new tools. Individual agencies can play a part in recasting their role but central government policies about the control and regulation of L&RED programmes are of greater importance. As Morgan (1997, p 92) has argued, it is possible to ensure public accountability "without compromising the need for economy, efficiency and relative autonomy".

There are a number of models for the funding of L&RED organisations potentially available that address the apparent conflict between the need for efficiency on the one hand and public accountability in L&RED on the other. Unfortunately there are no simple solutions as the tension between accountability and the establishment of a long-term funding structure that enables L&RED agencies to act as independent agencies is profound. However, some approaches enable practitioners and policy makers to manage this tension more effectively than other models. For example, L&RED agencies could be funded through formal agreements with central or local governments. These agreements could cover a relatively long period of time – five or more years – with the outcomes specified in greater or lesser detail. This approach is applied in some Australian states to the funding of regional development boards. It effectively separates the process of L&RED into an outcome negotiated between two parties, the purchaser (the state government) and the provider (the regional development board). This strategy has advantages in providing for a degree of independence for the L&RED agencies and in offering security of funding, but the nature of the contract may interfere with the development of broader partnerships for regional development. Such contracts may also be insufficiently flexible to deal with changed circumstances or new opportunities. Alternatively, in some parts of the US economic development activities are funded by local governments but administered by a semi-autonomous commission, with the commissioners appointed by the mayor. This model ensures a degree of distance from day-to-day politics and administration, but also guarantees accountability and relevance to community priorities. It is a more inclusive model, but one which is open to more substantial local political interference.

The determinant role of governance in the success of L&RED agencies helps us understand why conventional public policy evaluation instruments are often inadequate. There is no simple arithmetic for measuring success if effectiveness is a function of governance factors rather than inputs. Institutional factors cannot be reproduced or embedded within a new policy or programme in the same way greater funding or new development tools can be institutionalised. The importance of governance factors also helps explain why some regional development discourses place such a great emphasis on leadership, either within the community (McKinsey and Co, 1994; Kenyon and Black, 2001) or among development professionals.

Strategic selectivity and institutional thickness

In Chapter Two we considered the strategic and spatial selectivity of the state. That discussion recognised that central governments provide legitimacy and resources, and ultimately empower, L&RED agencies. Central governments have the capacity to select some organisations and approaches for continued operation while abandoning or superseding other approaches. This perspective appears particularly cogent in England where the national government plays such a dominant role. Elsewhere the explanatory power of this approach appears muted, as systems of governance with more diffuse power mean that L&RED agencies are not reliant on central governments. As Chapter Seven showed, the EU has been an important 'non-state' sponsor of community-based L&RED. In the US, the federal government is relatively unimportant for the operations of most L&RED organisations and state governments, local governments, community groups and local businesses ensure that a variety of different types of body are active in L&RED.

In federal systems, such as Australia and the US, state and local governments will often pursue place-based economic development strategies at odds with the policies of the national governments. The survey showed, for example, that industrial recruitment remains a common economic development strategy in the US, despite falling from favour among central government policy makers and academic economists (Loveridge, 1996). Industrial recruitment was a relatively unimportant local economic development strategy in England and Northern Ireland, but a range of 'new regionalism' policy instruments were common because they fit the current policy settings of the government. Under these circumstances, strategic selectivity is important both for determining the broad paradigm of L&RED evident in a country, and the detail of its implementation. Furthermore, strategic selectivity is also evident in the way central governments reserve some powers and policy options for their use. Both the UK government and state governments in Australia, for example, engage in industrial recruitment but limit the capacity of L&RED agencies to follow suit.

Strategic selectivity clearly affects the landscape of L&RED in any nation in complex ways. Under certain circumstances it results in the coexistence of competing perspectives on L&RED in a single region, as policy options abandoned by one tier of government are maintained by other tiers. It is worth noting that in all jurisdictions covered in this study there were appreciable differences between local government and non-local government agencies in their approach to L&RED, their objectives, attitudes and assessments. In part this was a function of the differing structural position of the two types of agencies, but differences in approach were also important.

In many ways power or capacity within L&RED appears to reside in diverse sources. In all four nations respondents to the questionnaire indicated that networking was one of their most effective strategies. This embraced networking with private businesses, but also the building of bridges with government bodies, community groups and/or Chambers of Commerce. L&RED bodies are too small to directly affect growth within their region and therefore must work in partnership with other agencies and the private sector. This is the institutional thickness identified by Amin and Thrift (1995), and our research adds weight to their contentions about its significance. Networking is clearly important for any L&RED organisation. They need to network in order to gain resources for firms within their region, to gather and distribute information within their region, to deliver programmes, and, perhaps most importantly, to advance the support of key stakeholders. The latter is an important consideration because agencies need to advance their own future in order to secure the future of their regions. In nations such as England where the institutional architecture for L&RED is characterised by a concentration of power within central government departments, and in places such as the US where a broader range of actors play a determinant role, agencies need to maintain an active profile to guarantee support. Networking and the maintenance of an 'institutionally thick' policy environment therefore play both a positive role in increasing a region's capacity, and a defensive role in securing the continuing operations of the agency.

Implications for policy, implications for practice

Our research has important implications for both the policy environment surrounding L&RED and its practice. To a certain degree our research challenges the way we think about L&RED. It suggests that if we aspire to better L&RED and improved outcomes for our regions, cities and towns, the policy solution will not necessarily lie in the development of new and better techniques, but may well reside in the improved delivery of established tools. The survey – of almost 900 economic development practitioners across four nations – clearly shows that some of the most effective actions for encouraging the growth of a region are some of the simplest. In all four nations practitioners nominated the provision of assistance or services to business as their most effective activity, and included networking and partnership building within their five most successful strategies. These are relatively low-cost activities, and can be effectively applied by both large and small organisations.

More expensive or more sophisticated approaches were not prominent among practitioners' nominations of what constituted their most effective actions. Within this context it is worth noting that Cloney (2003) observed that regional development policy in New Zealand in the 1990s was heavily influenced by Michael Porter's ideas on cluster building. Porter helped establish a policy framework that encouraged cluster building, but returned after five years to find relatively little substantive benefit with respect to key indicators such as employment growth, export development and increased international competitiveness. While five years is too early to base a judgement on, it does remind us of the need for caution in assuming 'advanced' approaches such as clusters will necessarily suit in all contexts. Indeed the whole point should be that new policies need to be devised and implemented in ways that are context-sensitive. This points to the need to be wary of those who seem to adopt a cargo-cult mentality and overlook the importance of well delivered conventional regional development interventions.

The assessments of practitioners of what is effective may well reflect what it is that an L&RED organisation can contribute to local and regional development. These organisations operate in an environment in which much larger agencies are responsible for the main sectors of the economy, such as agriculture and manufacturing, for the development of new industries in areas such as biotechnology, and for the provision of major physical and social infrastructure. L&RED organisations are most effective when they work in the gaps between these agencies. That is, they link activities across sectors, deliver services at a level that larger agencies cannot, undertake strategic planning across all sectors of their region, or act as a 'regional animateur', to return to Kevin Morgan's idea of an L&RED sector working to build trust, partnership and capacity within their region.

For example, business services that need to be physically accessible, or that require local knowledge, are best provided at the local level. This particularly applies to small business advisory services, which were rated as effective activities by our organisations, even when these services then link clients to programmes provided through the Internet. Business support strategies that involve businesses working together, whether to learn from each other or to solve common problems, also depend on proximity and the trust developed through personal relationships, and are best undertaken at the local level. Programmes for management or staff training, for export enhancement or for improving the use of IT are also most effectively delivered at the local level.

While we must be cautious about the potential benefits of new approaches, there is a strong case for policy transfer and learning between nations. England, Australia and Northern Ireland could all benefit from an investigation of the funding models used in the US. The independence and certainty in funding evident in the US has evident benefits for the delivery of L&RED assistance. The potential benefits are most clearly drawn in Northern Ireland where the sector is confronted by the prospect of the withdrawal of European Commission funding when the various programmes associated with the peace process come to an end. Local government is not currently a major participant in L&RED in Northern Ireland and the potential for provincial government funding is limited. Change in Northern Ireland's funding regime is inevitable, and the US model would be an appropriate starting point in any debate about the future shape of the sector. While making this recommendation we note that it may not be practical to attempt to apply the US model, either in part or in full, in other places. As noted in Chapter Two, governmental structures, cultural attitudes to private sector support for community-based action and the nature of public sector programmes determine what lies within the realms of possibility.

The US model, however, does represent a useful point of departure for any evaluation and reformulation of current practice.

L&RED in Australia may well be more effective if it was to broaden its range of policy instruments and objectives. As with the US, L&RED in Australia is notable for the absence of a strong social justice/equity element. The development and funding of social economy initiatives warrants attention, particularly in places with populations marked by long-term socio-economic disadvantage. The current emphasis within L&RED in Australia on facilitation has resulted in a limited engagement with the more sophisticated economic development tools applied in the US and England. Strategies such as the encouragement of supply chain associations, the establishment of business incubators, providing assistance to firms to meet ISO standards and assistance with venture capital could add to the substance of L&RED in Australia. We would argue that the restricted range of L&RED tools used currently is partly a function of the limited core funding for agencies, but also reflects the fact that regional policy in Australia is concentrated on non-metropolitan regions. The development of business incubators and assisting firms to gain access to venture capital are not practical solutions to the challenge of encouraging growth in the sparsely populated Australian countryside. However, they are relevant in Australia's cities, and their absence must limit the international competitiveness of these metropolitan regions, and the national economy as a whole.

In this study we used the simple device of asking respondents to provide an assessment of the effectiveness of their organisation. The results showed that people completing the questionnaire were willing to make critical judgements where they thought it appropriate. The results also make intriguing reading – indeed we are still trying to think through some of the issues raised by our findings. At heart what the results tell us is that most practitioners judge their success by how they operate, the process aspects of L&RED, rather than relying on the so-called hard outputs such as 'jobs created'. Indeed, practitioners are as intrigued as we are as academics in how they were compelled to certain actions rather than others and the implications for their ability to operate successfully. And that surely bodes well for the future of local and regional economic development. We are still learning – together.

References

Aglietta, M. (1979) *A theory of capitalist regulation*, London: New Left Books.

Allison, J. and Kwitko, L. (1998) 'Restructuring on the rural/urban cusp of South East Queensland: the role of local authorities in local economic development', *Regional Policy and Practice*, vol 7, no 2, pp 22-30.

Amin, A. (1994) 'Models, fantasies and phantoms of transition', in A. Amin (ed) *Post-Fordism: A reader*, Oxford: Blackwell, pp 1-39.

Amin, A. and Thrift, N. (1995) 'Globalisation, institutional "thickness" and the local economy', in P. Healey, S. Cameron, S. Davoudi, S. Graham and A. Madani-Pour (eds) *Managing cities: The new urban context*, New York, NY: John Wiley and Sons, pp 91-107.

Anderson, J. and Tuckey, W. (2002) *Regional Australia: A partnership for stronger regions*, Canberra: Department of Transport and Regional Services.

Audit Commission (1989) *Urban regeneration and economic development: The local government dimension*, London: HMSO.

Audit Commission (1999) *A life's work: Local authorities, economic development and economic regeneration*, Abingdon: Audit Commission.

Axford, N. and Pinch, S. (1994) 'Growth coalitions and local economic development strategy in southern England: a case study of the Hampshire Development Association', *Political Geography*, vol 13, no 4, pp 344-60.

Badcock, B. (1984) *Unfairly structured cities*, Oxford: Blackwell.

Barker, A.J. (1992) 'Decentralisation and regional business enterprise: the South-West Development Authority', in F. Broeze (ed) *Private enterprise, government and society: Studies in Western Australian history*, no 13, Perth: Centre for Western Australian History, University of Western Australia, pp 126-39.

Beer, A. (1998) 'Economic rationalism and the decline of local economic development in Australia', *Local Economy*, vol 13, no 2, pp 52-64.

Beer, A. (2000a) 'Regional policy in Australia: running out of solutions?', in B. Pritchard and P. McManus (eds) *Land of discontent: The dynamics of change in rural and regional Australia*, Sydney: University of New South Wales Press, pp 169-94.

Beer, A. (2000b) 'Listening, talking and acting: a new approach to regional policy and practice in Australia?', *Australian Planner*, vol 37, no 3, pp 114-19.

Beer, A. and Maude, A. (1997) *Effectiveness of state frameworks for local economic development*, Adelaide: Local Government Association of South Australia.

Beer, A. and Maude, A. (2002) *Local and regional economic development agencies in Australia*, Report prepared for the Local Government Association of South Australia, Adelaide: School of Geography, Population and Environmental Management, Flinders University.

Beer, A., Maude, A. and Pritchard, B. (2003) *Developing Australia's regions: Theory and Practice*, Sydney: University of New South Wales Press.

Bennett, R.J. and Krebbs, G. (1991) *Local economic development: Public–private partnership initiatives in Britain and Germany*, London: Belhaven.

Bennett R.J. and LGA (Local Government Assocation) (1998) 'Survey of local economic development in local government', www.lga.gov.uk/economicregeneration/survey.pdf (accessed 5 February 2003).

Birrell, D. and Hayes, A. (1999) *The local government system in Northern Ireland*, Dublin: Institute of Public Administration.

Blair, J.P. and Kumar, R. (1999) 'Is local economic development a zero-sum game?', in R.D. Bingham and R. Mier (eds) *Dilemmas of urban economic development*, Thousand Oaks, CA: Sage Publications, pp 1-20.

Blakely, E.J. (1994) *Planning local economic development: Theory and practice*, Thousand Oaks, CA: Sage Publications.

Blakely, E.J. (2001) 'Competitive advantage for the 21st century city: can a place-based approach to economic development survive in the cyber-space age', *Journal of the American Planning Association*, vol 67, no 2, pp 133-41.

Bradley, J. and Hamilton, D. (1999) 'Strategy 2010: planning economic development in Northern Ireland', *Regional Studies*, vol 33, no 9, pp 885-90.

Brazeal, S. and Finkle, J. (2001) 'Legislation opens new doors for economic renewal', *The American City and County*, vol 116, no 5, pp 38-42.

Brenner, N. (2000) 'The urban question as a scale question: reflections on Henri Lefebvre, urban theory and the politics of scale', *International Journal of Urban and Regional Research*, vol 24, pp 361-78.

Butlin, N., Barnard, G. and Pincus, J. (1982) *Government and capitalism*, Melbourne: Oxford University Press.

City of Onkaparinga (2003) accessed at www.onkaparinga.sa.gov.au

Clavel, P. (1986) *The progressive city: Planning and participation, 1969-1984*, New Jersey: Rutgers University Press.

Cloney, M. (2003) 'Regional development policy for Australia', Unpublished PhD thesis, Department of Political Economy, University of Sydney.

Cochrane, A. (ed) (1987) *Developing local economic strategies*, Milton Keynes: Open University Press.

Cohen, A.B. (2001) 'Community renewal tax relief act's incentives for investors – form over substance?', *The Tax Adviser*, vol 32, no 6, pp 383-4.

Collits, P. (1995) 'Balanced state development in NSW regional policy making – past glories and future prospects', Paper presented to the Australian and New Zealand Regional Science Association Annual Conference, Brisbane, December.

Cooke, P. and Morgan, K. (2000) *The associational economy: Firms, regions and innovation*, Oxford: Oxford University Press.

Cookstown District Council website, accessed at www.cookstown.gov.uk, 28 February 2003.

Cox, A., Alwang, J. and Johnson, T. (2000) 'Local preferences for economic development outcomes: analytical hierarchy', *Growth and Change*, vol 31, no 3, pp 341-66.

Cox, K. and Mair, A. (1989) 'Urban growth machines and the politics of local economic development', *International Journal of Urban and Regional Research*, vol 13, pp 137-46.

Danson, M., Halkier, H. and Cameron, G. (2000) *Governance, institutional change and regional development*, London: Ashgate.

Danson, M. and Whittam, G. (1999) *Regional governance, institutions and development* (a Regional Research Institute web book, www.rri.wvu.edu/WebBook/ Danson/contents.htm)

Dawkins, P. and Kelly, P. (eds) (2003) *Hard heads, soft hearts: A new reform agenda for Australia*, Sydney: Allen & Unwin.

Dean, M. (1999) *Governmentality: Power and rule in modern society*, London: Sage Publications.

DiGaetano, A. (1997) 'Urban governing alignments and realignments in comparative perspective: developmental politics in Boston, Massachusetts, and Bristol, England, 1980-1996', *Urban Affairs Review*, vol 32, no 6, pp 844-70.

DiGiovanna, S. (1996) 'Industrial districts and regional economic development: a regulation approach', *Regional Studies*, vol 30, no 4, pp 373-88.

DIIRD (Department of Innovation, Industry and Regional Development) (2002) *Community capacity building initiative, community action plan. Pilot project Ballan*, Melbourne: DIIRD.

EC (European Commission) (1993) *Growth, competitiveness and employment: The challenges and ways forward into the 21st century*, White Paper, COM(93) 700 final, Brussels: European Commission.

Eisinger, P. (1995) 'State development in the 1990s', *Economic Development Quarterly*, vol 9, no 2, pp 146-58.

Eisinger, P. (2002) 'Financing economic development: a survey of techniques', *Government Finance Review*, June, pp 20-3.

Esping-Andersen, G. (1990) *The three worlds of welfare capitalism*, Cambridge: Polity Press.

Forth, G. and Howell, K. (2002) 'Don't cry for me Upper Wombat: the realities of regional/small town decline in non-coastal Australia', *Sustaining Regions*, vol 2, no 2, pp 4-11.

Foucault, M. (1991) 'Governmentality', in G. Burchell, C. Gordon and P. Miller, *The Foucault effect: Studies in governmentality*, London: Harvester Wheatsheaf, pp 87-104.

Fulop, L. and Brennan, M. (1997) *Meeting the challenge: Regional Economic Development Organisations in Australia*, Canberra: Australian Local Government Association.

Gabe, T.M. and Kraybill, D.S. (2002) 'The effect of state economic development incentives on employment growth of establishments', *Journal of Regional Science*, vol 42, no 4, pp 703-30.

Gain, B. and Dunn, D. (2001) 'Fiber glut challenged as misperception', *EBN*, February, no 1292, retrieved 10 December from ABI/INFORM Global database.

Gallagher, A.M. (1991) *Majority minority review 2: Employment, unemployment and religion in Northern Ireland*, Coleraine: University of Ulster.

Geddes, M. (1999) 'Partnership and local development in the European Union', in G. Haughton (ed) *Community economic development*, London: The Stationery Office, pp 47-64.

Gleeson, B. (2001) *Towards a national framework for Australia*, Issues Paper no 8, Urban Futures Program, Sydney: University of Western Sydney.

Goodwin, M. and Painter, J. (1996) 'Local governance, the crisis of Fordism and the changing geographies of regulation', *Transactions of the Institute of British Geographers*, vol 21, pp 635-48.

Greer, J. (2001) *Partnership governance in Northern Ireland*, Aldershot: Ashgate.

Greer, J., Hughes, J., Knox, C. and Murray, M. (1999) 'Reshaping local governance in a divided society: district partnerships in Northern Ireland', in G. Haughton (ed) *Community economic development*, London: The Stationery Office, pp 79-94.

Guardian, The (2002) 'Irish paramilitaries linked with smuggling', 3 July.

Halkier, H. and Danson, M. (1998) 'Regional development agencies in western Europe: a survey of key characteristics and trends', in H. Halkier, M. Danson and M. Damborg, *Regional development agencies in Europe*, London: Jessica Kingsley/Regional Studies Association.

Halkier, H., Danson, M. and Damborg, C. (1998) *Regional development agencies in Europe*, London: Jessica Kingsley/Regional Studies Association.

Hall, P. (1989) *Urban and regional planning*, London: Unwin Hyman.

Harding, A. (1999) 'Review article: North American political economy, urban theory and British research', *British Journal of Political Science*, vol 29, pp 673-98.

Hatry, H., Fall, M., Singer, T. and Liner, B. (1990) *A manual: Monitoring the outcomes of economic development programs*, Washington, DC: Urban Institute Press.

Haughton, G. (1987) 'Constructing a social audit: putting the regional multiplier into practice', *Town Planning Review*, vol 50, no 3, pp 255-65.

Haughton, G. (1999a) 'Community economic development: challenges of theory, method and practice', in G. Haughton (ed) *Community economic development*, London: The Stationery Office, pp 3-22.

Haughton G. (1999b) 'Trojan horse or white elephant? The contested biography of the life and times of the Leeds Development Corporation', *Town Planning Review*, vol 70, no 2, pp 173-90.

Haughton, G. and Thomas, K. (1992) 'The role of local sector studies: the development of sector studies in the UK', *Local Economy*, vol 7, no 2, pp 100-13.

Haughton, G. and While, A. (1999) 'From corporate city to citizen's city? Urban leadership *after* local entrepreneurialism in the UK', *Urban Affairs Review*, vol 35, no 1, pp 3-23.

Haughton, G. and Whitney, D. (1994) 'Dancing to different tunes: the growth of urban development partnerships in West Yorkshire', in G. Haughton and D. Whitney (eds) *Reinventing a region: Restructuring and policy response in West Yorkshire*, Aldershot: Avebury, pp 107-26.

Haughton, G., Lloyd, P. and Meegan, R. (1999) 'The rediscovery of community economic development in Britain: the European dimension to grassroots involvement in local regeneration', in G. Haughton (ed) *Community economic development*, London: The Stationery Office, pp 209-23.

Haughton, G., Peck, J.A. and Strange, I. (1997) 'Turf wars: the battle for control of English local economic development', *Local Government Studies*, vol 23, no 1, pp 88-106.

Hay, C. (1995) 'Re-stating the problem of regulation and re-regulating the local state', *Economy and Society*, vol 24, no 3, pp 387-407.

Henton, D. (1994) 'Reinventing Silicon Valley: creating a total quality community', in *Cities and the new global economy: An international conference presented by the OECD and the Australian government*, Melbourne, 20-23 November, Canberra: Australian Government Publishing Service, pp 310-26.

Hill, S. (2002) 'Assessing the impact of regional development policies: towards the development of guidelines for good practice', Paper presented to the Australian and New Zealand Regional Science Association Conference, Gold Coast, October.

Hodgett, S. and Johnson, D. (2001) 'Troubles, partnerships and possibilities: a study of the Making Belfast Work Development Initiative in Northern Ireland', *Public Administration and Development*, vol 21, pp 321-32.

Hughes, J. (1998) 'The role of development agencies in regional policy: an academic and practitioner approach', *Urban Studies*, vol 35, no 4, pp 615-26.

Hull Cityvision (2002) *Hull community strategy*, Hull: Hull Cityvision.

Imrie, R. and Thomas, H. (eds) (1999) *British urban policy* (2nd edn), London: Sage Publications.

Industry Commission (1996) *State, territory and local government assistance to industry*, Melbourne: Productivity Commission.

Isserman, A. (1994) 'State economic development policy and practice in the United States, a survey article', *International Regional Science Review*, vol 16, nos 1&2, pp 49-100.

Jessop, B. (1990a) *State theory: Putting the capitalist state in its place*, Cambridge: Polity Press.

Jessop, B. (1990b) 'Regulation theories in retrospect and prospect', *Economy and Society*, vol 19, no 2, pp 152-216.

Jessop, B. (1995) 'The regulation approach, governance and post-Fordism: alternative perspectives on economic and political change?', *Economy and Society*, vol 24, pp 307-33.

Jessop, B. (1997) 'The entrepreneurial city: re-imaging localities, redesigning economic governance, or restructuring capital?', in N. Jewson and S. MacGregor (eds) *Transforming cities: Contested governance and new spatial divisions*, London: Routledge, pp 28-41.

Jessop, B. (1998) 'The rise of governance and the risks of failure: the case of economic development', *International Social Science Journal*, vol 155, pp 29-45.

Jessop, B. (1999) 'Reflections on globalization and its (il)logics', in K. Olds et al (eds) *Globalization and the Asia-Pacific*, London: Routledge, pp 19-38.

Jessop, B. (2000) 'The crisis of the national spatio-temporal fix and the ecological dominance of globalizing capitalism', *International Journal of Urban and Regional Studies*, vol 24, no 2, pp 273-310.

Jessop, B. (2002) 'Liberalism, neoliberalism and urban governance: a state-theoretical perspective', *Antipode*, vol 34, no 2, pp 452-72.

Judd, D.R. and Ready, R.L. (1986) 'Entrepreneurial cities and the new politics of economic development', in P.E. Peterson and C.W. Lewis (eds) *Reagan and the cities*, Washington, DC: Urban Institute Press.

Karmatz, L., Labi, A. and Levinstein, J. (1998) 'Corporate welfare', *Time*, 9 November, pp 29-47.

Keating, M. (2001) 'Rethinking the region: culture, institutions and economic development in Catalonia and Galicia', *European Urban and Regional Studies*, vol 8, pp 217-34.

Kenyon, P. and Black, A. (eds) (2001) *Small town renewal: Overview and case studies*, Publication No 01/043, Canberra: Rural Industries Research and Development Corporation.

Lambert, T. and Coomes, P. (2001) 'An evaluation of the effectiveness of Louiseville's Enterprise Zone', *Economic Development Quarterly*, vol 15, no 2, pp 168-80.

Lenihan, H. (1999) 'An evaluation of a regional development agency's grants in terms of deadweight and displacement', *Environment and Planning C: Government and Policy*, vol 17, no 3, pp 303-18.

Levy, J.M. (1990) 'What local economic developers actually do: location quotients versus press releases', *Journal of the American Planning Association*, Spring, pp 153-60, retrieved 10 December from ABI/INFORM Global database.

Logan, M. (1978) 'Regional policy', in P. Scott (ed) *Australian cities and public policy*, Melbourne: Georgian House, pp 23-39.

Logan, J. and Molotch, H. (1987) *Urban fortunes: The political economy of place* Berkeley, CA: University of California Press.

Loveridge, S. (1996) 'On the continuing popularity of industrial recruitment', *Economic Development Quarterly*, vol 10, no 2, pp 151-8.

Lovering, J. (1999) 'Theory led by policy: the inadequacies of the new regionalism', *International Journal of Urban and Regional Research*, vol 23, pp 379-95.

Mack Management Consulting (1998) 'Key performance indicators for regional development boards', Unpublished report prepared for the Local Government Association of South Australia and the South Australian Regional Development Association, Adelaide.

MacLeod, G. (2002) 'New regionalism reconsidered: globalisation and the remaking of political economic space', *International Journal of Urban and Regional Research*, vol 25, no 4, pp 804-29.

MacLeod, G. and Goodwin, M. (1999) 'Space, scale and state strategy: rethinking urban and regional governance', *Progress in Human Geography*, vol 23, no 4, pp 503-27.

MacKinnon, D., Cumbers, A. and Chapman, K. (2002) 'Learning, innovation and regional development: a critical appraisal of recent debates', *Progress in Human Geography*, vol 26, no 3, pp 293-311.

Mark, S.T., McGuire, T.J. and Papke, L.E. (2000) 'The influence of taxes on employment and population growth: evidence from the Washington, DC, Metropolitan Area', *National Tax Journal*, vol 53, no 1, pp 105-23.

Markusen, A (1999) 'Fuzzy concepts, scanty evidence, policy distance: the case for rigor and policy relevance in critical regional studies', *Regional Studies*, vol 33, no 9, pp 869-84.

McFarlane, A.G. (1999) 'Race, space and place: the geography of economic development', *The San Diego Law Review*, vol 36, no 2, pp 295-354.

McKinsey & Co (1994) *Lead local compete global*, Sydney: McKinsey & Co.

McManus, P. and Pritchard, B. (2000) 'Introduction', in B. Pritchard and P. McManus (eds) *Land of discontent: The dynamics of change in rural and regional Australia*, Sydney: University of New South Wales Press, pp 1-13.

Miranda, R. and Rosdil, D. (1995) 'From boosterism to qualitative growth: classifying economic development strategies', *Urban Affairs Quarterly*, vol 39, no 6, pp 868-79.

Monks, H. (1994) 'The interaction of government funders and management in regional development organisations', *Regional Policy and Practice*, vol 3, no 2, pp 7-13.

Morgan, K. (1997) 'The regional animateur: taking stock of the Welsh Development Agency', *Regional and Federal Studies*, vol 7, no 2, pp 70-94.

Morgan, K. and Nauwelaers, C. (eds) (1999) *Regional innovation strategies: The challenge for less-favoured regions*, London: The Stationery Office.

Morrissey, M. and Gaffikin, F. (2001) 'Northern Ireland: democratizing for development', *Local Economy*, vol 16, no 1, pp 2-13.

Munro, A. (1997) 'Local and regional governance: back to basics', *Australian Journal of Public Administration*, vol 56, no 3, pp 77-83.

Murdoch, J. (2000) 'Space against time: competing rationalities in planning for housing', *Transactions Institute of British Geographers*, vol 25, pp 503-19.

Murray, M. and Greer, J.O. (1993) 'Rural development in Northern Ireland', in M. Murray and J. Greer (eds) *Rural development in Ireland*, Aldershot: Avebury, pp 55-67.

National Commission of Audit (1996) *Report to the federal government*, Canberra: Australian Government Publishing Service.

National Statistics (2002) *ILO unemployment rates for June-August 2002*, accessed at www.statistics.gov.uk/statbase/, January 2003.

Nickel, D.R. (1995) 'The progressive city? Urban redevelopment in Minneapolis', *Urban Affairs Review*, vol 30, no 3, pp 355-77.

NIEC (Northern Ireland Economic Council) (1999) *A step-change in economic performance? A response to Strategy 2010*, Belfast: NIEC.

NIEC (2000) *Local development: A turning point*, Belfast: NIEC.

NSW (New South Wales) County Mayors Association (1993) *Towards balanced state development*, Australian Government Publishing Service, Canberra.

O'Dowd, L. (1995) 'Development or dependency? State, economy and society in Northern Ireland', in P. Clancy, S. Drudy, K. Lynch and L. O'Dowd (eds) *Irish society: Sociological perspectives*, Dublin: Institute of Public Administration.

OECD (Organisation for Economic Co-operation and Development) (1997) *Trends in regional policies in OECD countries*, Paris: OECD.

OECD (2001) *Best practices in local development*, Paris: OECD.

Office of the Attorney General for the State of Texas (2001) *Handbook on economic development laws for Texas cities*, vol 1, Austin, TX: Office of the Attorney General.

Olberding, J. (2002) 'Does regionalism beget regionalism? The relationship between norms and regional partnerships for economic development', *Public Administration Review*, vol 62, no 4, pp 480-91.

Paasi, A. (2002) 'Place and region: regional worlds and words', *Progress in Human Geography*, vol 26, no 6, pp 802-11.

Painter, J. (2002) 'Governmentality and regional economic strategies', in J. Hillier and E. Rooksby (eds) *Habitus: A sense of place*, Aldershot: Ashgate, pp 115-39.

Peck, J. (2002) 'Political economies of scale: fast policy, interscalar relations, and neoliberal workfare', *Economic Geography*, vol 78, pp 331-60.

Peck, J. and Tickell, A. (2002) 'Neoliberalising space', *Antipode*, vol 34, pp 380-404.

Pierre, J. and Peters, B.G. (2000) *Governance, politics and the state*, Basingstoke: Macmillan.

Poole, K.E., Erickcek, G.A., Iannone, D.T., McCrea, N. and Salem, P. (1999) *Evaluating business development incentives*, Washington, DC: National Association of State Development Agencies.

Pradzynski, J. and Yiftachel, O. (1991) 'Regional planning and economic development in the South West Region, Western Australia', *Urban Policy and Research*, vol 9, no 1, pp 110-22.

Randolph, B. and Judd, B. (2000) 'Community renewal and large public housing estates', *Urban Policy and Research*, vol 18, no 1, pp 91-104.

Ráth Mór Centre website accessed at www.rathmor.com, 28 February 2003.

Reese, L. (1997) *Local economic development policy: The United States and Canada*, New York, NY: Garland Publishing.

Reese, L. and Rosenfeld, R. (2002) *The civic culture of local economic development*, Thousand Oaks, CA: Sage Publications.

Regional Australia Summit, Summit Working Groups (1999) 'Report of Theme 5 – Government', accessed at www.dotars.gov.au/regional/summit/outcomes/reports/theme5_report.htm

Regional Development Taskforce (South Australia) (1999) *Report*, Adelaide: South Australian Government Printer.

Robson, B., Peck, J. and Holden, A. (2000) *Regional agencies and area-based regeneration*, Bristol/York: The Policy Press/Joseph Rowntree Foundation.

Rubin, H. (1988) 'Shoot anything that flies, claim anything that falls: conversations with economic development practitioners', *Economic Development Quarterly*, vol 21, pp 236-51.

Santopietro, G.D. (2002) 'Analyzing income convergence at the county level: the case of development in central Appalachia', *Journal of Economic Issues*, vol 36, no 4, pp 893-906.

Saxenian, A. (1994) *Regional advantage: Culture and competition in Silicon Valley and Route 128*, Cambridge: Harvard University Press.

Sellgren, J. (1989) 'Assisting local economies: an assessment of emerging patterns of local authority economic development activities', in D. Gibbs (ed) *Government policy and industrial change*, London: Routledge.

Sellgren, J. (1991) 'The changing nature of economic development activities: a longitudinal analysis of local authorities in Great Britain', *Environment and Planning C: Government and Policy*, vol 9, no 3, pp 341-62.

Shutt, J. (2000) 'Lessons from America in the 1990s', in P. Roberts and H. Sykes (eds) *Urban regeneration: A handbook*, London: Sage Publications, pp 257-80.

Shutt, J., Haughton, G. and Kumi-Ampofo, F. (2001) *Advancing community partnerships: The social economy in Yorkshire and Humber*, Leeds: Yorkshire Forward.

Stilwell, F. (2000) *Changing track: A new political economic direction for Australia*, Sydney: Pluto Press, chapter 20.

Stone, C.L. (1989) *Regime politics: Governing Atlanta 1946-1988*, Lawrence: University Press of Kansas.

Strozniak, P. (2002) 'Incentives stay – for now', *Industry Week*, vol 251, no 10, pp 51-3.

Suarez-Villa, L. (2002) 'Regional inversion in the United States: the institutional context for the rise of the sunbelt since the 1940s', *Tidjschrift voor Economische en Sociale Geografie*, vol 92, no 4, pp 424-42.

Taylor, M. (1998), 'Combating the social exclusion of housing estates', *Housing Studies*, vol 13, no 6, pp 819-32.

Taylor, M. (2000) 'The dynamics of Australian regional policy: lessons for Europe?', *Federal & Regional Studies*, vol 10, no 2, pp 107-25.

Teague, P. and Wilson, R. (1995) 'Towards an inclusive society', in P. Teague and R. Wilson (eds) *Democratic dialogue report: Social exclusion, social inclusion*, Belfast: Democratic Dialogue.

Tickell, A. and Peck, J. (1995) 'Social regulation after Fordism: regulation theory, neo-liberalism and the global-local nexus', *Economy and Society*, vol 24, no 3, pp 357-86.

Tietz, M. (1994) 'Changes in economic development theory and practice', *International Regional Science Review*, vol 16, no 1, pp 101-6.

Tonts, M. (1999) 'Some recent trends in Australian regional economic development policy', *Regional Studies*, vol 33, pp. 581-6.

Vipond, J. (1989) 'Australian experiments with regional policies', in B. Higgins and K. Zagorski (eds) *Australian regional developments: Readings in regional experiences, policies and prospects*, Canberra: Australian Government Publishing Service, pp 65-78.

Weinstein, B., Gross, H. and Clower, T. (1994) *Recommended performance measures for the Business Development Division of the Texas Department of Commerce*, Denton, TX: Center for Economic Development and Research.

Wheatbelt Development Commission (2002) 'Annual report 2002', www.wheatbelt.wa.gov.au

White, L., Hart, M. and Harvey, S. (2000) 'Towards internal cohesion? The role of local government in economic development under the EU Single Programme in Northern Ireland, *Local Economy*, vol 14, no 4, pp 357-69.

Wirtz, R.A. (2000) 'The crowed field of local economic development', *Fedgazzette*, vol 12, no 2, pp 3-8.

Wood, A. (1996a) 'The politics of local economic development: making sense of cross-national convergence', *Urban Studies*, vol 33, no 8, pp 1281-95.

Wood, A. (1996b) 'Analysing the politics of local economic development', *Urban Studies*, vol 33, no 8, pp 1263-80.

Woodward, D., Miley, H. Jr and Ulbrich, H. (2000) 'Education and economic development in South Carolina', *Business and Economic Review*, vol 46, no 4, pp 3-10.

Wong, C. (1998) 'Interrelationships between key actors in local economic development', *Environment and Planning C: Government and Policy*, vol 16, pp 463-81.

Index

Page references for figures and tables are in *italics*; those for notes are followed by n